FOLLIES

FOLLIES

BOOK BY

JAMES GOLDMAN

MUSIC AND LYRICS BY

STEPHEN SONDHEIM

THEATRE COMMUNICATIONS GROUP
NEW YORK

Preface & Acknowledgments

In the wake of the demise of *Realsozialismus* in the Soviet Union and Eastern Europe, the 1990s became an era of revisionism. It has become fashionable to question many commonly held beliefs of the past. In the case of the revolutionary Left in El Salvador, Nicaragua, and Guatemala some observers and protagonists who used to glorify the revolutionary movements have joined their most vocal critics. In Guatemala one encounters the argument that the Guerrilla Army of the Poor "provoked" the death of its supporters, prolonging a war that it knew had been lost.[1] In Nicaragua, some members of the revolutionary government of the 1980s have come to question the legitimacy of the elections held in 1984, which were recognized by the international community as "fair and free." Reevaluation is an exercise central to gaining a full understanding of the past; however, we need to be careful not to exchange old ideological blinders for new ones. While it is easy to criticize with 20/20 hindsight, Central American reality needs to be interpreted in the context of the conditions prevailing at the time. The guerrillas were never the glorified heroes of the 1980s, nor are they the villains of the 1990s. It is my hope that this study contributes to a more balanced assessment of the revolutionary Left's record.

As the title of the book suggests, the study compares El Salvador, Nicaragua, and Guatemala, three countries whose recent history was shaped by revolutionary struggles. I employ a gender perspective to analyze the transformation of the revolutionary Left from guerrilla movements into political parties. I want to inform the reader from the outset that all three countries are not analyzed in the same depth. The Salvadoran experience is at the core of this book. Nicaragua and Guatemala are examined in order to obtain a more comprehensive view and to put the Salvadoran record in context. A wealth of excellent studies has been published which examine the Sandinista record in Nicaragua.[2] Thus, I limit myself to exploring pertinent developments following the 1990 electoral defeat of the revolutionary government. In the case of Guatemala, the analysis has to be preliminary in nature, since the transformation of the Guatemalan guerrilla movement into a political party is so recent.

This book is based to a large extent on interviews. My analysis, therefore, is by necessity informed by the views and recollections of my informants. I have been careful, however, to take every individual's history and role in the struggle into account when drawing my own conclusions. The reader has to trust that more than fifteen years of field research in Central America have honed my analytical skills so that I can reach conclusions that are consistent with reality. I also do not pretend to be an "objective" observer. We all carry our own biases. My own views in favor of a transformation of the Central American societies toward substantive democratic political systems, based on equality for all citizens regardless of their class, gender, or ethnic background, inform my writing. Within this context I have done my best to evaluate and present the record of the revolutionary Left as objectively as possible.

The long-drawn-out military conflicts in Nicaragua, El Salvador, and Guatemala have finally ended. Following the demobilization of the Nicaraguan Resistance in 1990, the Salvadoran and Guatemalan guerrilla forces signed peace accords in 1992 (El Salvador) and 1996 (Guatemala) with their respective governments. In the wake of these agreements, Central America presents a new reality. The focus has shifted from war strategies to the consolidation of emerging democratic structures. The revolutionary Left, one of the main protagonists in the conflict that ravaged the region during the 1980s, now confronts a new challenge: it must demonstrate to its supporters and the general public that it indeed presents a viable political alternative.

The guerrilla movements of El Salvador, Nicaragua, and Guatemala waged their struggle under the banner of social and economic justice for the people. Many women who sought to participate in the construction of a new society joined their fight. Now it is important to establish whether the strong participation of women during the war is being translated into effective representation in the political structures that have emerged or are still developing. I seek to establish the extent to which the revolutionary Left has instituted a gender perspective in its policies, seeking to affect the process of internal and societal democratization in the direction of increased equality between women and men. I maintain that gender equality is a central indicator in assessing whether the revolutionary Left is fulfilling its promises toward its female constituents and continues to fight for a society based on greater justice.

Gender can be understood as a socially produced category, defined in Terrell Carver's terms as "the ways that sex and sexuality become power relations in society."[3] Equality is used as a twofold concept. It includes "formal equality, which can be achieved by means of legislation" and "substantial equality, which aspires to being able to deal with relations between individuals in different original positions."[4] Further, Carver makes a crucial point by emphasizing that "gender is not a synonym for women." Gender analysis is not directed against men but seeks to understand relations between the two sexes. In the prevailing societal relations both women and men are negatively affected. This view also leads to the conclusion that only men and women together can transform the inherited power relations. This conviction is at the core of the current emphasis on "mainstreaming" gender. Sustainable development and democracy require the explicit integration of a gender perspective: women and men have to be in the mainstream of development. I argue that sustainable development requires substantive democracy and can be achieved only if equality between men and women becomes an integral part of societal development.

In this book, I explore the following central research question: How do gender politics illuminate the process of democratic consolidation in Central America? Specifically, I seek to establish whether the revolutionary Left in Nicaragua, El Salvador, and Guatemala has instituted a gender perspective in its policies. My book is a case study of the role political parties play in the process of democratic consolidation. In light of the argument that "one of the principal fault lines of democracy in the hemisphere is to be found in the exclusion of women from participation in the political systems of many countries,"[5] it is essential to assess women's role in Central American politics. I intend to show that women are assuming an increasingly important role in the development of Central American society. Their active participation as combatants during the civil wars that ravaged the region has now been translated into significant representation in political parties and social movements.

The key analytical concepts that I rely on in exploring my central research question are formal versus substantive democracy and formal versus substantive gender equality. These concepts inform my analysis of several key issues that are an integral part of the literature on democratic transition and consolidation. I specifically address the legacy of women's participation in the Central American guerrilla movements, the gender dimension of the peace accords, the conflict between neoliberal policies and democratization, and the transformation of military organizations into political parties with its inherent difficulties in achieving internal democratization. I conclude with an examination of the electoral politics of these newly established political parties.

This study examines gender politics and democratization both at the national level (electoral politics) and at the level of party politics. I maintain that a gendered analysis of democratization is essential to obtaining a meaningful picture of the social and political reality confronting societies in transition toward more democratic forms of government. In order to make such an analysis, the study explores several key questions: Are female party members successful in changing gender relations within the revolutionary Left and in moving toward substantive equality? What strategies do they employ? For evidence that gender relations have undergone change, I examine women's participation in the Central American revolutions and their inclusion or exclusion from the peace accords. I further study the representation of women in party structures, in candidate lists for public office, and in the composition of legislative assemblies. In addition to this focus on quantitative indicators, I look at women's strategies for achieving greater female representation to provide the context in which to examine their struggle to achieve substantive equality. Thus, my study contributes to our understanding of the challenges faced by the ex-combatants of the revolutionary Left as they build political parties to advance the process of democratization in their respective societies. It provides evidence of the crucial role women play in this process. It is a key argument of my study that democracy can not be successfully consolidated without the full incorporation of women into the political process at both party and societal levels. Women's rights have to be recognized, whether in their role as party militants or as citizens. In their role as militants, women contribute to the internal democratization of their parties, which in turn is a precondition for a more inclusive democratic political system. I demonstrate that the increased role of women in party politics can be translated into increased participation for women in decision-making structures at the national level.

A central thesis that runs throughout the book holds that meaningful democratization at the national level requires that the key political actors, that is, political parties, observe the basic norms of internal democracy. The construction of "effective democratic governance depends fundamentally on the quotidian building, exercise, and maintenance of democratic political practice."[6] The revolutionary Left confronts a particularly difficult task because it has to transform itself from authoritarian, hierarchical, military organizations into democratic political parties. The Left has to learn to accept dissent within its ranks. Otherwise, internal division rooted in ideological differences and opposing views on how to increase a party's political strength and gain political power limit and constrain the development of internal party democracy. The struggle to achieve internal democracy is complex. Indeed, the Salvadoran experience indicates that the Left has to navigate between Scylla and Charybdis: the Scylla of repressing dissent and the Charybdis of allowing for "too much democracy," that is, institutionalizing norms and procedures that invite division and are impossible to adhere to at early stages of party development.[7]

Latin America in the 1990s was characterized by two main trends: a continuation of the transition to democracy initiated in the previous decade and economic reforms guided by the dominant paradigm of neoliberalism. Politicians and academics alike, particularly in Western Europe and the United States, have celebrated the "globalization of democracy." The advance of liberal constitutionalism has led some to talk of "the end of history." Yet this celebratory mood is not replicated among the poor majorities in Central America. It is central to ask the important question, what does this "democratization" mean for them. What are the real changes from a substantive as opposed to a formal democratic perspective?

An extensive body of literature on democratization analyzes the "third wave" of democratization, which started in the 1970s.[8] Whereas these studies initially focused on the breakdown of authoritarian regimes, they subsequently emphasized democratic consolidation. Some writers in this tradition tend to equate democracy with liberal constitutionalism. This leads analysts to emphasize the absence or existence of competitive party politics as the main indicator of democratic consolidation instead of looking at the wider distribution of power in society. This narrow focus allows them to ignore gender inequalities.[9] More sophisticated analysts agree that democracy cannot be reduced to the holding of elections.[10] Instead, we need to focus on a comprehensive concept of democracy. Larry Diamond describes such a concept as encompassing "extensive protections for individual and group freedoms, inclusive pluralism in civil society as well as party politics, civilian control over the military, institutions to hold office-holders accountable, and thus a strong rule of law secured through an independent, impartial judiciary."[11] Similarly, Jorge Domínguez and Marc Lindenberg understand the process of democratization as "the shift to free, fair, and competitive elections, held at regular intervals, in the context of guaranteed civil and political rights, responsible government (i.e., accountability of the executive, administrative, and coercive arms of government to elected representatives), and political inclusion (i.e., universal suffrage and nonproscription of parties)."[12] Further, as Felipe Agüero and Jeffrey Stark have emphasized, the concept of consolidation itself is controversial since it "comprised the idea that the democratic nature of post-transition regimes ceased to be problematic."[13] The authors concur with Diamond and Andreas Schedler who seek "to replace the focus from the endurance of situations of precarious democratic credentials to the problems of becoming fully democratic."[14] Still there is a lack of gender analysis.

A growing number of students of democratic transitions maintain that only a gendered analysis of democratization provides a meaningful picture of the social and political reality prevailing in a society in transition. Female political theorists have long recognized that "philosophical discussions of political democracy have been carried on largely in the absence of a discussion of women's rights or the impact of gender inequities on the function of a democratic political order."[15] In the Latin American context, Marysa Navarro and Susan C. Bourque, while acknowledging some positive trends for increased female participation during the last two decades, have argued that "equal access to political participation and leadership remain distant goals for women in the region's newly constituted democracies."[16] The two authors criticize that "in the flurry of scholarly works on redemocratization in Latin America, and more specifically on the subject of democratic consolidation, relatively little attention has been paid to the question of women's participation."[17]

My own work is based on a comprehensive view of democracy and seeks to address key obstacles to democratic consolidation that have been raised in the literature. In particular, I start with the premise that "inclusive pluralism in civil society as well as party politics" requires gender equality. Thus, I seek to fill in some of the lacunae in the literature about democratization.

The emphasis on the challenge of transforming the revolutionary Left from armed movements into democratic political parties, seen from a comparative perspective and through a gender lens, helps us to see Central American reality in a new light. The end to the military conflicts in Nicaragua, El Salvador, and Guatemala adds an important dimension to the region's process of democratization that deserves further study. Few would argue the merits of a move toward more democratic forms of government, efforts to correct the severe economic problems endemic in the region, or peace as opposed to war. In order to evaluate these significant regional developments, however, we need to examine what these changes entail for the people of Central America.

Cynthia Arnson has demonstrated that there is much to learn from a systematic analysis of the peace processes underway in Nicaragua, El Salvador, and Guatemala. In postwar situations, the successful reintegration into society of the former combatants has to be a central part of the process of building peace and democracy.[18] In the Nicaraguan context, Rose Spalding has argued that political space for ex-combatants and the state's capacity to attend to their (and society's) needs are key factors in the peace building process.[19] Most ex-combatants belong to traditionally marginalized sectors and are thus particularly affected by the policies implemented by their respective governments. Further, these groups challenged their governments militarily in order to bring about changes in the political system. Thus it is essential to establish whether the emerging political structures reflect their interests and to what degree the ex-combatants have been able to establish themselves as political actors in the postwar era.

I argue that much of the optimism found in the literature on democratic transitions is premature. It is justified only if we focus on formal democracy.[20] From this perspective, elections held during the 1990s in Central America were crucial steps toward the consolidation of democracy in the region. Yet the institutionalization of electoral democracy is by no means a sufficient guarantee that the emerging political structures will reflect popular interests. Abraham Lowenthal and Jorge Domínguez, recognizing that "democratic political norms and procedures are increasingly common throughout Latin America and the Caribbean," emphasize that "effective democratic governance—the daily practice of constitutional law with stable political institutions that mediate among power contenders, restrain the dominant and protect the weak—is far from consolidated; in many countries it is not even gaining strength. In fact, effective governance has yet to be construed in most countries of the region."[21] Carlos Vilas concurs and affirms that democratization in Central America requires "fuller and more effective [citizen] participation" as well as "a broad-based process of institution-building that includes honest and independent courts, effective safeguards for constitutional guarantees and human rights, and real subordination of the armed forces and security forces to civilian authority."[22] Susanne Jonas argues that in the case of Guatemala, it is this broader political process that has to be the focus of the analysis rather than the occurrence of elections as such.[23] Rachel McCleary affirms this view, arguing that the democratization of Guatemala requires a broadening of political participation.[24]

In order to facilitate and guarantee political participation, the Central American countries need effective political parties that are "autonomous, stable, and powerful enough to express and aggregate social interests."[25] Alan Angell maintains that the evolution of the Latin American Left "will inevitably affect the nature of the transition to democracy, especially in regard to two central challenges: consolidating democratic rule and complying with popular demands for socioeconomic development and distributive justice."[26] The challenge is especially great for the revolutionary Left in Central America, which represents a constituency that once sought to achieve its objectives through violence and has to build new parties in countries with weak party systems. In Guatemala, Edelberto Torres-Rivas argues, the weakness of the political party system "is explained not only by its precarious temporal existence but also by its programmatic void and, even more, by its weak social implantation."[27] Parties tend to be created for electoral purposes, winning parties tend to lack a strong mandate, and the previous governing party is often reduced to insignificance. Torres-Rivas maintains that "the experience of Guatemala is clear proof that democracy cannot function without political parties: government, a sense of order, and institutional stability will elude consolidation unless political parties rigorously shape the collective private sphere."[28] It is essential that political parties "learn from past experiences and introduce democratic practices and procedures into the life of each party."[29]

From a gender perspective, parties have the responsibility for providing avenues for the previously underrepresented sectors of society, particularly women, to be heard. Although many political parties claim to share a commitment to gender equality, there is evidence that women continue to be excluded from important decisions and are underrepresented in party structures. Concerning public office, Georgina Waylen has argued that few women were "being chosen as candidates by political parties in the first competitive elections" following a transition from authoritarian rule.[30] On the other hand, a recent study by the Inter-American Development Bank maintains: "Democratization gives women and other groups formerly excluded from the political process greater opportunity to participate. It opens space for women in governance, within both state and civil institutions."[31] It is time to establish whether these opportunities do indeed exist and are being realized.

In order to advance democratization, the former guerrilla movements have to democratize themselves and effectively "articulate the demands and perspectives emerging from the newly-mobilized sectors."[32] Women are at the core of this new social movement as evidenced by the proliferation of a strong women's movement throughout the region. Women's demands have traditionally been neglected by a male-dominated party system. Starting in the late 1980s, the women's movement has publicly challenged the political parties to incorporate its demands into their political programs. The revolutionary Left has been more receptive than other political forces in heeding women's call for justice. I argue that the fight for gender equality has to be a central part of the program of any modern party on the Left. In the wake of the demise of real socialism, the revolutionary Left needs to reflect on its identity and formulate an agenda for societal change that brings to the fore the essence of its revolutionary heritage—

the fight for a society based on justice for all. At a time when the possibility for immediate radical economic change appears remote, the fight for gender equality is an essential part of a political agenda that demonstrates to its militants and potential new supporters that the Left has not abandoned its ideological principles and represents a viable political alternative. Can the Central American Left rise to this challenge? If it does not, the epitaph of the Left in the new millennium will read no differently from this assessment from the 1990s: "It is true that the Left in the 1990s has no distinctive policies to offer that are politically attractive and represent a true alternative to those of the neo-liberal Right."[33]

Before we examine the record of the Central American revolutionary Left vis-à-vis its female constituents, a brief historical background is useful. The discussion focuses on three parties: the Salvadoran Frente Farabundo Martí para la Liberación Nacional (Farabundo Martí National Liberation Front, or FMLN) the Nicaraguan Frente Sandinista de Liberación Nacional (Sandinista National Liberation Front, or FSLN), and the Guatemalan Unidad Revolucionaria Nacional Guatemalteca (Guatemalan National Revolutionary Unity, or URNG).

The FMLN became a legal political party in 1992, following the Chapúltepec peace accords signed by representatives of the guerrillas and the Salvadoran government. It faced its first electoral test in 1994, when it participated in the first democratic elections in El Salvador's history. The former guerrilla movement obtained a respectable 21 percent of the popular vote, making it the second-largest party after the governing Alianza Republicana Nacionalista (National Republican Alliance, or ARENA). Since 1994, ARENA and the FMLN have been the two main protagonists of the Salvadoran political process. In March 2000, the former guerrillas became the strongest party in the Salvadoran parliament.

The Sandinista movement in Nicaragua enjoyed considerably greater experience as a political actor than its Salvadoran counterpart. It came to power on July 19, 1979, following the overthrow of the Somoza regime. The FSLN governed Nicaragua until the 1990 elections, when it was defeated by a multiparty coalition, the Unión Nacional Opositora (National Opposition Union, or UNO) led by Violeta Barrios de Chamorro. In 1990, the FSLN received 40 percent of the vote and continued to be the strongest single political party in Nicaragua. The UNO later disintegrated, and the

FSLN's main rival in the October 1996 elections was the Alianza Liberal (Liberal Alliance). In that contest, the FSLN failed to regain power and remained the strongest opposition party.

On December 29, 1996, the guerrilla forces of the URNG and the Guatemalan government, headed by president Alvaro Arzú, signed historic peace accords, which ended a conflict that had traumatized Guatemala for thirty-six years. In the wake of the peace accords, the URNG started the process of becoming a legal political party, seeking to provide political representation for its supporters. In October 1998 the URNG was officially registered as a new party. The process of legalization was completed six months later when the URNG held its constituent assembly. Formal recognition, however, was a necessary but by no means sufficient step in the arduous process of transforming the URNG's military, hierarchical structures into those of a democratic party of the people. In October 1999, the new party competed in its first elections, which were won by the right-wing Frente Republicano Guatemalteco (Guatemalan Republican Front, FRG).

The analysis in Chapter One focuses on women's participation in the Central American guerrilla movements. I examine the relative strength of women at the time of demobilization in El Salvador and Guatemala, where records are available, and analyze the various roles women performed during the struggle from a gender perspective. I also explore the reasons that women joined the guerrilla movements and their view of gender relations during the war. The chapter concludes with an account of the human dimension of the war and the process of reintegration into society, emphasizing the difficulties women encountered because of their gender.

Chapter Two presents a gender perspective in discussing the various programs established under the peace accords to facilitate the former combatants' transition into civilian life. The first important test for the armed groups seeking to transform themselves into democratic political parties was the successful integration into society of their combatants and political cadres. From a substantive democratic perspective, it is essential to establish whether the female combatants who had contributed significantly to the war effort were incorporated into civilian life on the same terms as their male counterparts. In the case of El Salvador, I maintain that early instances of overt discrimination and sexism were mostly corrected. However, since the gender differences between male and female FMLN members were not taken into account in the design and implementation of the programs, female militants suffered. In Nicaragua, where the FSLN completed its reintegration as the governing party in the early 1980s, I evaluate the more recent reintegration into society of the Nicaraguan Resistance or Contras, focusing on the controversial property issue. The data for the Resistance are not separated by sex, which makes it impossible to compare the male and female record. Nevertheless, I am able to take women's postwar reality into account, since they form part of the families that were given land. I conclude with an analysis of the ambitious Guatemalan accords and the factors that impeded their full implementation.

Chapter Three provides a grass-roots perspective on the reintegration into society of the Salvadoran revolutionary Left. It gives voice to ex-combatants and FMLN supporters living in three Salvadoran towns: San José Las Flores in the department of Chalatenango, Meanguera in Morazán, and San Esteban Catarina in San Vicente. It is impossible to fully understand the reality of the Salvadoran peace process without listening to the voices of the individuals who participated in the process. I begin the discussion by examining the background of the people interviewed in the three towns. Next I explore their reasons for joining the revolutionary struggle and assess to what degree they have benefited from the reinsertion programs. I then establish whether the former combatants continue to be active in the party and present their views on gender relations during and after the war. I conclude with the beneficiaries' expectations for the future.

Chapter Four explores the challenges posed by the difficult transformation of secretive, hierarchical guerrilla movements into democratic political parties. Internal democratization is a sine qua non if the revolutionary Left is to become a viable political option. Issues related to internal democracy that tend to lead to conflict within the revolutionary Left concern the question of "renewal" and the nature of the political agenda to be pursued. I focus on the Salvadoran case and contrast this experience with Nicaragua and Guatemala. In the case of Nicaragua my analysis is centered on the FSLN's process of internal democratization subsequent to its 1990 electoral defeat. For comparative purposes I also discuss the attempt of the Nicaraguan Resistance to transform itself into a political movement. In Guatemala, I examine the first steps of the URNG, which became a legal political party in May 1999.

The participation of female militants in the emerging party structures is the subject of Chapter Five. The significant female participation in the Central American guerrilla movements raises the question of whether women continue to play an important role now that these movements have evolved into political parties. It is common for female militants to express the fear that women have lost their influence as a result of the transition from the popular revolutionary struggle of the 1970s and 1980s, which was characterized by mass participation, to a return to the traditional party politics in the 1990s, when the grass roots were only activated for election campaigns.[34] What are the consequences of this transition? Have women obtained significant representation in the parties' political structures? What is the impact of the female militants on the formulation of the Left's political projects?

Chapter Six analyzes recent elections in Nicaragua, El Salvador, and Guatemala from a gender perspective. I focus on the revolutionary Left and discuss the record of the governing parties in the three countries to provide a context for the analysis. I examine the strategies used by female militants to increase women's representation on the candidate list for parliament and reflect on the relations between party militants and the women's movement. The discussion of the Guatemalan experience is limited to an overview of the November 1999 elections, the first time that the URNG competed in a national election.

I conclude with evaluation of the Central American revolutionary Left's record concerning its female militants and seek to draw general conclusions from the experience of the three individual countries in my study. My work provides evidence for the crucial role women play in the process of consolidating democracy. Further, a focus on substantive as opposed to formal democracy shows that the democratic consolidation of Central American society is far from complete. I emphasize that only joint efforts by both sexes will lead to meaningful democratization.

THE RESEARCH FOR THIS MANUSCRIPT WAS MADE POSSIBLE by grants from DIAKONIA and Lutherhjälpen in Sweden, the European Commission, and the substantial support provided by Virginia Tech in the form of numerous grants and several teaching releases. I am especially grateful for the support the two Swedish organizations have given to my work. In particular, I want to express my gratitude to Tomas Jonsson from Lutherhjälpen and Ewa Widén and Ia Katarina Adolfsson from DIAKONIA-Sweden.

I want to thank all of my informants who have shared their insights and given me their valuable time. Sofía Montenegro, María Teresa Blandón, Nidia Díaz, Deysi Cheyne, Lorena Peña, Ana Gertrudis Méndez ("Lety"), Salvador Sánchez, Francisco Jovel, Gerson Martínez, Facundo Guardado, Luz Méndez, and Ana Leticia Aguilar were especially helpful. I am particularly indebted to Ana Francis Góngora, a knowledgeable and astute observer of Salvadoran reality for her contribution to the chapter on the Salvadoran grass roots. Ana Francis headed a team of researchers that carried out most of the interviews in the three towns discussed in Chapter Three. We conceived the questions together, and Ana Francis wrote summaries based on the interviews. In this particular chapter, her contribution goes beyond the work of a research assistant and comes closer to that of a coauthor. I would also like to thank my copy editor, Kennie Lyman, for an excellent job on the manuscript.

Finally, I am grateful to my wife, Jane Goette, and my son, Carl David, for understanding that I had to be away from home on numerous occasions. It is their support and love that inspires me.

Excerpts from Chapters One, Two, Four, and Five originally appeared in "Gender Equality in the Salvadoran Transition," *Latin American Perspectives* 26, no. 2 (March 1999), © 1999 Latin American Perspectives, and in *Género y Cultura en América Latina*, edited by María Luisa Tarrés (Mexico City: El Colegio de México, 1998).

An earlier version of Chapter Six appeared in "Gender Equality and Electoral Politics on the Left: A Comparison of El Salvador and Nicaragua," *Journal of Interamerican Studies and World Affairs* 40, no. 1 (Spring 1998). A Spanish version of this material was published as "Izquierda revolucionaria, igualdad de género y democratización: una comparación entre El Salvador y Nicaragua," *Pensamiento Propio* 3 (January–April 1998).

Excerpts from several chapters were also included in my contribution to *Radical Women in Latin America: Left and Right*, edited by Victoria González and Karen Kampwirth (University Park: Penn State University Press, 2001), and in "Democracy and Its Discontents: Life in Post-conflict Central America," *Development* 43, no. 3 (September 2000).

This material is protected by copyright and is used here with permission from the publishers.

My work has been conducted with the financial assistance of the European Union. The views expressed in this book are my own and in no way reflect the official opinion of the European Union.

Methodological Note

My analysis is based on field research carried out over a number of years. This research was not conducted by "remote-control." I have visited all three countries numerous times and have personally observed many of the events I discuss. In many instances my work is based on participant observation. I interviewed 103 key officials in the three countries. These were structured interviews that I taped. Thirty-three of these officials were interviewed at least twice (several up to five times) in order to get their perspective over time. In addition, I coordinated a team of interviewers who carried out a survey of 200 ex-combatants in El Salvador.

Field research has its own perils. Interrogation for several hours by the Salvadoran police, the contraction of severe hepatitis, and the theft of important interview materials in both Nicaragua and Guatemala need to be absorbed with stoicism. The writing for this book was initially informed by field visits to Nicaragua during the Sandinista revolution. I worked in Nicaragua from October 1984 to July 1985 as a guest professor and conducted research from December 1985 to February 1986 as well as July–August 1988, July–August 1989, and November–December 1989. Following the 1990 electoral defeat of the Sandinistas, I observed meetings and conducted interviews during June and July 1992, August 1993, January 1996, January and February 1997, November 1997, June 1998, and February 2001. Field research in Guatemala was carried out in June 1989, July 1993, February 1997, April 1997, November 1997, March 1999, and May 2001. Finally, I began field research in El Salvador in June 1988 while the war was still going on. Subsequently, I made field visits in July–August 1993, March 1994, April–May 1995, December 1995, February 1996, April 1996, February 1997, March 1997, November 1997, June 1998, March 1999, March 2000, and February 2001.

Unless otherwise noted, all translations of both written and oral material are mine.

Acronyms

AMNLAE	Asociación de Mujeres Nicaragüenses, Luisa Amanda Espinoza (Association of Nicaraguan Women)
ANN	Alianza Nueva Nación (New Nation Alliance, Guatemala)
ARENA	Alianza Republicana Nacionalista (National Republican Alliance, El Salvador)
CIAV	Comisión Internacional de Apoyo y Verificación (International Commission on Support and Verification, Nicaragua)
DIA	Desarrollo Integral Auténtico (Authentic Integral Development, Guatemala)
DRU	Dirección Revolucioniaria Unificada (Unified Revolutionary Directorate, El Salvador)
EGP	Ejército Guerrillero de los Pobres (Guerrilla Army of the Poor, Guatemala)
ERP	Ejército Revolucionario del Pueblo (Revolutionary Army of the People, El Salvador)
FAL	Fuerzas Armadas de Liberación (Armed Forces of Liberation, the armed forces of the Communist Party, El Salvador)
FDNG	Frente Democrático Nueva Guatemala (New Guatemala Democratic Front)

FMLN   Frente Farabundo Martí para la Liberación Nacional
                (Farabundo Martí National Liberation Front,
                El Salvador)

FPL   Fuerzas Populares de Liberación (Popular Forces
                of Liberation, El Salvador)

FRG   Frente Republicano Guatemalteco (Guatemalan
                Republican Front)

FSLN   Frente Sandinista de Liberación Nacional
                (Sandinista National Liberation Front,
                Nicaragua)

MAM   Movimiento de Mujeres "Mélida Anaya Montes"
                (Mélida Anaya Montes Women's Movement)

MINUSAL   Misión de Naciones Unidas en El Salvador (United
                Nations Mission in El Salvador)

MRS   Movimiento de Renovación Sandinista (Sandinista
                Reform Movement, Nicaragua)

OEA   Organización de Estados Americanos (Organization
                of American States)

ONUSAL   Misión de Observadores de las Naciones Unidas
                en El Salvador (United Nations Observer Mission
                in El Salvador)

ORPA   Organización Revolucionaria del Pueblo en Armas
                (Revolutionary Organization of Armed Citizens,
                Guatemala)

PAN   Partido de Avanzada Nacional (Party for National
                Advancement, Guatemala)

PD   Partido Demócrata (Democratic Party, El Salvador)

PGT   Partido Guatemalteco de Trabajo (Guatemalan Labor
                Party)

PRN	Partido Resistencia Nicaragüense (Nicaraguan Resistance Party)
PRTC	Partido Revolucionario de Trabajadores Centroamericanos (Revolutionary Party of Central American Workers, El Salvador)
PSD	Partido Social Demócrata (Social Democratic Party, El Salvador)
RN	Resistencia Nacional (National Resistance, El Salvador)
UNAMG	Unión Nacional de Mujeres Guatemaltecas (National Union of Guatemalan Women)
URNG	Unidad Revolucionaria Nacional Guatemalteca (Guatemalan National Revolutionary Unity)

After the Revolution

I

The Gender Composition of
the Central American Guerrilla Movements

War is men's business and as hard as women try,
they will never play the same role.
—Facundo Guardado, FMLN leader

In his comprehensive study of Latin American guerrilla movements, Timothy Wickham-Crowley found that female participation during the first wave of revolutions (1956–70) varied greatly. At the leadership level, exclusively male structures were not uncommon, although in some instances women represented up to 20 percent of the leadership. There were no cases of "female predominance in either numbers or power within a movement [and not] a single case of a female peasant joining as an arms-bearing guerrilla."[1]

It was obviously the Cuban revolution that shaped the first revolutionary wave. Che Guevara, a key protagonist of the Cuban struggle, codified the lessons of guerrilla warfare learned in the Sierra Maestra in his book, *Guerrilla Warfare*. It became the bible for a generation of revolutionaries. Che recognized the importance of the potential contribution women could make to the revolutionary struggle. He emphasized that "the part that the woman can play in the development of a revolutionary process is of extraordinary importance."[2] Indeed, a number of women held leadership positions in the early days of the Cuban war. In 1957, the urban leadership represented in the National Directorate of the July 26 movement included Celia Sánchez, Vílma Espín, and Haydée Santamaría. At that time, Che

himself had yet to join the exclusive rank of the Directorate.[3] The first female volunteer to join the guerrilla forces in the mountains in July 1957
was seventeen-year-old Oniria Gutiérrez.[4]

In Che's view, "The woman is capable of performing the most difficult
tasks, of fighting beside the men; and despite current belief, she does not
create conflicts of a sexual type in the troops. In the rigorous combatant life
the woman is a companion who brings the qualities appropriate to her sex,
but she can work the same as a man and she can fight; she is weaker but no
less resistant than he. She can perform every class of combat task that a
man can at a given moment, and on certain occasions in the Cuban struggle she performed a relief role."[5] In the Cuban context of the 1950s, in
which societal relations were characterized by machismo, this was an enlightened position. Che maintained that "naturally the combatant women
are a minority."[6] He saw the primary role of women as being in "communications between different combatant forces," and other support roles,
such as teachers, social workers, and nurses attending to the guerrilla fighters and the population living in the zone of operations. Guevara's traditional gender views come through when he argues for women to perform
the "habitual tasks of peacetime . . . The woman as cook can greatly improve the diet and, furthermore, it is easier to keep her in these domestic
tasks; one of the problems in guerrilla bands is that all works of a civilian
character are scorned by those who perform them; they are constantly trying to get out of these tasks in order to enter into forces that are actively in
combat."[7]

Central American women encountered the same stereotypes when they
joined the Central American revolutionary movements in the 1970s.
Much had changed since the early days of the Cuban revolution, yet the
basic challenges remained the same. It took fifteen years following the triumph of the Cuban revolution before women started to participate in
greater numbers and served as regular combatants. The ascendancy of the
international feminist movement provided a context that was conducive
to increased interest in the role of women in revolutionary struggles. The
success of the Sandinista revolution in 1979 highlighted the significant role
women had played in the insurrection. It was reported that at the high
point of the Nicaraguan insurrection, women constituted between 25 and
30 percent of the combatants.

The Central American guerrilla movements should be held to a high standard in terms of their position vis-à-vis the female members. After all, they thought of themselves as a vanguard representing the values of a new society. However, it is important to keep in mind when examining gender relations during the war period that the struggle for women's rights was not a factor motivating women to join the Central American guerrilla movements; and, in the final analysis, the men and women of the FMLN, FSLN and URNG embodied and reflected the prevailing culture.

Women in the FMLN: Social Justice versus Gender Equality

In El Salvador, the guerrillas opposed the hegemony of the United States and its Salvadoran allies. Until 1995, the FMLN was made up of five distinct groups: the Fuerzas Populares de Liberación (Popular Forces of Liberation, or FPL); the Ejército Revolucionario del Pueblo (Revolutionary Army of the People, or ERP); the armed forces of the Communist Party, the Fuerzas Armadas de Liberación (Armed Forces of Liberation, or FAL); the Resistencia Nacional (National Resistance, or RN); and the Partido Revolucionario de Trabajadores Centroamericanos (Revolutionary Party of Central American Workers, or PRTC). Tommie Sue Montgomery and other students of the Salvadoran revolution have maintained that in the 1980s women represented 30 percent of the FMLN's combatants and about 40 percent of the total membership.[8] There have been long-standing arguments over the reliability of the figures cited in studies assessing women's participation in revolutionary movements, since they could not be independently verified. In the Salvadoran case, we can at last have an informed debate, because we now have reliable data.

Upon the signing of the peace accords, the FMLN forces were supposed to demobilize in a five-stage process between May 1 and October 31, 1992. The demobilization was supervised by the United Nations Observer Mission in El Salvador (ONUSAL), which processed and registered the FMLN membership that had been concentrated in camps throughout the country. FMLN members were registered according to their status as combatants, wounded noncombatants, or *políticos* (FMLN militants who were engaged in political work on behalf of the guerrillas both in El Salvador and abroad). Due to various delays, the combatants were actually demobilized between

Table 1.1   Gender Composition of FMLN Membership by Demobilization Category

Category	Women	%	Men	%	Total	%
Combatants	2,485	55.3	6,067	57.7	8,552	57.0
Wounded Noncombatants	549	12.2	1,925	18.3	2,474	16.5
Political Personnel	1,458	32.5	2,525	24.0	3,983	26.5
Total	4,492	100.0	10,517	100.0	15,009	100.0

Source: ONUSAL, Proceso de desmovilicación del personal del FMLN (San Salvador: Imprenta El Estudiante, n.d.).

June 30 and December 15, 1992, while the wounded noncombatants were registered between October 15 and November 20, 1993. The políticos were processed on March 25, 1993.[9] Their demobilization, not foreseen in the original accords, was negotiated by the FMLN in order to be able to provide these cadres with some minimal material benefits.

ONUSAL collected a variety of data regarding the FMLN members, including their affiliation with one of the five groups making up the FMLN, their sex, educational level, age, and place of origin. According to the 1994 data, a total of 15,009 FMLN members were registered: 8,552 combatants, 2,474 wounded noncombatants, and 3,983 political cadres. The number of women in the FMLN was 4,492.

Some caution is in order when examining the ONUSAL figures, since knowledgeable sources report that about 10 to 15 percent of the FMLN's membership was not processed.[10] There were a variety of reasons an individual might decide not to register. Several high-ranking FMLN officials, including members of the FMLN National Council, chose not to go through official channels because they did not want to be perceived as taking advantage of the benefits every registered person was entitled to. Other militants were not prepared to reveal themselves as such after having successfully infiltrated state institutions during the war. By far the most important reason was simple fear. Many former combatants had little faith in the viability of the peace accords. Having survived years of clandestine struggle, they were understandably reluctant to be officially registered as having been part of the guerrilla movement. The memories of death lists of "subversives" that were read by the late Major Roberto d'Aubuisson and others on national TV was still too fresh in their minds. With these limitations,

Table 1.2   Gender Composition of FMLN Groups

Group	Women	%	Men	%	Total	%	Women as % of Total
ERP	1,156	25.7	2,774	26.4	3,930	26.2	29.4
FAL	734	16.3	1,516	14.4	2,250	15.0	32.6
FPL	1,397	31.1	3,685	35.0	5,082	33.8	27.5
PRTC	356	7.9	892	8.5	1,248	8.3	28.5
RN	849	18.9	1,650	15.7	2,499	16.7	34.0
Total	4,492	100.0	10,517	100.0	15,009	100.0	29.9

Source: ONUSAL, *Proceso de desmovilicación del personal del FMLN.*

the ONUSAL data reveal that women made up from 27 to 34 percent of the membership of the five armies (Table 1.2). In terms of the three demobilization categories, women were strongest among the political cadres, where they represented 36.6 percent.

Table 1.3 provides a detailed picture of the FMLN's gender composition by FMLN group and demobilization category. Of the 8,552 combatants that were processed, 2,485 or 29.1 percent were female. Among the five groups, the Resistencia Nacional had the highest percentage of women in its ranks with 35.2 percent. The Partido Revolucionario de Trabajadores Centroamericanos had the lowest rate of participation with about 24 percent. The Ejército Revolucionario del Pueblo and the Fuerzas Populares de Liberación had numerically the largest number of women in their ranks, 754 and 696 respectively, and ranked in the middle in terms of the percentage of women in their ranks. Finally, the armed forces of the Communist Party, the Fuerzas Armadas de Liberación had a female participation rate of 30.1 percent and a total of 334 women fighters.

In the case of the FMLN políticos, the data indicate that 3,983 FMLN members were processed as being part of political structures. Among them were 1,458 women, representing 36.6 percent of the total. Female participation ranged from a high of 40 percent in the case of the ERP, to 34 percent for the FPL. The FPL had by far the largest number of políticos. Their political cadres included 951 men and 488 women, compared with 615 male and 381 female políticos for the FAL, which had the second largest overall number. The dominance of FPL and FAL members among the

Table 1.3   Gender Composition of Demobilized FMLN Members by FMLN Group
and Demobilization Category

Group	Women	%	Men	%	Total	%	Women as % of Total
A: FMLN Combatants							
ERP	754	30.3	1,899	31.3	2,653	31.0	28.4
FAL	334	13.4	776	12.8	1,110	13.0	30.1
FPL	696	28.0	1,887	31.1	2,583	30.2	26.9
PRTC	154	6.1	498	8.2	652	7.6	23.6
RN	547	22.2	1,007	16.6	1,554	18.2	35.2
Total	2,485	100.0	6,067	100.0	8,552	100.0	29.0
B: FMLN Political Personnel							
ERP	185	12.7	278	11.0	463	11.6	40.0
FAL	381	26.1	615	24.4	996	25.0	38.3
FPL	488	33.5	951	37.7	1,439	36.1	33.9
PRTC	168	11.5	261	10.3	429	10.8	39.2
RN	236	16.2	420	16.6	656	16.5	36.0
Total	1,458	100.0	2,525	100.0	3,983	100.0	36.6
C: FMLN Wounded Noncombatants							
ERP	217	39.5	597	31.0	814	32.9	26.6
FAL	19	3.5	125	6.5	144	5.8	13.2
FPL	213	38.8	847	44.0	1,060	42.8	20.1
PRTC	34	6.2	133	6.9	167	6.8	20.4
RN	66	12.0	223	11.6	289	11.7	22.8
Total	549	100.0	1,925	100.0	2,474	100.0	22.2

Source: ONUSAL, Proceso de desmovilicación del personal del FMLN.

FMLN's political personnel was an important basis upon which these two groups built their strong positions within the political party that emerged out of the guerrilla movement.

In addition to the combatants and the políticos, 2,474 wounded non-combatants were processed by ONUSAL. Of these, 549 (22.2%) were women. This latest category comprised "noncombatant personnel who had been injured in the war and belonged to the FMLN."[11] According to Gerson Martínez (Orlando Quinteros legalized this nom de guerre), a senior

FMLN official, some members of this group were not FMLN militants but civilians who had been caught in the crossfire without having expressed negative or positive views about the guerrillas.[12] The various FMLN groups apparently included them out of a sense of responsibility, thus making them eligible to receive some benefits.

When examining the gender composition of the five groups at the time of demobilization in detail, it is important to keep in mind that the data refer to the rank order of the five groups in 1992. The relative rankings tended to change somewhat over the course of the war. Norma Guevara, a senior FMLN official, proudly maintained that in the mid-1980s the FAL had the most female members in its ranks, while some students of the Salvadoran revolution argued that the ERP had the greatest number of female combatants and officers.[13] The different views can be attributed largely to the particular statistics that are being used. According to 1993 internal ONUSAL data, the ERP had indeed the largest *overall number of female combatants* (754), whereas the Communist Party's 334 female fighters represented the *second highest percentage of female combatants* (second only to the RN) among the five groups. Thus the FAL forces could easily have had the highest percentage of women at some point in the war.

The data are consistent with the estimates of the 1980s on women's participation as combatants. The estimate was 30 percent compared with the actual 29.1 percent at the time of demobilization. The ONUSAL figure of 29.9 percent women members, however, does not accord with the wartime claim that women represented 40 percent of the FMLN membership.

Another aspect of the data on the FMLN combatants deserves further scrutiny: If we examine the age distribution of male and female members, it is evident that not all of them were arms-bearing fighters. According to 1993 ONUSAL data, 60 FMLN members processed as combatants (0.75%) were younger than thirteen, while 170 (2.1%) were older than sixty. It is reasonable to assume that at least those over sixty years of age did not serve as armed combatants.

The group of combatants over sixty years of age included 41 females. The FPL had 4 women fighters at the biblical age of ninety-two. The ERP had only 4 women over sixty, and the PRTC's records show 1 ninety-one-year-old female combatant. The RN had 22 women over sixty, the oldest being eighty-five, and the FAL lists showed 10 women over sixty, with the

Table 1.4   Age Distribution of FMLN Combatants

A: Distribution of Combatants by Gender

Age Group	Female	Male	Total	%
0–13	31	29	60	0.75
14–20	972	1,859	2,831	35.15
21–25	527	1,055	1,582	19.64
26–30	342	699	1,041	12.93
31–35	169	563	732	9.09
36–40	128	440	568	7.05
41–45	69	349	418	5.19
46–50	60	233	293	3.64
51–55	37	161	198	2.46
56–60	25	135	160	1.99
61–70	27	97	124	1.54
71–80	8	22	30	0.37
81–90	1	3	4	0.05
91–93	5	7	12	0.15
Total	2,401	5,652	8,053	100%

B: Distribution of Female Combatants by Group

Age Group	ERP	FAL	FPL	PRTC	RN	Total
0–13	10	5	3	3	10	31
14–20	276	127	359	74	136	972
21–25	188	59	140	35	105	527
26–30	136	41	69	16	80	342
31–35	63	18	39	9	40	169
36–40	40	29	12	5	42	128
41–45	19	8	5	5	32	69
46–50	61	1	6	4	33	60
51–55	7	9	2	1	18	37
56–60	4	5	2	0	14	25
61–70	4	9	—	—	14	27
71–80	—	1	—	—	7	8
81–90	—	—	—	—	1	1
91–93	—	—	4	1	—	5
Total	753	322	641	153	532	2,401

Source: ONUSAL.

Note: Data for 453 combatants were not available.

oldest being seventy-two. Older guerrilla supporters were not the exclusive domain of the FMLN. In the case of Guatemala's URNG, demobilized personnel included a number of senior citizens. Indeed, 77 combatants or political cadres[14] were older than sixty-one, while 7 had passed the age of seventy-six.[15]

The Salvadoran records also indicate that a one-year-old baby and a six-year-old girl were processed as FAL combatants, while the RN had a five-year-old female fighter, and the ERP also demobilized a one-year-old baby girl. The infants were obviously children who were born in one of the fifteen sites where FMLN members were assembled to await demobilization. In the case of the young children, it seems likely that combatants, lacking alternative child-care options, had brought them along to the camps.

Some FMLN officials have questioned whether there were indeed "biblical-age women" in the ranks. Nidia Díaz (María Marta Valladares legalized this nom de guerre), one of the top PRTC officials and then the FMLN's vice-coordinator, claimed that she had absolutely no knowledge of a ninety-one-year-old woman in the ranks of the PRTC. In this instance, it could easily be that a civilian collaborator was demobilized as a combatant. The apparent discrepancies could also be the result of the precariousness or nonexistence of a decent civil register in the rural areas of El Salvador.[16] This makes it possible for people to invent their ages. The difficulties in the data collection process are conveyed in the following story told by ONUSAL officials: a fifty-five-year-old man, when asked his age and date of birth during the verification, answered that "only the midwife could know it, since she had helped him to come into this world."[17] In short, the data have some limitations. Gerson Martínez explained that women over ninety years old were processed as combatants at their insistence so that they would be recognized as having actively participated in the guerrilla struggle. A typical argument would be: "We have cooked and cared for the muchachos [boys] for many years. We have earned the right to be considered combatants."

In terms of the overall numbers of male and female fighters, the very old and very young FMLN members who were processed as combatants are not significant. Almost 90 percent of all female combatants and 82 percent of all male combatants were between fourteen and forty years old. Thus, the excellent data we have in the Salvadoran case permit us to deepen our understanding of the social composition of guerrilla movements. It is obvious that in the eyes of the guerrillas themselves, the category of "combatant" was not limited to the arms-bearing fighter. Instead, as in any other army in the world, it included males and females in support roles. Yet many academic sources discussing women's participation in guerrilla movements distinguish between arms-bearing combatants and women in support roles. The latter group is considered part of the guerrilla membership but is not included in the estimates of the combatants. This artificial distinction tends to obscure and denigrate the important role played by women and men who provided logistical support.

During the first wave of Latin American guerrilla movements (1956–70), female participation was indeed largely restricted to the traditional roles of women as cooks, caretakers for the wounded, or messengers. It appears that when women started to participate in combat, some observers considered it important to distinguish between actual fighters and those women in support positions in order to stress the change that had occurred. Medardo González, one of the FMLN's early members, who held the position of secretary of organization, estimated the number of arms-bearing female combatants to have ranged between 15 and 20 percent.[18]

His views were supported by the findings of a representative study of one third of all women registered by ONUSAL. According to this survey somewhat less than 30 percent of the women affiliated with the FMLN during the war worked in the kitchen, while 15 percent were engaged in health-related tasks. About 15 percent were actual fighters with an additional 11 percent acting in support roles. The remaining 40 percent had tasks of a different type.[19] Finally, it is significant that based on the gender composition of those FMLN fighters over sixty years old, more men were in support positions than women.

The controversy over the part female combatants played is part of the larger question of gender relations during the war. There is a tendency among some protagonists and students of the Central American revolutions to glorify male-female relations during the war. Although there were important changes in gender relations, on the whole, the subordination of women prevalent in prewar society continued. When women speak freely of their participation in the war, critical testimonies tend to predominate.

FMLN supporters in North America and Europe have expressed admiration for the guerrilla movement for having shown creativity and courage in resisting the Salvadoran army and the United States. This admiration appears to have extended to the FMLN's handling of gender relations during the war. In contrast to the guerrilla movement's success in the military and political sphere, however, there were "serious deficiencies in the discourse and practices of the FMLN in internal matters, [such as] the private sphere of life, gender relations, and women's subordination."[20] FMLN commanders experienced great difficulties when forced to reflect on gender relations in the camps. They believed in a "revolutionary utopia," which pretended "that the equality desired for the future existed already in the revolutionary nuclei, where all types of differences were decreed eliminated, for example, those existing between men and women . . . With such a conviction, the leadership of the guerrilla groups rejected the validity of an analysis [focusing] on the different situations of men and women within the group."[21]

With few exceptions, women linked up with the FMLN out of a sense of social justice, to escape the repression of the army and police forces, or because a family member had joined or was in the process of joining. Often women joined for a combination of these reasons. This is exemplified in the statement of a former combatant who joined the FMLN with her family:

Really, it was my father who joined in 1979 when I was eight years old. I remember that he started to work clandestinely, specifically with the FPL. In 1980, when I was nine years, people started to notice that we belonged to this group [the FPL] and we were forced to leave this place. That is, we had to leave our houses because there was already a lot of repression developing against my family. They knew we were guerrillas, and thus the repression began and we had to leave our place of origin, and we started to flee. The operations [search and destroy missions] started, and we had to run. The war began in serious. I was always with my mother and my three sisters and for three years we walked around together in the zone of conflict and then, well, we stayed with the Front.[22]

After joining the FMLN, female combatants were confronted with traditional gender views. Women faced these difficult situations alone. This isolation was conducive to the belief that they deserved to be mistreated due to personal failures and weaknesses. The following testimony is representative:

> During the war, we, the women, were always thought of as a supporting force. Even when we assumed military command positions, it was difficult for us to get the top command. In my case, for a long time, I interpreted this as being my problem or a problem with me, and not a problem that happened to all women. I continued to feel this way when I did the work and others reaped the rewards. I saw it in my case but also in the case of other women. Well, for example, a women's organization that emerged in Guazapa in 1982 provided impressive logistical support in the military arena. An important military operation took place in which these women played a decisive role. At the hour of the military communiqués, which served as both propaganda and moments of recognition, they were not mentioned. This bothered me a lot. Still I did not make the connection that this was a problem of female discrimination.

Those women who did manage to obtain a leadership position in the military hierarchy paid a high price. The demands were different on men and women. The situation was particularly difficult for female leaders who had family responsibilities:

> Not only did one have to do everything right, but one had to demonstrate that one knew how to do it right. I remember that I was a lot tougher, that is more demanding than other [male] leaders so that the combatants would respect me, so they would accept me as the leader. In general, the men didn't need to be tougher or more demanding to have their leadership respected.
>
> I think that the breaking of my role as a mother tore me up. To be a leader at that time, or to assume a command position or tasks of military leadership was in absolute contradiction to being a mother. It is not like this for men because the father-son relationship is different in this society. I wish it would be equal, but it is not. I remember this price I had to pay. On one occasion one of my daughters had broken her arm, and I was notified that the arm was broken and that she called for me from the hospital. I asked the leadership for permission to leave and they told me: "Look, you know that

none of us can leave here without authorization of the *compañeros* that are at the Guazapa volcano. Since within a month we will go to a meeting with them, it's better to wait." Well, O.K., I arrived at the meeting—it was in the western part of the country—full of hope that I would get permission to go and see my children. It had been almost four years since I had seen them. I state this and they told me: "Well, you have the right to leave, but we have a problem. We have to open a logistical corridor in the West. If you leave, the strategic work to open the corridor is halted. But we can not deny you permission. You decide." I remember how I cried that night and I said to my-self: "What do I do, oh, what do I do, I want to go and see my daughter. For so long has she had a broken arm." But there was the urgent task. And be-sides, I knew the price I would have to pay if I opted to go. So I stayed. I couldn't see my daughter until a year later.

Unlike its Nicaraguan counterpart, the FMLN did not explicitly address women's rights in its early programs and pronouncements. FMLN militants attribute this to several factors: strong religious influence, the predomi-nantly rural background of the FMLN base, and the culture of machismo that inhibited even strong female leaders. Other studies have confirmed that religion, in the form of Liberation Theology, had a considerable im-pact on gender relations within Central American guerrilla movements. Liberation Theology, a rethinking of traditional Catholic doctrine, was popular throughout Central America. It resulted from the 1968 meeting of the Latin American bishops in Medellín, Colombia. The bishops spoke of the need to liberate human kind from cultural, social, economic, and po-litical slavery, declaring that it was the role of the Church to take "a pref-erential option for the poor." They broadened the concept of sin to include an entire social system if it did not guarantee the right to a decent standard of living for all people. Liberation Theology led many to criticize the cap-italist system and support guerrilla movements that fought to bring about change to unjust economic and political conditions. Norma Vázquez and her colleagues have reported that "although it had a very positive influence in many spheres, in the case of issues related to sexuality and maternity, it was very conservative, especially in its impact on the role of women."[23]

In addition to these factors, women in the FMLN lacked organization. In the early days of the war few women participated in the guerrilla movement, and those who did were not organized around women's issues. This changed in the late 1970s, when women's groups emerged within the various Salvadoran guerrilla groups. For example, Tula Alvarenga, the wife of the FPL's eminent leader Salvador Cayetano Carpio, favored women's organizing efforts. She was marginalized, however, following the assassination of Mélida Anaya Montes and the 1983 suicide of Carpio, who was accused of having ordered the murder of his number two commander. As a consequence of these events, the FPL women's group first split into two and eventually dissolved.

In general, female FMLN commanders did not focus their energy or thoughts on women's rights. Mélida Anaya Montes, the most eminent woman during the early years of the struggle, is remembered for her lack of support for women's organizing. "Maybe she was in the first meeting of AMES [a precursor of FMLN women's groups]. But after that I never saw her in the work that we did," said one key female FMLN organizer. Even though some female militants considered Anaya Montes supportive, it was clear that women's issues were not high on her list of priorities. Nidia Díaz and Ana Guadalupe Martínez, two other high-ranking commanders, were thought of in the same light: "Even in 1987, 1988, the highest ranking female FMLN leaders did not listen to one on the woman's question." Women who served in leadership positions at the intermediate level were no different in their attitudes. Those female leaders who were outspoken in their support for women's rights tended to have spent some time outside of the country, where they were exposed to and influenced by the international dialogue on women's rights.

The early efforts of female organizing in the FMLN were greatly influenced by external factors. FMLN cadres engaged in political work in other countries, particularly Mexico, were exposed to the international discussion on women's rights. They, in turn, talked to their compañeras who served as urban commandos or were active in guerrilla forces operating in the Salvadoran countryside. Opportunities for such meetings arose when the political cadres entered the country or the combatants left El Salvador for periods of training or recuperation. One political cadre remembers that these conversations "were very tenuous, very soft. I was talking with several female FMLN leaders in Mexico in order to motivate them, so they would be sensitized to the woman's question and I was not heard." It was common that FMLN militants who tried to introduce a gender perspective met with great resistance. "I gave training exercises with a gender perspective. There were two or three workshops where the FMLN women asked me to leave because they thought I wanted to divide the revolution, since in what I was saying was a gender analysis that was not compatible with class analysis. My reasoning, on the other hand, was that the woman's situation has to be looked at from a class and a gender perspective. Well, the compañeras still remember that at that time they pulled me out of the workshops."

Women's special needs were rarely taken into account in the mountains. For example, it is reported that male commanders showed little understanding of why precious financial resources should be allocated for the purchase of articles of female hygiene. On the other hand, birth control pills were readily available, since they were essential to the FMLN's policy on reproductive choice. In general, sexual relations between combatants were also characterized by a double standard for male and female behavior. "For example, the male military leaders seduced, or used their power, or it was easier for them to establish sexual relations. For the women, it was not like this. The fact that a woman in a leadership position would slip up was grounds for a scandal that had costs when her political performance was evaluated."

According to the testimony of many female combatants, sexual harassment was a common phenomenon for the women who served in the guerrilla forces. Significantly, it was not only frequently condoned by superiors, but some FMLN leaders were among the transgressors. Female combatants tolerated this difficult climate with the help of a variety of rationalizations. Some claimed that things would improve after the war with a return to normalcy, arguing that the war situation facilitated the hostile climate. With only a few women in any particular camp, there was great pressure on them to give in to demands for sexual favors. Men and women tended to rationalize their behavior with the thought, "I might die tomorrow." Women, in particular, had few alternatives to dealing with their difficult situations in a stoic fashion. For the majority, packing up and leaving the FMLN was not a viable option. In some instances sexual abuses were denounced, but the individuals in question were almost never punished. Morena Herrera recounted such an incident: "In 1987 I lodged a complaint that a Comman-

der had sexually harassed a compañera over a long period of time. I brought
it to the attention of the highest authority of the organization, and they told
me that they would take the necessary measures, but they never did."

Very few combatants dared to challenge FMLN authorities so openly,
and most decided to remain silent. Only in the final days of the Salvadoran war, and then only in the case of a limited number of female FMLN
members, was the fight for social justice expected to include a conscious
emphasis on the struggle for gender equality.

The Female Insurrection in Nicaragua

The most widely reported estimates of female involvement in the Sandinista movement in Nicaragua state that women constituted between 25
and 30 percent of the combatants.[24] Patricia Chuchryk, for example, has
maintained that in Nicaragua the "rate of women's participation in armed
combat during the insurrection was the highest of any Latin American
revolutionary movement."[25] Unfortunately there are no hard data to support these estimates. While it is clear that women participated in great
numbers in the revolutionary struggle, the FSLN never released official figures on the composition of its guerrilla force at the time of demobilization.
For this reason, we are left with considerable variations in the reported estimates of female participation.

Carlos Vilas, basing his estimates on a review of Sandinista combatants'
death certificates, found that women constituted only 6.6 percent of Sandinista forces.[26] His findings differ considerably from the predominant image of a force that was one-third female. Two observations are helpful in
reconciling this conflict: One point, already made earlier, has to do with
the concept of *combatant*. Vilas's data obviously emphasize arms-bearing
combatants, while the definition of combatant employed by most other
studies tends to be much broader and includes support personnel. Secondly,
it is important to distinguish between women's participation during the final insurrectional phase and their involvement in the revolutionary struggle in general. Almost all studies reporting a 30 percent participation rate
refer to the final stage of the struggle.[27]

Whereas women did participate in significant numbers and came to occupy important leadership positions by the later stages of the conflict, fe-

male participation in the early years of the revolutionary struggle was very limited. This becomes evident when one listens to the accounts of women who joined the FSLN early on. They share the view that few men considered it important to incorporate women into the guerrilla movement.[28] Women who were sympathetic to the FSLN's revolutionary goals started to organize in the 1960s. In 1963, a group of women sharing a left-wing ideology formed the Federación Democrática (Democratic Federation). These were mainly militants from the Socialist Party and female students who supported the FSLN.[29] In 1967, women organized the Alianza Patriótica Nicaragüense (Nicaraguan Patriotic Alliance), which served as a recruiting pool for FSLN cadres.

In 1967, the FSLN leadership decided to integrate women into the rural guerrilla forces.[30] Until then, women had served only in support roles, acting as messengers, providing safe havens, and preparing the peasantry for the impending creation of a guerrilla *foco* (a center of guerrilla activity that would, according to Che Guevara's theory, eventually spark an uprising) in their area. The first woman to join the FSLN as a full-time armed combatant was Gladys Báez, who had been active in the Nicaraguan Patriotic Alliance. Báez was conscious of the responsibility of being the first female combatant: "In the first place, to accept the presence of women was a new experience for the men. The challenge in my case was that it depended on me whether more women would be brought to the mountains. I understood this clearly, that it depended on me. The compañeros were accustomed to see us arrive as messengers, to see us engaged in logistical support, but our full-time permanent presence, this was a different story." Out of this belief, Báez refused to leave the mountains even when she became ill and was advised to do so by medical personnel. At the time she suffered from, among other ailments, seven different types of parasites. When she was finally captured, it took her three years to recover her health.

Dorotea Wilson, a member of the FSLN National Directorate (1994–98), joined in 1977–78 motivated by strong religious beliefs. She experienced the socioeconomic injustices oppressing the Nicaraguan people in her own home. Her father, a miner, struggled to feed her and her nine brothers and sisters. After having collaborated for a number of years as a courier inside and outside the country Wilson became an FSLN combatant: "I had to do it, since I was pursued by the Guardia, which was already looking for me everywhere because they had information that I had contact with the guerrilla in the mountains."[31] As a combatant, Wilson continued her work in communications. An account of her years in the mountains depicts a challenging situation.

Men and women were required to carry the same forty-pound backpacks with ammunition and also shared in traditionally female tasks such as food preparation. Men, however, dominated the command structures. "I didn't know a single female commander of a column," Wilson emphasized, although she maintained that women held lower-level command positions. Information and authority were restricted, "but at the hour of combat men and women were in the first line of fire." Eventually a number of women assumed leadership positions. At the time of the FSLN triumph in 1979, Dora María Telléz, Doris Tijerino, and Leticia Herrera were high-ranking commanders, just below the nine-member FSLN National Directorate.

Gender relations in the Sandinista guerrilla forces were not different from those in the Salvadoran FMLN. Leticia Herrera, the fifth woman to join the Sandinistas as a full-time combatant, affirms that joining the guerrillas as a woman was a difficult experience. "It was very hard. I always say that this is one of the things few people take into account and value. We as women joined the movement, maybe not because of gender consciousness, but with the realization that we would fight for substantive, profound changes. We did not foresee that we would have to face a dual struggle—the struggle against the system of government and the fight against the men in the movement."[32] In Herrera's view, gender inequality was reflected early on: even though the FSLN gained a public profile between 1961 and 1963, female figures did not emerge until 1967. Even then women were not accepted as full-time members. At that time the predominant thinking was that a "woman was useful only to cook the meals in the house where those who were in the underground lived, wash their clothes, run their errands, [and] serve as cover for clandestine personnel. It was never contemplated that a woman could be an officer in charge of an underground structure. This is where the gender issue manifested itself, and this quadrupled the complexity of our efforts as women."[33]

Gladys Báez remembers that her brothers-in-arms "thought that when a woman joined, they had their meals and laundry taken care off. I said that if this is what I had to do, I would prefer to stay in my house and take care of my children's meals and laundry. I didn't join for this." The struggle against sexist attitudes had many dimensions and included subtle challenges like the concept of the "new man." The male leaders talked about "'the new man,' and I said, 'the new woman.' They said by saying 'man' everyone is included, and I said, No, señor, if one gives birth to a male child it is male, and when one gives birth to a female it is a female." Báez was aware how important it was to challenge sexist attitudes from the very beginning. "If I start to serve him the first day, I will always remain in that role."

Women obviously resented being used by their male companions but were reluctant to talk about these problems. As a rule, female combatants did not evaluate their experiences from a gender perspective, and women rarely discussed the sexist attitudes of their male companions among themselves. This should not be surprising because, as in El Salvador, women did not join the struggle to advance a feminist agenda but were motivated by a much broader desire to fight for social justice.

Mónica Baltodano, who joined the FSLN in 1972, represented an exception to the rule that women joining the FSLN lacked gender consciousness. In Baltodano's words: "I went underground with a female, feminist motivation. I had read some books that discussed female emancipation and equality—women's rights." She immediately confronted sexist attitudes in her male companions. In one incident, she was asked to wash a male militant's pants. She reacted as follows: "I told him I would not, because I had not gone underground to wash pants. He became very annoyed and told me that he had asked me because we were in a peasant's house and it would appear strange if he went out to wash the pants, that this was not suitable for a man according to the culture of the environment." Based on this explanation, Baltodano agreed to her companion's request. He, however, was no longer interested in having his laundry done, being very offended by her views.

On another occasion, when she was in guerrilla training school, Baltodano could not take the hard training and readily gave up when the trainers gave her the option. She was admonished for her attitude by Ana Julia Guido (who later became a commander of the Sandinista police), a woman of peasant origin who was physically more suited to the challenges of guerrilla training. Guido told her: "Look, it is for this reason that the men say we are not equal to them." Upon reflection, Baltodano answered: "It is true,

I am taking advantage of being a woman in order not to put forward the greatest effort."[34] Thus, women had to be careful not to overreact or take advantage of traditional gender views while struggling to convince their male companions that they should be treated as equals.

By 1974, the men in the FSLN had come to accept women's participation as an integral part of the movement. Yet, in the eyes of female militants, this acceptance was rooted in the FSLN's appreciation for the contributions women could make to the struggle rather than an understanding of women's rights. Bayardo Arce, for example, a member of the FSLN directorate, appreciated women's talent for political work or for the recruitment of new members, characteristics especially important for the growth of urban guerrilla structures.[35] This recognition of women's potential was self-serving and was not grounded in support for women's rights. The leadership's lack of understanding of women's issues was surprising in light of the strong support for women's rights stated in the 1969 *Historic Program of the FSLN*.[36] The discrepancy between programmatic statements and practice led some female militants to conclude that the passages on women's rights were written by an *internacionalista*, a foreigner who supported the FSLN. Officially, Carlos Fonseca, the FSLN's eminent intellectual leader, was given credit for the Sandinista Program.

Women proved themselves as combatants in a variety of fashions. Three women were part of the FSLN commando group that captured a number of foreign dignitaries and Somozista officials in the December 1974 raid on the house of Chema Castillo. By that time, women had proved their valor in combat at a considerable cost. Luisa Amanda Espinosa had been killed, while Gladys Báez and Doris Tijerino had been captured and tortured. Repression was particularly fierce in the wake of the 1974 FSLN raid, and women proved invaluable in maintaining the communication lines between the urban and rural FSLN forces. During this difficult period, traditional gender views were exploited to the FSLN's advantage. Realizing that "maybe the only part of the woman that they [the National Guard] would not search was the vagina . . . we made the messages in the form of a tampon. Then the task was to explain to a peasant woman who had never used a sanitary napkin what a tampon was, teach her how it was introduced and how it should be taken out, and how to make this tampon safe so that it would not be destroyed."[37]

In summary, women's participation in the Sandinista guerrilla movement can be analyzed in terms of three distinct phases. During the first phase, lasting from the origins of the FSLN in 1961 to the early 1970s, few women participated and only in exceptional cases did they serve in combat roles. During this period FSLN forces were extremely small, numbering only a few dozen fighters. Women joined in greater numbers during the second phase, which lasted from 1973 to 1977. This period marked a growing guerrilla movement with women mainly in support roles. The last stage, 1977 to 1979, witnessed the massive incorporation of women and coincided with popular uprisings in support of the FSLN. According to Baltodano, "These uprisings served as the seed, supplying people—combatants and women [to the small force of FSLN fighters]."[38] When the FSLN staged its strategic retreat from Managua to Masaya in June 1979, the number of female combatants was considerable. To showcase female participation, the FSLN staged a parade in the town of Carazo of an exclusively female squadron consisting of 150 women.[39] The contribution of female leaders to the triumph of the revolution was most prominent in the case of the FSLN's western front. Its general command was headed by Dora María Téllez and of its seven members, five were women. This command would take credit for the first major military victory of the guerrilla forces—the liberation of the provincial capital of León.

Women's participation in Nicaragua's armed movements was not limited to the revolutionary Left. In the 1980s, a number of women who opposed the Sandinista revolution joined the counterrevolutionary Resistencia Nicaragüense (Nicaraguan Resistance, or Contras) as combatants. Women also occupied political positions within the Nicaraguan Resistance. In a 1997 interview, Azucena Ferrey, the only woman in the Contra directorate recounted the difficulties of being a woman in an otherwise completely male structure, although she emphasized that "jealousy over leadership [positions] and clashes between political adversaries" were more problematic.[40]

When the Nicaraguan Resistance was disarmed in 1990, the Comisión Internacional de Apoyo y Verificación (International Commission on Support and Verification, or CIAV), whose officials were appointed by the Organization of American States (OEA), was in charge of demobilization. It reported that a total of 22,413 fighters,[41] with 58,721 family members were

Table 1.5   Number of Demobilized Nicaraguan Resistance Fighters
and Families by Zone of Demobilization

Zone	Demobilized		Family Members		
	Number	% Total	Number	% Total	Average Family Members
1 Amparo	2,894	12.91	4,715	8.03	1.63
2 Kubali	1,671	7.46	3,656	6.23	2.19
3 San Andres	3,019	13.47	7,631	13.00	2.53
4 La Piñuela	3,164	14.12	8,463	14.41	2.67
5 El Almendro	6,626	29.56	18,885	32.16	2.85
6 Bilwaskarma	1,785	7.96	6,233	10.61	3.49
7 Alamikamba	171	0.76	518	0.88	3.03
8 Yolaina	1,745	7.79	5,394	9.19	3.09
9 Los Cedros	1,338	5.97	3,226	5.49	2.41
Total	22,413	100.00	58,721	100.00	2.62

Source: CIAV-OEA, "Cuadros Estadísticos del Proceso de Desmovilización y Repatriación en Nicaragua."

processed in nine different security zones established throughout the country. Unfortunately the data collected by CIAV-OEA were not separated by sex. Thus, as in the case of the Sandinistas, we have to rely on estimates and indirect methods of data collection in order to determine the gender composition of the counterrevolutionary forces. It is established that there were a number of female fighters among the Contras, although the popular image holds that it was basically a male force. Karen Kampwirth, an authority on the gender composition of the Contras, has emphasized that female participation in the Nicaraguan Resistance "has been consistently ignored in the literature."[42] Based on interviews with Contra commanders and on news reports, Kampwirth has concluded that women constituted 7 to 15 percent of Contra combatants.[43] Indirect evidence suggests that female participation was at the lower end of this spectrum. CIAV-OEA also registered the family members of the fighters who lived in camps in Honduras. The data show the relationship of the demobilized family members to the fighters themselves. It is revealing that there were 7,300 wives and 3,132 common-law wives among the family members but only 236 husbands and 238 common-law husbands. Thus the male partners waiting in the camps for their loved ones to return from the war represented less than

5 percent of the female partners. This raises the interesting question of whether the majority of female combatants were single, whether their companions were active fighters, or whether they were somewhere else than in the camps. The evidence, however, while difficult to interpret and not conclusive, could also suggest a relatively low female participation rate. Since it was arguably even more dangerous for a male Nicaraguan with a spouse or companion in the Resistance to remain in Nicaragua, such a person would have been likely to seek refuge in Honduras.

It is interesting that the socioeconomic profile of the right-wing Resistance did not differ significantly from those of the left-wing guerrilla movements discussed in this chapter. The general demobilization records present a picture of a predominantly young, poorly educated force with a rural background. Of the actual combatants 1,832 (8.2%) were ten to fifteen years of age and 6,235 (27.8%) were between sixteen and twenty. Only 2,183 (9.7%) fighters were over forty. The great majority (84%) had three years or less of primary education. Not surprisingly, only 42 Contras had university diplomas. More than 70 percent shared a rural background, yet less than 24 percent owned property.[44] These statistics illustrate the challenge of incorporating such a force into civil society.

The Guatemalan Experience: Two Generations of Female Combatants

The Guatemalan guerrillas initiated their struggle around the same time that the Sandinistas set up their movement. While the Sandinista struggle ended in 1979 with the overthrow of the Somoza regime, however, the URNG's fight continued on for close to two decades. The Guatemalan experience encompasses thirty-five years of struggle, and this had repercussions on the gender composition of the URNG. While female participation during the 1960s and 1970s was limited, it started to increase in the 1980s. There is no question that the Salvadoran conflict, with its strong incidence of female FMLN fighters played a role in this development. In addition, the international context of the 1980s favored increased female participation.

When the URNG signed the 1996 peace accords, the Guatemalan guerrilla movement was composed of four different groups: the Ejército Guerrillero de los Pobres (Guerrilla Army of the Poor, or EGP), the Organización Revolucionaria del Pueblo en Armas (Revolutionary Organization of Armed Citizens, or ORPA), the Fuerzas Armadas Revolucionarias (Revolutionary Armed Forces, or FAR), and the Partido Guatemalteco del Trabajo (Guatemalan Workers' Party, or PGT). Throughout the struggle there was much speculation as to the strength of the respective groups, with the Guatemalan army claiming several times to have eliminated the guerrillas. Most observers agree that the URNG was considerably weakened by the end of the 1980s. According to Jack Spence and his coauthors, "In the last years of the war the URNG was estimated to field no more than 1,000–1,500 guerrillas and militarily became only a nuisance to the Guatemalan army."[45] While speculation will continue regarding the URNG's strength during the war, we have detailed records of URNG personnel at the time of demobilization.

In an accord signed in Oslo on December 4, 1996, as part of peace negotiations, the URNG agreed to a definitive cease-fire.[46] While the implementation of the peace accords was supervised and facilitated by the United Nations Mission for Human Rights Verification in Guatemala (MINUGUA), the demobilization and disarmament of URNG personnel was monitored by a United Nations peacekeeping mission. A group of 155 military observers, authorized by the United Nations Security Council, was in charge of security for the eight camps, located on six sites, where URNG combatants were concentrated and processed. The URNG agreed to demobilize its forces in three phases beginning on March 3, 1997, and continuing over a period of two months.[47]

By the end of March, all URNG forces had been concentrated in the established camps. According to Lieutenant Colonel Araujo Lima from Brazil, who was in charge of the demobilization camp located at Finca Claudia, Esquintla, the URNG presented an initial list of 3,614 combatants. This list was eventually revised down to 3,250. The actual number of demobilized combatants was somewhat lower still because some URNG members had no interest in going through the demobilization process. Some were already integrated into civilian life, while others did not want to appear in the official demobilization list.[48] As had been the case in El Salvador, some guerrilla fighters had little faith in the viability of the peace agreement. In light of the extreme political violence of the past, they were

Table 1.6   Composition of URNG Combatants
by Group, 1997

Group	Total	%
FAR	1,211	41.2
EGP	1,479	50.3
ORPA	250	8.5
Total	2,940	100.0

Source: MINUGUA.

not prepared to endanger their lives by officially registering as a member of the URNG.

To complicate matters further in terms of the reliability of the data we have, the URNG members who did congregate in the camps were not always actual combatants. In addition to those URNG fighters who went to the camps from their areas of operation inside Guatemala, a considerable number of URNG supporters were brought back from refugee camps in Mexico. Not all in the latter group were URNG combatants, a fact manifested by the considerable number of children among them. Based on United Nations records, 125 children under the age of fourteen were demobilized, several of them infants.[49] Some observers maintained that only about half of the URNG personnel in the camps were "actual former combatants."[50] In light of these observations one needs to take the membership statistics with a grain of salt.

According to United Nations data, 2,940 URNG combatants officially demobilized. The EGP and FAR constituted the great majority of the fighters, with 50 and 41 percent, respectively. The ORPA forces constituted less than 10 percent of the total, while the PGT (according to the official record) had no military forces at all. Ricardo Rosales, the head of the PGT since 1974, explained that although the number of PGT combatants was indeed small, the Communist Party did have a military force. In 1984 the PGT had established its own military front. When the army destroyed this front in December 1985, however, the Central Committee of the Communist Party decided to offer the party's personnel and military resources to the remaining guerrilla groups.[51] Thus a number of PGT combatants were integrated into the military forces of the other URNG groups. For example, the Frente Unitario (Unified Front) established in 1993 and originally consisting of only ORPA fighters, included 16 PGT combatants.[52]

In addition to the combatants concentrated in the various camps, the URNG demobilized 2,813 additional members. This latter group consisted of 493 people who had served as URNG international cadres, while the rest were URNG leaders and other personnel who had served as political cadres inside the country. Thus, according to United Nations records, the total URNG membership at the time of demobilization was 5,753.[53]

Unfortunately, the Guatemalan data, particularly in regard to the URNG's gender composition, are not as complete as those from El Salvador.[54] This situation reflects the continued climate of fear within the country at the time of demobilization and the extremely secretive nature of the URNG.[55] Nevertheless, a European Union–sponsored study of the socioeconomic background of the URNG membership gives a reasonably accurate picture of the URNG's gender composition. URNG members carried out this study during the demobilization process. The study is based on a survey of 2,778 URNG combatants (of the 2,940 concentrated in the camps) and 1,410 of the 2,813 political cadres. Although only half of the political cadres were surveyed, we have an almost complete picture of the URNG combatants.

According to Table 1.7, women represented 410 (15%) of the 2,778 combatants interviewed and 356 (about 25%) of the 1,410 political cadres. These data demonstrate that compared to their involvement in El Salvador and Nicaragua, female participation in Guatemala's revolutionary struggle was rather limited.[56] Among combatants (where we have the most complete data), the percentage of women in the URNG was only half as great as the percentage of women in the Salvadoran guerrilla movement.

While lower levels of female participation distinguished the Guate-

Table 1.7   Gender Composition of URNG by Demobilization Category, 1997

Category	Women	%	Men	%	Total	%
Combatants	410	14.8	2,368	85.2	2,778	100.0
Political Cadres	356	25.2	1,054	74.8	1,410	100.0
Total	766	18.3	3,422	81.7	4,188	100.0

Source: URNG, Personal Incorporado, 2–4.

malan guerrilla movement from its Central American counterparts, similarities were evident in other areas. For example, the reasons that women joined the guerrillas and the nature of gender relations during the war are both comparable to the situations in Nicaragua and El Salvador.

The reasons female combatants gave most frequently when asked why they joined the URNG had little to do with their gender interests. Instead they were similar to those given by their male counterparts. Many women joined out of a conviction that conditions in Guatemala had to be changed, some sought greater safety following the assassination of family members, while others joined the guerrillas together with their family. Representative reasons include "the need to move the country forward"; "the knowledge that Guatemala suffered severe repression"; "the death of my mother in combat in 1981"; "because of ethnic discrimination and the economic situation at the time and the advice of my father, who was a member of the revolutionary party." One combatant said, "my parents were organized before I was born. I joined conscientiously at the age of thirteen."[57]

In the early years of the Guatemalan guerrilla movement, female participation was very limited. In 1962, says former guerrilla Aura Marina Arriola, "the armed struggle was initiated with the organization of the first Rebel Armed Forces (FAR). In these [forces] a number of us women participated who also initiated our struggle for the liberation of women. Then we didn't know it, but in a society as machista as the Guatemalan, we were true pioneers."[58] This female participation, however, was largely restricted to the urban areas and involved support activities. URNG leader Juan José Hurtado has affirmed that during the 1960s "the revolutionary movement of the time failed to fully incorporate women. In fact, there were almost no women combatants in the guerrilla ranks."[59] Even in the early 1970s women were largely excluded. For example, Yvon Le Bot has emphasized that the initial group that started the EGP guerrilla front in 1972 consisted of fifteen men and not a single woman.[60] Indeed, "Comandante Lola" (Alba Estela Maldonado), the most senior female URNG commander at the time of demobilization, recounts that when she joined the EGP in 1974 she found only two women among her group. It was only in 1978–80 that women started to join in greater numbers, but at no time did women constitute more than 25 percent of the membership.[61] In the 1970s, an increasing number of indigenous women became part of the guerrilla move-

ment. Military leadership functions, however, were almost exclusively reserved for male Ladinos.[62] No woman held a rank higher than captain.[63]

The leadership initially strictly regulated sexual relations. Couples had
to go through a trial period and had to prove themselves before they could
seek permission to form a family. These stringent norms broke down as the
guerrilla movement grew in numbers. Many of the new recruits lacked
the political education and awareness of the old cadres. In the opinion of
the old guard, they exhibited a different level of commitment. Whereas the
original cadres held the view "if we join, it is for life" the new recruits
viewed their experience differently, announcing "I'll join the guerrillas for
one year."[64] Once the movement started to grow, the strict discipline enforced during the early years of the conflict started to break down. Indeed,
the level of female participation in the URNG fluctuated because of the
number of fighters who had to leave the mountains because they were pregnant. Interestingly, experience in the guerrilla movement not only affected
gender relations but was an important factor in breaking down ethnic barriers. According to Maldonado, members of different indigenous groups got
to know each other for the first time in a context where "ethnic differences
did not play a role in amorous relations."[65]

Traditional gender relations were reinforced and challenged at the same
time. As noted above, women in the military command structure were the
exception. Those women who had power were often resented. For example, in the ORPA, the wives of the commanders formed a tight network
that enabled them to exercise influence. Mid-level commanders resented
the informal power that their status and networking granted these
women.[66] Most female combatants were active in communications, logistics, and rear-guard activities. Traditional domestic activities, however,
such as preparing meals, washing clothes, cutting fire wood, or cleaning,
were more equally shared between the sexes. These experiences established
important precedents for the postwar period. Many female combatants
were reluctant to (re)assume traditional gender roles upon demobilization.
Others accepted the traditional gender roles assigned to them in the household as if their experiences in the guerrilla movement had never occurred.

Between April 15 and May 3, 1997, the ex-combatants left the camps
to reintegrate themselves into civilian life. The process of reintegration

promised to be complex and challenging. The URNG demobilized a predominantly young force, which was "demanding opportunities in education, training, and work."[67] Almost two-thirds of the former combatants
were between the ages of sixteen and thirty. Of particular concern was the
fact that many fighters had lost their local roots. For example, 600 URNG
members had to be put into temporary housing upon leaving the camps,
since they had no place to go. Many had lost their entire families in the
war, while others were afraid to return to their village of origin, since they
would be stigmatized as official URNG combatants.[68] The Ixcán incident
of May 1998 was ample proof that their fears were justified. The incident
occurred when a group of demobilized ex-combatants sought to return to
their communities and some villagers used violent means to prevent them
from doing so. This became a high-profile case because these communities
were considered sympathetic to the URNG.[69]

Conclusion: The Human Dimension

The data presented in this chapter clearly demonstrate the increased
role women came to play in Latin American guerrilla movements. In general, neither the revolutionary Left nor the Nicaraguan Resistance had an
"enlightened" position regarding women's emancipation during the days of
the military struggle. Thus, it is not surprising that only in exceptional cases
did women join the guerrillas because they considered these movements to
be fighting for women's rights. Instead, concerns for a better future for their
children or a more just society motivated them.[70] Nevertheless, the
counter-traditional nature of the revolutionary Left made it easier for
women to get accepted, while the Nicaraguan Resistance's counterrevolutionary struggle tended to uphold and reinforce traditional values, which
had obvious implications for potential female participation.[71]

All women, regardless of their ideology, suffered discrimination during
the reintegration phase. Their experiences during the war had raised the
expectations of many female combatants as to their role in the construction of their postwar societies. Having experienced the relative freedom
and equality of combat, which was characterized by the predominance of
nontraditional values, many women were reluctant to return to the

straightjacket of gender inequality imposed by traditional societal norms. The former combatants paid a high price for their newly acquired gender consciousness.

Female combatants seeking to rejoin their families were treated as outcasts by their own parents, siblings, and children for having abandoned their children during the war and chosen the revolutionary struggle over their families.[72] Not surprisingly, the feelings of guilt these women experienced were foreign to fathers in similar situations. Whereas women were seen as "having betrayed their families" men were recognized for "their heroic struggle." A number of female combatants felt deeply humiliated because at the war's conclusion, their spouses, who started relationships with younger women, abandoned them. Although this caused great resentment among the women, the men's decisions were not openly criticized. The Central American societies, like other cultures, applied different standards to men and women.

The personal stories of many combatants illustrate the high price women paid for joining the struggle. Nidia Díaz's personal difficulties are representative of the challenges that many female guerrilla leaders faced during and after the war. Díaz, one of the most senior female commanders in the FMLN, played an important role in the negotiations ending the war. She continued to hold important leadership posts in the FMLN following its conversion into a political party and was nominated the FMLN's vice-presidential candidate in 1998.

Felix Rodriguez, a Cuban-American advisor to the Salvadoran armed forces, had captured Díaz in 1985. She was imprisoned and tortured for eight months. Rodriguez, infamous among the Left for his role in the capture and execution of Che Guevara, managed to prolong Diaz's humiliating experience long after she regained her freedom by putting her brassiere on exhibit in his Miami house.[73] After she was exchanged for the daughter of President Napoleón Duarte, who had been abducted by an FMLN commando, Díaz went to Nicaragua. Her mother had fled to Sweden with Díaz's four-year-old son Alejandro when Díaz was captured. When Díaz and her son were reunited, Alejandro failed to recognize his mother. With her hair burned and her body scarred from bullet wounds she seemed a stranger to him. Alejandro, whose father was disappeared in 1985 in Guatemala, was raised by his grandmother in Sweden and Cuba. For many years, he considered his grandmother his real mother. Even after the peace accords, Alejandro, by then a teenager, was afraid to return to El Salvador. This was not surprising in light of the attempts on his mother's life and the general climate of violence prevailing in the country.

After the peace accords, Díaz continued to be a prime target for assassination attempts. Being close to her was considered so risky that her own family initially refused to share a house with her. Considered "the psychological author" of the assassination of a group of U.S. Marines in an event known as the Zona Rosa incident, Díaz was on repeated occasions refused a visa to the United States, despite having become a member of the Salvadoran parliament and being in charge of her party's department of international relations.

During Díaz's campaign as the FMLN's vice-presidential candidate for the March 1999 elections, Felix Rodríguez reappeared in her life. Four days before the elections, Rodríguez came to El Salvador. In interviews with the local media, he recounted the story of Díaz's capture, claiming that children had been among the FMLN fighters who had accompanied her at the time. Two days later, Díaz finally had a chance to view a tape of the interview. The interview brought back unpleasant memories; and after a night of nightmares, Díaz awoke on election eve physically ill. She perceived the purpose of Rodríguez's visit as a "psychological operation" intended to cast the FMLN in a bad light with the voters. Uncertain of the former CIA agent's intentions, she was particularly concerned about her son's security. Knowing that San Salvador was swarming with U.S. agents preparing for the impending visit of President Clinton did nothing to allay her fears. The March 1999 presidential election ended on a sadly personal note for Díaz. The FMLN ticket headed by Facundo Guardado was defeated by ARENA candidate Francisco Flores.

2

Gender Equality and
the Central American Peace Accords

Of all those who shouldered a rifle,
only to the women did they give back a broom.
—Julio Manuel Canales-Cerro de Guazapa

Peace and democracy have returned to Central America. This is the view held by many policymakers in the West who focus on the end to the civil wars that were ravaging the region during the 1980s. Is it really the case that El Salvador, Nicaragua, and Guatemala have now joined the "third wave of democratization?"[1]

The Resistencia Nicaragüense[2] was disarmed between April and June 1990, in the wake of the electoral defeat of the Sandinistas in Nicaragua. The conflict between the revolutionary government and the United States–sponsored counterrevolution led to 30,865 Nicaraguans being killed.[3] These casualties were in addition to the 50,000 people who had died during the Sandinista struggle to oust dictator Anastasio Somoza from power. The Nicaraguan peace agreement was followed on January 16, 1992, by the historic peace accords, signed at Chapúltepec Castle, Mexico, between the government of El Salvador and the guerrilla forces integrated in the Farabundo Martí National Liberation Front. This agreement ended a twelve-year conflict (1979–92) that had traumatized a whole nation. The war ravaged the country, creating 1.5 million refugees and claiming the lives of more than 70,000 people, most of them civilians. In the wake of the accords, optimism regarding El Salvador's future was widespread. On

December 29, 1996, the final Central American peace accord was completed. The guerrilla forces integrated into the URNG and the Guatemalan government, headed by President Alvaro Arzú, signed an agreement that ended the conflict that had engulfed Guatemala for thirty-six years. The human suffering during this period defies imagination. According to the report by the Commission for Historical Clarification, charged under the peace accords with establishing the truth about Guatemala's violent past, more than 200,000 Guatemalans were killed or disappeared over the course of the conflict.[4] In addition, hundreds of villages were destroyed and 1.5 million people were internally displaced or sought refuge in Mexico.[5]

In all three wars, the United States government was a major player, either backing repressive governments or sponsoring counterrevolutionary forces. In March 1999, President Bill Clinton acknowledged the destructive role played by the United States in the Guatemalan conflict. In an unprecedented gesture, President Clinton formally apologized to the Guatemalan people at a meeting held in Antigua, Guatemala: "For the United States, it is important that I state clearly that support for military forces and intelligence units which engaged in widespread repression was wrong, and the United States must not repeat that mistake."[6]

A comparison is useful for understanding the scope of the human tragedy caused by these wars. The Vietnam War, in which 58,000 North American soldiers were killed, led to the Vietnam Syndrome. The impact of the war on the North American public was so great that it took years to rebuild public support for open foreign interventions involving U.S. troops. Yet the human cost incurred by the United States in the Vietnam War pales in comparison to the suffering wrought on the Central American societies. In terms of the U.S. population, the victims of the Nicaraguan revolutionary and counterrevolutionary wars would amount to a staggering 7.3 million. The conflict in El Salvador would correspond to 3.5 million deaths and 75 million refugees. Finally, the genocide in Guatemala would have been the equivalent of 6 million dead North Americans.

Despite the end of the Central American wars, I argue that the prevailing optimism regarding the future of democracy in Central America might be premature.[7] First, we have to question whether the Central American countries should have been considered democracies before the civil conflicts intensified. They were ruled by military or authoritarian civilian gov-

ernments, which frequently violated established norms of formal democracy and did little to satisfy the basic needs of their people. Thus it makes
little sense to talk about a "return" to democratic rule. Further, the current
emphasis on democratization is justified only if we focus on formal democracy.[8] While the institutionalization of electoral democracy[9] in the wake
of the peace accords is encouraging, it is by no means a sufficient guarantee that the emerging political structures will reflect popular interests. The
political transitions taking place in Central America have to be analyzed
in light of the wars that ravaged the region for so many years. The definitive resolution of these conflicts, a precondition of sustainable peace and
democracy, requires more than an end to armed struggle. Rose Spalding has
emphasized that "peace building is not an inevitable extension of regime
transition, and it should not be subsumed under an electoral process."[10]

Instead we need to focus on substantive (real) democracy, which requires social and economic justice. From this perspective, a successful implementation of the Central American peace accords was a sine qua non
for democratization in the region to have any meaning. In postwar
Nicaragua, El Salvador, and Guatemala, the successful reintegration of the
former combatants into society had to be a central part of the process of
building peace and democracy. In the Nicaraguan context, Spalding has argued that political space for ex-combatants and the state's capacity to attend to their (and society's) needs were key factors in the peace-building
process.[11] Most ex-combatants belonged to traditionally marginalized sectors and were thus particularly affected by the policies implemented by
their respective governments.

The Evolution of the Peace Agreements

The Central American peace process was driven by the need to find a
solution to the war between the revolutionary government in Nicaragua
and the U.S.-sponsored counterrevolutionary forces. The eventual disarming of the Nicaraguan Resistance required agreements far more comprehensive than any negotiation between the Sandinista government and the
counterrevolutionary forces could achieve. Accords between the Sandinistas and the Resistance became possible only after all the countries in the
region had agreed on the necessity of finding a peaceful solution to all con-

flicts ravaging Central America. The most important breakthrough occurred at the second reunion of the Central American presidents, held August 6–7, 1987, in Guatemala.[12] The agreements reached at this meeting became known as the Arias Plan. The fundamental points of the treaty included the recognition of the legitimacy of the Sandinista revolution by the other Central American governments. Further, the agreement called for an end to U.S. aid for the Nicaraguan Resistance and Soviet aid to the Sandinistas as well as an amnesty program and the promise of a dialogue between the two hostile camps.[13]

Negotiations between the Central American presidents began in 1986 in Guatemala, after the efforts of the Contadora group (consisting of Colombia, Panama, Mexico, and Venezuela) had failed to bring about peace in the region. The process concluded after six meetings on April 3, 1990, in Montelimar, Nicaragua. On this occasion, peace seemed finally at hand. The Sandinista government, defeated in the elections of February 1990, was in the process of transferring power to the newly elected Chamorro administration. This opened the space for the disarming of the Resistance.

Following the initiation of the regional negotiations, the Sandinista government had started a dialogue with the Contras. Initial contacts between the two sides began in 1987, but little progress was made. The first significant breakthrough occurred in March 1988, when an important agreement was signed in Sapoá, Nicaragua. The two sides established procedures for a cease-fire, disarmament, and an amnesty; and the Contras agreed to accept only humanitarian aid from the United States.[14] Subsequently the Resistance went through a divisive stage, characterized by internal struggles over the issue of negotiations with the Sandinistas.[15] While moderate leaders recognized the need to end the armed struggle, an intransigent sector opposed any accommodation with the revolutionary government. This left the Resistance without decision-making capability and impeded further progress at the negotiating table. In the end, the moderates won out. The support provided by the United States to the Contras' cause was a crucial factor prolonging the war, although the U.S. government became increasingly reluctant to continue funding in the wake of the Iran-Contra scandal. According to Jack Child, it was only after Violeta Chamorro had been elected president of Nicaragua that U.S. officials stated publicly that "the United States expected the Contras to disarm."[16] Representatives of the newly elected government met with the Contra leadership during March 1990 in Toncontín, Honduras, and in April in Managua. On these occasions, a definitive cease-fire was agreed upon, and the mechanism for the demobilization process was worked out. The indigenous forces integrated into Yapti Tasba Masraka nanih Aslatakanka (Organization of the Nations of the Motherland) and the Frente Sur (Southern Front) of the Resistance signed separate accords.[17]

The disarming of the Contras began on April 16, 1990, and was completed on July 5. The main institution entrusted with verifying the demobilization process was the CIAV-OEA. The CIAV-OEA was created with the mandate of overseeing the demobilization of insurgent forces in Central America and providing humanitarian assistance.[18] In return for agreeing to disarm, the Nicaraguan government promised the Resistance "cash, housing, health centers, schools, personal security and support for their full reintegration into civilian life."[19]

The initial government plan consisted in the creation of *polos de desarrollo* (development areas). The Resistance was supposed to receive land in several regions of Nicaragua. The idea behind the areas was that they would offer protection (they were supposed to be controlled by a new rural police force consisting mainly of former Contras) and allow the government to attend to the needs of the Contras in a coherent fashion.[20] Yet these areas were never created. The government simply lacked the resources to make them a reality. In addition, the land to be set aside for the ex-Resistance was already occupied by peasants who were not willing to give up their properties.[21] Joaquín Lovo, vice-minister of Government, expressed a widely held belief when he argued that the planned development areas were economically and politically not viable.[22] Thus, the members of the Resistance were dispersed throughout the country. This situation complicated their efforts to organize into a unified political force.

Developments in El Salvador were influenced by events in Nicaragua. With the Sandinistas out of power, the FMLN had lost its main supporter in the region. Further, the post–Cold War reality, following the demise of the Soviet Union, represented a context that forced the main protagonists of the Salvadoran conflict to see the benefits of a negotiated settlement. Peace talks between the guerrillas and the government had been initiated in 1984 under President Napoleon Duarte. Little progress was made during the subsequent five years of "war with dialogue," since the military option still appeared viable to both sides.[23]

In November 1989, the FMLN began an offensive against the Salvadoran government, hoping that the people would support it with a mass uprising. Despite significant battle successes (the guerrillas even occupied large parts of the capital for days) mass support failed to materialize. In the end, the FMLN was forced into a strategic retreat. The failure of this offensive led the FMLN leadership to rethink the possibilities of continued armed struggle. It became clear that the war could not be won militarily. In particular, core FMLN supporters were growing increasingly tired of the war. Morena Herrera, an FMLN leader, recounted that after the offensive the leadership started to realize "that people no longer wanted war. People who loved us a lot, including me personally, told us: 'Look, I collaborate with you in whatever you want, but this has got to end.' This was the first time that the war had been experienced here [in the capital]. People got scared. This led us to reflect on the possibilities of continuing the armed struggle."[24] The Salvadoran government and the Bush administration, on the other hand, which had claimed that the guerrillas had ceased to be a military threat, were greatly embarrassed that the FMLN succeeded in occupying parts of the capital. The offensive was countrywide and led to attacks on all the country's major cities.[25] In the wake of the offensive a final two-year period of "war with negotiation" began.[26]

At the beginning of 1990 when the United Nations assumed a direct role in facilitating the peace talks between the FMLN and the government, prospects for a settlement improved.[27] With negotiations making progress, the Security Council authorized the May 1991 deployment of ONUSAL, the United Nations Observer Group in El Salvador. ONUSAL's mission consisted in supervising the implementation of the accords between the Salvadoran government and the guerrillas.[28] The final breakthrough came with the signing of a cease-fire on New Year's Eve 1991 in New York, followed by the January signing of the Chapúltepec peace accords. As part of the comprehensive peace accords, the guerrillas agreed to demobilize their military structures, and the Salvadoran government committed itself to reducing the size of its armed forces. The FMLN demobilized its fighters in five stages beginning on June 30, 1992, and ending on December 15.

The accords that ended the Guatemalan war were the result of negotiations that were conducted over seven years and involved three successive administrations. The first accord concerned democratization and was signed in Querétaro, Mexico, on July 25, 1991. Interestingly, it was the government of Jorge Serrano, a conservative, who took this first important step. When Serrano instigated a failed coup in May 1993, however, and was subsequently forced from office, the negotiation process stalled. It was resurrected in 1994 under President Ramiro de León Carpio, with the United Nations assuming the role of moderator. Further, a group of countries—Norway, Colombia, Venezuela, Spain, Mexico, and the United States—officially organized as the Group of Friends of the peace process, exerted pressure on the two parties to resume talks.[29] It took two more years and a third Guatemalan administration, under President Alvaro Arzú, before the government signed the final peace agreement with the leadership of the URNG on December 29, 1996. The guerrilla movement agreed to demobilize its forces in three phases over a period of two months. The disarming of the combatants started on March 3, 1997. It was completed in August of the same year, in a final, originally not programmed, fourth phase.

In contrast to the accords process in Nicaragua and El Salvador, civil society contributed greatly to the successful initiation and conclusion of the negotiations. The talks held between various sectors of Guatemalan society, including the business sector, the religious community, and the labor unions that preceded the signing of the first accord were essential because, as Edgar Gutiérrez has pointed out, they "legitimized the idea of a negotiated end to the armed conflict."[30] The role of civil society in the peace process was institutionalized by an accord that established the Asamblea de la Sociedad Civil (Assembly of Civil Society, or ASC). The ASC consisted of ten diverse organizations representing the main sectors of Guatemalan society and derived its legitimacy from the January 1994 framework agreement, giving it "official recognition as an interlocutor by the parties to the peace talks."[31] Specifically, the ASC was charged with the mandate "of transmitting to the UN moderator, the government and the URNG, nonbinding recommendations" and "of acting as guarantor for bilateral agreements to give them the character of national commitments."[32]

El Salvador

Women's issues received scant to no attention in the peace negotiations in El Salvador, although Nidia Díaz, Lorena Peña, and Ana Guadalupe Martínez, all high-ranking female commanders, participated in this process. At the time, none of the three women could have been considered an advocate for women's rights. Peña has affirmed that the special problems of women were simply not discussed during the negotiations. Now a committed feminist, she recognizes that women's emancipation was not an issue during the war and that she had had no idea of gender consciousness at the time of the demobilization.[33] Díaz strongly supported women's rights within the FMLN but tended to keep a low public profile on gender issues, a habit she maintained during the negotiations.[34] Martínez, on the other hand, was the least likely supporter of a women's rights agenda. Although she expressed support for the inclusion of women in all party activities, she considered the organized women's movement extremist and radical.[35]

The lack of a gender perspective evident in the design of the reintegration programs translated into discrimination when female combatants initially did not receive equal treatment in the allocation of crucial resources such as land.[36] The reasons were many, ranging from machismo to lack of support from the male-dominated leadership of the guerrilla movement. Nidia Díaz, the FMLN official originally in charge of the land program, has said that while the exclusion of female combatants was not officially sanctioned or designed, the sociocultural context often made it a reality.[37] Lorena Peña concurs: "I believe that the principal problem that we have experienced is that the reintegration of the female combatant into civilian life has taken place under the classical sexist concepts that have predominated in all political forces of the country, including the FMLN."[38] This was particularly evident in the case of the Land Transfer Program established to provide land to ex-combatants.

Early appraisals of the Land Transfer Program were quite pessimistic. In 1993, Lorena Peña claimed that an estimated 70 to 80 percent of female combatants did not receive the benefits allocated to them.[39] She based her opinion on the findings of a study sponsored by UNICEF that recorded the difficult situation female ex-combatants faced a year after the signing of the peace accords.[40] Later data on the reintegration programs, however, revealed that the early instances of discrimination had largely been rectified. The concern over the treatment of female FMLN militants regarding their access to land under the reinsertion program was definitely justified. Land was a particularly scarce resource in El Salvador.

Many observers considered the conflict over land a key issue that had fueled the civil war. Mitchell Seligson has noted that many studies associate the country's "high population density, greater than that of India, extreme concentration in the distribution of land," and the masses of "landless, land-poor, and tenant populations" with the prolonged confrontation between the FMLN and the government.[41] He himself suggests that the agrarian question was less problematic than commonly believed and argued that a "relative decline (not disappearance) of the agricultural sector has occurred and with it a decline in the proportion of the population that is landless and land-poor."[42] Although there is controversy regarding the degree to which the land issue was a central cause underlying the Salvadoran conflict, there is no question that living conditions in the countryside—including access to land—were precarious. It is important to briefly analyze the situation of land tenure in order provide a context for the Land Transfer Program.

Under pressure from the U.S. government, the military junta headed by José Napoleon Duarte announced an agrarian reform in March 1980. Conceived by U.S. advisors, the reform—on paper—was much more radical than the 1981 Sandinista agrarian reform law in Nicaragua. It consisted of three phases. Under Phase 1, all properties over 714 manzanas (500 hectares) were to be expropriated (in Nicaragua, there was no limit on the amount of land an individual could hold). Phase 2 would have expropriated holdings between 143 (100 hectares) and 714 manzanas, while Phase 3 involved a "land-to-the-tiller" program.[43]

The reform suffered from many deficiencies: in addition to having been designed from above without input from the intended beneficiaries, it had internal contradictions, lacked ideological clarity, and could not overcome the resistance of the dominant interests.[44] Phase 2, which would have affected the interests of the powerful coffee growers, was modified in 1983. In order to protect the coffee oligarchy, the new rules stated that those properties with less than 350 manzanas could not be expropriated.[45] The expropriations called for by Phase 1 were the catalyst for the formation of death squads financed by the former owners, which plunged the country into the insanity of the early 1980s when forty thousand people were murdered. Finally, Wim Pelupessy has observed that Phase 3 was "more an exercise in establishing a permanent reserve labour force of smallholders than an effort to meet their needs or to restructure the agrarian sector."[46]

With the land issue unresolved during the 1980s, it naturally became an important point of discussion during the peace negotiations. It has been argued that although "the FMLN chose, or was forced to choose, to rectify political and military issues rather than socio-economic problems" in the negotiations, the land question is the "chief exception to vagueness in the reconstruction section of the accords."[47]

The accords established that outside the zones of conflict, properties in excess of the 350 manzanas limit established in Phase 2 of the 1980 agrarian reform as well as state-owned lands were to be transferred to benefit those peasants and small farmers who needed land.[48] For the zones of conflict, the FMLN was supposed to present an inventory of occupied properties. This inventory eventually came to comprise a list of 4,666 properties, representing 375,714 manzanas or 18 percent of the country's arable land.[49] Following many arguments, the government and the FMLN agreed that seventy-five hundred FMLN combatants, twenty-five thousand *tenedores* (squatters generally considered supportive of the FMLN), and fifteen thousand demobilized members of the Armed Forces, were to receive land under the Land Transfer Program.[50]

The program was plagued by difficulties, and several deadlines passed before its various phases were successfully completed. There was more than enough blame to go around. Officials from the United States Agency for International Development (USAID), which financed a large part of the program, accused the FMLN of not providing beneficiary lists on time. The FMLN, on the other hand, criticized USAID for being overly bureaucratic[51] and faulted government agencies for the exceedingly slow implementation of the program.[52]

As Table 2.1 indicates, by March 1994, only limited progress had been made. Based on data supplied by the United Nations, 10,619 beneficiaries had received title to 41,709 manzanas of land. Of those, 7,748 were former FMLN combatants and tenedores, while 2,871 were former soldiers. In ad-

Table 2.1 State of Land Transfer Program, March 1994

	Number of Properties	Area in Manzanas[1]	Number of Beneficiaries	Millions of Colones
A: FMLN				
Private properties negotiated	333	38,647	9,056	261.8
Private properties titled	234	24,672	6,410	178.9
Private properties not approved by Land Bank	18	1,445	350	10.5
State properties negotiated	53	25,866	5,359	
State properties titled	21	6,777	1,338	0[2]
B: FAES				
Private properties negotiated	133	12,720	3,180	93.0
Private properties titled	74	8,367	2,457	42.7
Private properties not approved by Land Bank	0	0	0	0
State properties negotiated	12	2,984	674	0[2]
State properties titled	8	1,893	414	0[2]
C: Total				
Private properties negotiated	466	51,367	12,236	354.8
Private properties titled	308	33,039	8,867	221.6
Private properties not approved by Land Bank	18	1,445	350	10.5
State properties negotiated	65	28,850	6,033	0
State properties titled	29	8,670	1,752	0[2]

Source: ONUSAL.

[1] 1 manzana = 0.7 hectares = 1.75 acres.

[2] Cost of titled state properties not included.

dition, FMLN officials had successfully negotiated the sale of 80,217 man-zanas, benefiting 18,269 people, but legal proceedings had not been com-pleted. The titling process was cumbersome indeed. A year later, on April 30, 1995, when the ONUSAL mission was downgraded to MINUSAL (United Nations Mission in El Salvador)[53] and yet another deadline for the completion of the program had passed, the number of beneficiaries had almost doubled to 20,790. It now comprised 3,818 former guerrillas, 13,121 tenedores, and 3,851 members of the Armed Forces.[54] Although the rate of the titling process had increased, more than three years after the signing of the accords, the needs of less than 50 percent of the intended 47,500 beneficiaries had been met.

The slow implementation of the Land Transfer Program created serious problems for the former combatants and tenedores. They were generally impoverished and thus could not afford being idle while waiting until all legal hurdles had been cleared. Those who wanted to farm the land despite the legal uncertainties could not do so due to lack of credit, which was only available to those with a secure title.[55] As a result, many beneficiaries aban-doned the properties that they had occupied and were in the process of ne-gotiating. According to MINUSAL, when the mission was about to con-clude its mandate in March 1996, these problems had reduced the number of beneficiaries from 7,500 FMLN combatants to 5,896 and from 25,000 tenedores to 22,525. Interestingly, the greatest decrease could be observed in the case of the Armed Forces. Of the 15,000 soldiers entitled to receive land, there were only 8,130 final beneficiaries.[56]

By mid-1996, about 90 percent of the final beneficiary population had received land, yet only 50 percent had completed the process of legally reg-istering their properties. Several officials involved in the program main-tained that the process should not be rushed. They pointed to neighbor-ing Nicaragua, where the insecurity of land tenure contributed to the violence engulfing the countryside, and argued that the more orderly, al-beit slow, process in El Salvador was the preferable way to proceed. A shortcoming of the Salvadoran program was that it discriminated against young FMLN fighters. Only guerrillas who were sixteen years old on Feb-ruary 1, 1992, were eligible to receive land, which excluded an estimated 700 teenagers.[57]

As of March 1996, a total of 4,282 ex-combatants and 14,652 tenedores

Table 2.2   Gender Distribution of the Land Transfer Program Beneficiaries—Titled Private Properties, March 1996

Department	No. of Properties	Area in Manzanas	Ex-combatants		Total Ex-combatants	Tenedores		Total Tenedores	Total Beneficiaries
			Men	Women		Men	Women		
San Miguel	163	8,940	244	73	317	1,034	561	1,595	1,912
Usulutan	379	17,738	718	301	1,019	2,978	1,526	4,504	5,523
La Union	5	502	32	17	49	32	39	71	120
Morazan	184	3,910	305	120	425	314	202	516	941
San Salvador	47	3,504	125	24	149	512	178	690	839
La Libertad	2	311	42	7	49	16	3	19	68
Chalatenango	604	14,353	634	217	851	1,362	953	2,315	3,166
Cuscatlan	234	11,159	486	152	638	1,391	780	2,171	2,809
San Vicente	199	10,473	345	81	426	1,228	681	1,909	2,335
La Paz	26	1,175	7	2	9	239	83	322	331
Cabañas	147	3,788	216	128	344	254	187	441	785
Sonsonate	1	5	0	0	0	1	0	1	1
Santa Ana	6	472	6	0	6	88	10	98	104
Total	1,997	76,330	3,160	1,122	4,282	9,449	5,203	14,652	18,934

Source: Land Bank.

had received titles to private properties. From a gender perspective, the central problem in the implementation of the land program was that initially many women were excluded. By the time the program neared its completion, however, one could not detect evidence of gender discrimination. Of the universe of 18,934 beneficiaries who obtained private properties, 1,122 ex-combatants and 5,203 tenedores (33.4%) were female. In terms of gender equality, the case of the ex-combatants is most illustrative. Women represented 29.1 percent of the FMLN's combatants at the time of demobilization. Since the 1,122 female militants receiving land titles made up 26.2 percent of the beneficiary population, the data no longer supported the earlier reports of gender discrimination. Further, according to Antonio Alvarez, the FMLN official in charge of the reintegration programs, an additional 677 former combatants received properties owned by the state. In this case too, about one third of the beneficiaries were female.[58] Thus women received land according to their relative strength in the FMLN at the time of demobilization. In light of this evidence the question must be raised why the perception of widespread discrimination continues to prevail among female FMLN officials as well as rank-and-file members.

While the later record of the land-titling program contradicts claims of massive discrimination, evidence from the early stages of the reintegration programs indicated that women were indeed discriminated against.[59] A 1993 study of the Land Transfer Program concluded: "A good part of the tenedoras, particularly those that are *acompañadas* (common-law spouses) or married, remain at the margins of the benefits of the Land Transfer Program, because the communal leaders apply discriminatory criteria to women."[60] Indeed, senior FMLN officials confirmed that there were problems, particularly in the departments of Cuscatlán and San Salvador. According to Alvarez, these problems were due to actions taken by local officials and not the product of official FMLN policy.[61] These instances of discrimination took a variety of forms.

In cases in which both husband and wife were tenedores, frequently only the husband was registered as a potential beneficiary, a practice in direct violation of the official guidelines. Alvarez argues that local officials misinterpreted the rules and allocated land per *family group* and not per *individual* as established in the guidelines. An opportunity to correct these problems presented itself when the official universe of potential beneficiaries was revised in 1993, and 7,280 people were added.[62] Thus, women who had been excluded originally could be incorporated into the new lists.

Yet women faced other hurdles as well. Communal leaders established their own requisites for potential beneficiaries, such as knowing how to read and write or possessing birth certificates or voter registration cards.[63] Since women were more likely than men to be illiterate and to lack proper documentation, these measures were discriminatory. For example, Michelle Saint-Germain has estimated that of the seventy-five thousand Salvadorans who did not succeed in obtaining their voter registration cards in 1994 because their personal identification papers were missing or not in order, 75 percent were women.[64] Further, those women who were successful in obtaining land "had more problems in securing loans and technical assistance than the men did."[65] Another manifestation of these subtler and therefore hidden forms of discrimination could be found in the poor quality of the land that was often assigned to women. In addition, many potential female beneficiaries excluded themselves, feeling they were incapable of assuming the responsibility of repaying the assumed debt. Others argued that they were too old or lacked farming experience.[66]

The statistics on the remaining reintegration programs showed little evidence of gender discrimination. According to Table 2.3, which summa-

Table 2.3   Gender Composition of Reinsertion Programs

Beneficiaries	Women	%	Men	%	Total
A: Agricultural Credit Program Beneficiaries (Ex-Combatants)					
6,504	1,669	25.7	4,835	74.3	6,504
B: Study Grant Program Beneficiaries (Demobilized FMLN Personnel)					
699	294	42.0	405	58.0	699
C: Industry and Services Program (FPL only)					
467	190	40.7	277	59.3	467

Source: FMLN internal document.

Note: The universe of beneficiaries in the three tables differs. Table A refers only to ex-combatants; Table B to ex-combatants, political personnel, and wounded noncombatants; and Table C shows data only for demobilized members of the FPL. The total number of FMLN beneficiaries in the Industry and Service Program is 880.

Table 2.4   Gender Composition of Economic Reinsertion Program for FMLN Leaders and Middle-Level Officers

A: Allocation of Financing According to Category

Category	Women	%	Men	%	Total	%
A	16	13.4	123	25.7	139	23.2
B	47	39.5	131	27.3	178	29.8
C	56	47.1	225	47.0	281	47.0
Total	119	100.0	479	100.0	598	100.0

B: Condition of Projects

Beneficiaries	Women	%	Men	%	Total	%
Registered credit	97	86.6	384	88.3	481	88.0
Suspended credit	3	2.7	26	6.0	29	5.3
Credit refused	5	4.5	12	2.7	17	3.1
Application withdrawn	7	6.2	13	3.0	20	3.7
Total	112	100.0	435	100.0	547	100.0

Source: FMLN internal document.

rizes the agricultural credit program for ex-combatants, about one quarter of the beneficiaries were female. Although this percentage is somewhat lower than the percentage of female FMLN members at demobilization, the data do not support claims of institutionalized discrimination.

In the Study Grant and Industry and Services programs, women were in fact somewhat over-represented, constituting about 40 percent of the beneficiaries. However, the analysis of yet another program, which provided for financing of small economic projects to help FMLN leaders and middle-level officers with their reintegration into society, reveals that one needs to go beyond the statistics to understand the gender dynamics of the peace process.

The program for FMLN officers provided financing to 119 female FMLN leaders, who represented 20 percent of the 598 beneficiaries (Table 2.4). This number corresponds to the wartime estimate of women holding 20 percent of the military leadership positions.[67] Financial awards were made according to the level of responsibility held during the war. The 16 women at the highest level represented 11.5 percent of the total in that category. The remaining women were split rather evenly between the two lower levels but made up a somewhat greater percentage of the total. It is not surprising that so few women were to be found in the highest category, considering that the 15-member Unified Revolutionary Directorate (DRU) included only 3 women during the war.

While the overall number of women who participated in this program corresponded to their respective strength in leadership positions, arguments arose over the relative rankings of particular women. The testimony of Morena Herrera, a former FMLN leader and head of Las Dignas, an important women's organization, is representative of the sentiments of other women in her position:

> A friend came and told me: "Look, Morena, they are making a list [of beneficiaries] for 600 FMLN leaders, and you can be part of it" . . . There were three levels, A, B, and C, according to the leadership position one had occupied, and they asked me, "At what level are you?" "Show me the criteria for how these categories are established," I said to the girl who was registering, and she explained it to me. "Put me in level A," I told her. But it [the list] was checked by the leaders, the Political Commission of the Front . . . and they left me in category B. However, they proposed initially to take me out [of A] and put me in category C.[68]

Whether Herrera was justified in her self-appraisal is beside the point. What is significant about her story is that female FMLN leaders felt that their contribution to the cause was not sufficiently valued by their male counterparts and that they suffered discrimination in the implementation of the reintegration programs. Morena Herrera emphasized in a recent conversation that her story should be understood in light of the struggle for autonomy being waged at the time of the demobilization by several women's groups affiliated with the FMLN. Because of this struggle, relations between male and female leaders tended to be tense.[69]

Male and female FMLN members alike faced enormous challenges in their efforts to reintegrate themselves into society. Yet, according to a representative FMLN study of beneficiaries of the accords, female combatants were confronted with additional hurdles "due to their gender, since society in general restricts the opportunities for development of women as such and because of this there is greater discrimination toward FMLN women who did and do not conform totally with the stereotypical roles assigned to women."[70] Also, the programs failed to consider the special needs of women. FMLN women who gathered for a national meeting in August 1993 emphasized this problem: "The reintegration plans did not take women's specificity into account and because of this the benefit for women ex-combatants has been minimal. Also, there are programs that were implemented with a stereotypical vision of women. There has been no responsible follow-up of widows, wounded ex-combatants, or the orphan children of the war."[71] This reality explains the frustration and anger encountered in interviews with female militants.

Women were allowed a "counter-traditional role" as long as it was in the interests of the struggle. After the war, when their new identities threatened traditional gender relations, an attempt was made to relegate them to the private sphere and disempower them.[72] A 1993 study of 1,100 FMLN women provided evidence that this was indeed the case. In one important indicator, 57 percent of the women interviewed reported that they had worked primarily in the household before the war, while barely a year after the peace accords 95 percent said they were engaged in domestic work.[73] With no immediate remedies available to address the resulting psychological traumas and emotional scars, women focused their energies on challenging the discriminatory practices encountered within the FMLN. As we will see, eventually their efforts translated into increased gender equality within the party. This suggests that many women who had joined the FMLN in their early teens and had experienced relative freedom to establish their gender identity during the war were forced back into traditional roles.

Nicaragua

The central issue complicating the reintegration into society of the Nicaraguan resistance was the ongoing dispute over property rights. Unlike El Salvador, Nicaragua was blessed with low population density. Although land scarcity was a problem in the densely populated pacific regions of Nicaragua, it was the insecurity of land tenure that was the crux of the problem. According to 1992 estimates, more than 165,000 rural households that owned property had some defect in their titles.[74] Many of these problems stemmed from the days of the Sandinista government.

The Sandinista revolution profoundly changed Nicaragua's land tenure structure. Almost 50 percent of the country's arable land was affected by the agrarian reform. The percentage of large farms (those over 500 manzanas)[75] was reduced from 36.2 to 6.4 percent. At the same time, new productive relations, comprising state enterprises and production cooperatives, emerged. In 1989, these new types of producers controlled about 23 percent of total arable land.[76] According to Jaime Wheelock, the Sandinista official in charge of the agrarian reform, a total of 59,200 families received 1,495,953 manzanas of land between 1981 and 1990. Further, thousands of squatters in the agricultural frontier were given title to their land.[77]

The agrarian reform suffered from a major deficiency—the land distribution program was not definitive. At the time of the Sandinista electoral defeat on February 25, 1990, many cooperatives and individual producers who had received land under the agrarian reform lacked legal titles. The problem was quite extensive. Although the Sandinistas accelerated the pace of the land titling process during the election campaign of 1989–90, a considerable number of agrarian reform beneficiaries remained without secure property rights. The revolutionary government sought to address this issue during the transition period. According to official data, 76 percent of all land distributed to individuals before April 1990 was titled between August 1989 and April 1990. In the case of cooperatives the corresponding figure was 49.6 percent.[78]

Between February 25 and April 25, 1990, the Sandinistas passed laws 85, 86, and 88, which legalized urban and rural properties that had been distributed while the revolutionary government was in power but whose owners had not received legal titles. Yet the Sandinistas also transferred new land during this period. Critics of the revolutionary government maintained that during the two-month transition more than 750,000 manzanas were distributed to supporters of the revolutionary government. Official data released by the Chamorro government show that during March and April 1990, 399,846 manzanas were titled to 8,583 families.[79] Wheelock, however, acknowledged the distribution of only 130,000 manzanas of new land. He claimed that the rest concerned the titling of previously distributed land.[80] The distribution of new land and the misappropriation of state property by Sandinista officials during the transition period (events known as the *piñata*) damaged the reputation of the revolutionary authorities and did little to solve the insecurity of land tenure. While the Sandinistas could pass last-minute laws, which provided agrarian reform beneficiaries with titles, they were not able to get these titles registered. Without having their properties legally registered, the beneficiaries frequently faced challenges to their ownership by parties who held titles to the same property and, in some instances, had their titles legally registered.

It was in this difficult climate that a new group with land demands emerged—the demobilized Nicaraguan Resistance. Its members from rural areas were originally promised about 70 manzanas each in the above-mentioned development areas.[81] Having left these faltering centers, the ex-combatants requested land in the communities where they had eventually settled down. Since land was not made immediately available, the ex-Contras invaded private properties, cooperatives, and state farms. The Contras were part of a wave of land invasions, initiated in 1990 by farm workers occupying state farms. By 1994, over a thousand invasions had taken place, destabilizing the Nicaraguan countryside.[82] In northern Nicaragua, where the departments of Matagalpa and Jinotega are located, twelve hundred ex-Contras occupied thirty-three private farms in the first year following their demobilization.[83] Overall, members of the Resistance occupied more than half a million manzanas, including state, private, and cooperative farms.[84] Sandinista production cooperatives were prime targets of attacks. In 1990 members of the Resistance invaded over 220 cooperatives.[85] Although many cooperatives became battlegrounds between Sandinista peasants and Contras, there were numerous examples of cooperatives that gave part of their land to ex-combatants. According to the Unión Nacional de Agricultores y Ganaderos (National Union of Farmers and Ranchers), over 30,000 manzanas were given to demobilized Contras.

The number of land invasions started to decline once the Chamorro government's agrarian reform program began to be implemented. Although the new government was justified in claiming credit for distributing a considerable amount of land during its first two years in office, the manner in which land was distributed was not definitive, that is, titles were often provisional and conflicted with existing property claims. By March 1992, 701,500 manzanas had been distributed benefiting 24,038 families. According to official data, 80 percent of the distributed land went to members of the ex-Resistance. Overall, more that half a million manzanas were given to 15,691 families. This left about 7,000 Contras without land. It is reasonable to assume that a considerable number of the 22,500 demobilized fighters were not interested in engaging in agricultural production, since 29 percent did not have rural backgrounds. Further, almost one-fourth had been property owners prior to joining the Resistance. Nevertheless, the continued pressure for land indicated that the land issue had not been successfully settled.

In addition to the ex-Resistance, several other groups demanded land. Foremost were over 77,000 members of the Sandinista army and security forces who had to find means of subsistence, having lost their jobs when the army was restructured between 1990 and 1992.[86] Another group in need was agricultural workers who had been laid off when the state farms were privatized. By March 1992, over 35,000 agricultural workers were unemployed as a consequence of the privatization program.[87] It is reasonable to assume that some members of this group returned to their original land and were not in need of land allocated under the reintegration program. Finally, there were about 22,000 peasants without land or with insufficient land whose needs had not been satisfied under the Sandinista government.[88] In light of the considerable number of people demanding land, it is surprising that José Boanerges Matus, minister of Agrarian Reform, ar-

Table 2.5   Land Distributed under the Chamorro Government, April 1990–March 1992

Regions	Ex-Resistance		Traditional Claims		Other		Total	
	Area	Families	Area	Families	Area	Families	Area	Families
I	17,041	841	7,096	689	457	33	24,594	1,563
II	4,338	0	34,471	1,759	688	14	39,496	1,772
III	6,137	0	3,356	415	9,098	334	18,591	748
IV	3,961	165	3,650	2,466	468	292	8,079	2,923
V	225,740	7,842	20,038	805	0	0	245,779	8,647
VI	200,244	5,265	7,567	376	0	0	207,811	5,641
RAAN	17,397	345	4,953	83	275	22	22,625	449
RAAS	48,378	758	4,265	427	0	0	52,643	1,185
ZE III	40,723	475	16,719	204	24,440	430	81,882	1,109
Total	563,961	15,691	102,114	7,223	35,425	1,125	701,500	24,038

Source: Data obtained by author from the Minister of Agrarian Reform, José Boanerges Matus.

gued in 1992 that the land distribution program was basically completed, since all state land accumulated under the Sandinistas had been distributed.[89]

Although most members of the Nicaraguan Resistance did receive land, access to land by itself did not guarantee their economic subsistence. Many other problems remained to be solved. Former owners frequently succeeded in their efforts to dispossess beneficiaries because the distribution program was badly designed and violated existing property rights. In addition, many Contras had little experience in production, having joined the Resistance as teenagers. Further, as agricultural producers were quick to point out, the new farmers lacked the resources to use their land productively.[90] The central problem revolved around the access to credit. Under the agricultural development policies of the Chamorro government, large capital-intensive production units were given priority over small-scale producers who were typical of the beneficiary population. Further, the banking system itself was under severe strain and had little capital to lend. Another problem was the lack of a legal title, a prerequisite for obtaining agricultural credit. The overwhelming majority of the ex-combatants had no legal title. Government officials acknowledged the problem in 1992 and promised an efficient titling process for the future. Yet the titling process proceeded at a snail's pace.

The data in Table 2.6 indicate the extent of the problem. By July 1993, only 16 percent (111,809 manzanas) of the 700,000 manzanas distributed by 1992 had been titled. Members of the Resistance received about one-third of all titles, representing 45,742 manzanas. The titling process continued at a slow pace. A year and a half later, in December 1994, a little over 300,000 manzanas had been titled, again with one-third going to the Resistance.[91] Considering that the Contras had received more than half a million manzanas, the titled area was insignificant. Under these circumstances, it is not surprising that the instability in the Nicaraguan countryside continued.

Following the October 1996 election of Arnoldo Alemán as president of Nicaragua, the property issue remained the key area of conflict between the government and the Sandinistas. The magnitude of the problem was impressive, and there was evidence of it every day. Announcements in the news section of the main Nicaraguan newspapers warned potential buyers

Table 2.6   Titled Properties by Department, September 1992–July 1993

| Region | Department | Number of Titles | | AREA | | Number of |
		Total	Resistance	Total	Resistance	Families
I	Nueva Segovia	327	28	6,465	810	1,635
I	Madriz	81	10	997	502	405
III	Managua	3	1	722	428	153
IV	Carazo	96	7	573	412	480
IV	Granada	14	7	1,128	108	70
IV	Rivas	77	5	1,465	53	385
V	Juigalpa	633	278	31,970	13,517	3,165
V	Boaco	85	62	3,222	2,557	425
VI	Jinotega	310	135	5,512	2,567	1,550
VI	Matagalpa	1,098	645	36,890	21,978	5,490
ZE III	Rio San Juan	497	57	22,865	2,810	2,485
	Total	3,221	1,235	111,809	45,742	16,105

Source: Nicaraguan Institute of Agrarian Reform (INRA) internal data.

that several parties contested the rights to certain properties advertised for sale. With the Alemán government taking the position that it would not "negotiate" the property question with the Sandinistas, relations between the government and the main opposition party remained acrimonious during 1997.[92] The reality behind the tough rhetoric on both sides, however, was different. By September 1997, it became public knowledge that the FSLN leadership and the Alemán government had been secretly negotiating the property question for seven months. The September public announcement of a draft for a new property law, elaborated by the FSLN and government officials, caused strong reactions. During Spring 1997, the government and the FSLN agreed to convoke a meeting with representatives from all major sectors of civil society. This conference, called the Diálogo Nacional (National Dialogue) was charged with helping to find solutions to Nicaragua's most pressing problems.[93] Not surprisingly, the property question headed the agenda. When the deal struck between the two main political forces became public, key participants in the Dialogue (in which the FSLN had refused to participate) wondered aloud whether the Dialogue had been relegated to a sideshow. While the participants had been working between July and September 1997 to achieve a societal consensus to solve the thorny property issue, the FSLN and the government had created a faît accompli. The National Assembly, with the votes of the FSLN and Liberal Alliance, approved the new property law in December.

The sense of betrayal extended to high-ranking Sandinistas. Henry Ruiz, one of the historic FSLN commanders and a member of its National Directorate felt so deceived that he announced, "the draft for a new property law was for me the point to leave."[94] In his view, the Sandinista leadership had abandoned its core constituency, the poor majority: "We have lost the meaning of the historic mission that we carried and because of that I no longer want to continue in this Sandinismo."[95] In the opinion of many observers, a pact among the elites had once again protected their interests while abandoning the poor. The Contras were part of this disenfranchised majority whose needs were not taken into account. The reintegration into society of the Nicaraguan Resistance had encountered many problems. As a result, Nicaragua continued to be plagued by high levels of rural violence.

Guatemala

In Guatemala, a vocal women's movement supported the efforts of a few high-ranking female URNG officials to put gender equality on the agenda of the peace negotiations.[96] For example, Luz Méndez, a member of the URNG's commission negotiating the peace accords, was conscious of the importance of incorporating women's rights into the agreements.[97] She had learned from the Salvadoran experience. As discussed, the FMLN leadership had paid little attention to women's rights in the peace negotiations. Although Méndez and several other officials advocated the necessity of incorporating a gender perspective into the accords, this view was not representative of the URNG in general. Awareness of gender issues was limited in the guerrilla movement. This made it imperative for the advocates of women's rights to be supported from sectors within society at large.

The Assembly of Civil Society particularly played an important role in advocating the inclusion of women's rights into the accords. A highly visible group within the ASC was the Women's Sector. URNG official Comandante Lola affirmed that "the Women's Sector, practically the only one with a permanent presence in the Assembly of Civil Society, influenced . . .

the coordination and the content of some of the accords."[98] As a result, women's rights were specifically addressed in four of the seven substantive agreements that were reached between July 1991 and September 1996. This fact was publicized only days after the signing of the accords in a study of the accords' gender content conducted by researchers from the University of San Carlos and released in January 1997.[99] The emphasis on gender issues in the Guatemalan peace accords indicates that the level of gender awareness in the region had changed since the 1992 Salvadoran agreement.

Indeed, there were a number of important passages on women's rights in the accords. In the accord establishing procedures for the resettlement of populations uprooted during the war, the parties agreed "to emphasize in particular the protection of families headed by women, as well as the widows and orphans who have been most affected."[100] Further, the Guatemalan government "committed itself to eliminating all forms of discrimination, factual or legal, against women, and to make it easier [for them to have] access to land, housing, [and] credit and to participate in development projects. A gender perspective will be incorporated in the policies, programs and activities of the global development strategy."[101] In the important agreement on the rights of Guatemala's indigenous peoples, considered one of the key achievements of the URNG leadership, indigenous women were given special protection. For example, sexual harassment of an indigenous woman was to be punished particularly severely under Guatemalan law.[102] Women's political rights were also addressed. The accord concerning the strengthening of civil society advocated the introduction of measures of positive discrimination to increase female participation. The agreement required the signatory parties "to take the corresponding measures in order to ensure that organizations of political and social character adopt specific policies tending to encourage and favor women's participation as part of the process of strengthening civilian power."[103]

Luz Méndez emphasized the importance of the international climate during the peace negotiations. For example, discussions on the socioeconomic and agrarian accord coincided with the 1995 Fourth World Conference on Women in Beijing. Having gender issues on the forefront internationally made it easier to incorporate provisions favoring women's rights into this accord.[104] A key passage of the agreement stated:

Recognizing the insufficiently appreciated contribution of women in all spheres of economic and social activity, particularly their work in favor of improving the community, the [signatory] parties recognize the necessity of strengthening women's participation in economic and social development on terms of equality. To this end the government commits itself to take the specific economic and social situation of women into account in the strategies, plans and development programs and to train civil servants in the analysis and planning based on this perspective. This includes: recognizing the equality of rights between women and men in the home, the workplace, production, as well as in social and political life and assuring them the same possibilities as men, in particular concerning access to credit, the awarding of land and other productive and technological resources.[105]

Thus, the Guatemalan accords were unique in addressing the role of women in society and advocating change toward greater gender equality. The accords reflected a rethinking of women's role in society. At least at a formal level, women were acknowledged as key protagonists in Guatemala's future development.[106] Yet the challenge remained to implement the provisions in the accords in a way that would transform Guatemalan society.

Jack Spence and his colleagues have emphasized that "the Guatemalan agreement contains more wide ranging language on social and economic areas, by far, than the Salvadoran accord, but a great many of the provisions are stated in sufficiently general terms as to make them virtually unenforceable."[107] The authors point to this as the Achilles' heel of the accords. David Holiday has argued that the guerrillas were considered "relatively weak actors with minority support within society" and therefore "lacked the kind of leverage exerted by revolutionaries in neighboring El Salvador."[108] There is strong consensus that the URNG's weakness at the bargaining table made it impossible for the guerrilla leadership to negotiate more specific, enforceable agreements, a reality that impeded the full realization of the provisions in the accords.

The challenge of reintegrating the URNG combatants into civilian life was enormous. Of particular concern were the poverty and the ethnic backgrounds of the ex-combatants. The majority of the URNG's personnel came from Guatemala's twenty-one indigenous peoples and belonged to the most marginalized sectors of society. Among URNG combatants, indigenous people represented 82 percent of the total, while they made up about 50 percent of the political cadres.[109] Communication between URNG members was difficult due to significant language barriers within the indigenous community. According to Rachel McCleary, "among the rank-and-file supporters of the URNG, 16 indigenous languages [were] spoken."[110] The living conditions of Guatemala's indigenous communities were appalling. The people had little access to the most basic human needs, including health care, housing, and education. World Bank data reveal that in the countryside, where the overwhelming majority of the indigenous population is located, 90 percent lived in conditions of abject poverty.[111] In the case of URNG personnel, government statistics indicated that in the zones of origin of the majority of URNG members, 82 percent of the population lived in poverty or absolute poverty.[112]

In a few areas, the socioeconomic profile of URNG members was remarkably different from that of the population in general. For example, 84 percent of the ex-combatants and political cadres were literate, and an equally large group had some form of technical or university education.[113] In the general population, on the other hand, the literacy rate was only 66 percent.[114] In most regards, however, the URNG members shared the characteristics of the general population. The majority of the former combatants was of peasant background without access to land or stable jobs.[115] Thus, the URNG leadership, seeking to provide for the needs of its supporters in the wake of the peace accords, confronted an enormous challenge.

Not surprisingly, early evaluations of the peace accords' impact sounded a pessimistic note. Leaders of the women's movement argued that "the demands of women in respect to the implementation of the accords lack tangible results. Fourteen months after they took effect, it is difficult to perceive how these commitments have been converted into actions; the reality is that six out of every ten Guatemalan women live in rural areas, and the absence of public services is common."[116] The government was criticized for "failing to have an idea of how to attend to women's historic problems" and for lacking a strategy of action designed to ensure that the provisions of the accords would not remain empty words.[117]

Unlike the Salvadoran accords, the accords in Guatemala did not entitle ex-combatants to receive land. The URNG leadership criticized the lack of "an immediate and effective solution" for URNG cadres with a farming background.[118] Whereas most ex-combatants shared a peasant background, only 16 percent indicated they had any land.[119] Their predicament reflected the conditions prevailing in Guatemala's rural sector: extreme inequality in land tenure and extensive insecurity over property rights. Not surprisingly, the situation was particularly precarious for URNG women. Only 25 female ex-combatants had any land, while 635 (out of the total 766 interviewed) had responsibility for the support and survival of their families. The burden of responsibility was particularly heavy in the case of the 141 single mothers.[120]

The prospects for URNG militants were bleak because the "URNG was unable to get agreement in the negotiations for provisions calling for a land reform that would have been a pale version of that legislated by the Arbenz government forty five years earlier because the issue is anathema to the government and the large landholders that back it."[121] Due to the resistance of the rural bourgeoisie, it was believed that only "small numbers of former combatants" would be able to obtain "land and credit for purchasing it under the accords."[122] The positive exception to the bleak situation was the successful distribution of land to returning refugees.[123]

The initial stage of reintegrating URNG forces into Guatemalan society—under the shared responsibility of the government, the URNG, and a group of countries supporting the accords—concluded in May 1998.[124] The reintegration program was multifaceted and included economic, educational, human rights, family reunification, documentation, health care, housing, and training components. Interviews conducted with political cadres and former URNG combatants between August 1997 and June 1998 show that the great majority of URNG personnel had received some benefits under the reinsertion programs.[125] Overall the international community pledged close to $2 billion to aid Guatemala with the implementation of the peace accords.[126] Obviously, URNG members received only a fraction of these funds. Most were given about $600 to cover their immediate monetary needs following their demobilization. They also received an equivalent amount in agricultural inputs. The most fortunate obtained credit to buy land. Those not interested in farming received training in various vocations or obtained study grants to continue their education. Inevitably, some URNG members fell through the cracks. A local URNG leader complained that "there are historic fighters who have been left out [of the reinsertion programs]." As in El Salvador there were instances of gender discrimination in the allocation of benefits. María, a young female combatant, complained that she had received no land "because they gave it to my compañero."

After years in the mountains, URNG combatants had to start over under precarious circumstances. Despite these difficult circumstances, ex-combatants expressed hope that they had not fought in vain. Doña Virginia, formerly an armed combatant explained, "Many of us had nothing or we lost everything in the war. In fact, we needed something in order to live with dignity, and for this we fought—not only for us but for a lot of people who will also benefit from the productive projects." Several combatants emphasized the enormous difficulty they faced in making a new life. Dozens of former fighters had to spend more than a year in hostels following their demobilization because they had nowhere to go. Almost all URNG cadres had problems obtaining the legal documents required for a successful reintegration into society. Expectations generally exceeded the limited benefits. Disappointment and the pressures of daily life made many former combatants reluctant to continue their militancy in the URNG.

As in El Salvador and Nicaragua, the URNG leadership had problems in maintaining close relations with its supporters from the war days. Several party leaders affirmed, and personal interviews with URNG cadres confirmed, that the URNG had lost part of its rank and file during the transition from a military organization to a political movement. Grass-roots leaders, sympathetic to the ideas of the revolutionary Left, complained that their constituents who had fought with the URNG were not aware of the content of the URNG's political project.[127] For several months following the signing of the peace accords, the URNG lacked the organic structures necessary to maintain contact with the grass roots. The military structures from the war days had been dissolved, and the structures of the emerging political party were still under construction at the local and regional level.

Once the ex-combatants returned to their communities, they struggled to make a new life. The great majority had no economic resources or support from their families. According to a 1999 study, 19 percent of the URNG militants interviewed felt rejected by their communities and 80 percent reported being unemployed.[128] The daily fight for survival left them little time for activities involving the emerging party. This was particularly true for female militants.[129] Also, a number of URNG militants were disillusioned with the peace accords and showed little interest in becoming part of a new political movement. Other old cadres were simply left out, a development that caused great resentment. Those militants who were active in party-building were accustomed to taking orders from the leadership and had a difficult time adjusting to the new "democratic" reality, where the neatness of following the directions from the leadership was replaced by messy participatory decision-making.

At the same time there was an influx of new people who frequently lacked the commitment to the political project that had originally given rise to the Guatemalan guerrilla movement. One of the advantages these newcomers had was that their documentation was in order while many longtime URNG supporters lacked the legal documents required to officially join a political party. Once again, this was especially the case for female militants. It was a common practice in the Guatemalan countryside not to register female children.[130] The lack of birth certificates subsequently impeded women from fully exercising their political rights. Women were confronted with a variety of societal norms and expectations that were discriminatory in nature. Most importantly, female cadres were expected to resume their roles in the private sphere of the household following their demobilization. Since they were not supposed to be politically active, few became legal members of the emerging party. In this regard Guatemala followed a pattern similar to the one we encountered in El Salvador.

Conclusion

The peace agreements of Guatemala and El Salvador failed to resolve the fundamental problems that led to the wars in the first place; and the Contras, who never had a coherent objective apart from overthrowing the Sandinistas, were marginalized in postrevolutionary Nicaragua. The success of the three armed movements in reintegrating their former combatants into civilian life varied from country to country. The Salvadoran experience differed significantly from the experiences in Nicaragua and Guatemala. While the Contras demobilized *after* the 1990 elections that brought Chamorro to power, the 1992 peace accords permitted the Salvadoran guerrilla movement to establish itself as a political party in time to participate in the 1994 elections. The URNG had a similar advantage, since it became a legal political party in time for the 1999 elections. But the Guatemalan and Salvadoran peace accords differed significantly. The 1992 Salvadoran accords constituted, in the words of United Nations negotiator Alvaro de Soto, "a negotiated revolution." Under its terms, the Salvadoran government agreed to many demands made by the FMLN. The URNG, on the other hand, lacked a comparable bargaining position, with the Contras playing the weakest hand by far.

The Contra leaders lacked a political vision for the postwar era and suffered from internal division. Thus, they proved incapable of forging a political movement that could defend the interests of their former rebel force. The Contra field commanders, while adept at warfare, had little or no political experience. On the other hand, key civilian members of the Contra directorate, such as Alfredo César and Azucena Ferrey, chose to rejoin the political parties they had belonged to previously instead of dedicating themselves to the task of building a new party. Once the demobilization sites were abandoned and the Contra army dispersed throughout the country, the Nicaraguan Resistance ceased to exist as a coherent force at the military level. Without a shared ideology and with its military structure dissolved, the Resistance was easily marginalized.

These weaknesses impeded the Resistance from playing an active role in the design and implementation of the government programs intended to ease the ex-combatants' transition into civilian life. Abandoned by their leaders, the members of the Resistance were left to fend for themselves except for the help offered by CIAV-OEA. It is not surprising that this situation, particularly in the context of a poor economy and a crisis over property rights, resulted in high levels of political violence. The state of anarchy that characterized several regions of Nicaragua during the early 1990s severely damaged the Chamorro government's credibility and highlighted the unique challenges of regime transitions in postwar situations. Many peasants had voted for Violeta Chamorro in the expectation that she would bring about a climate of peace and security in the countryside. The president's failure to deliver on the promise of peace was a key factor in the rise to power of Alemán's Liberal Alliance in the 1996 elections.

Five years after the peace accords, it was too early to provide a definitive assessment of the URNG's success in reintegrating its forces into civil society. Compared to the attempted integration of the Nicaraguan Resistance, the process was orderly. The URNG leadership maintained control over their forces but lacked the clout to pressure the government to live up to its commitments. Progress was slow for the ex-combatants with even greater hurdles remaining for the implementation of the overall accords. By 2001, the emphasis given to women's rights in the accords had not translated into concrete improvements for the female population.

On May 16, 1999, Guatemala held a referendum on the constitutional reforms necessary to fully implement the peace accords. The referendum failed to gain the support necessary to change the constitution and raised serious questions regarding the viability of the accords. In a victory for voter apathy, 81 percent of the registered 4.08 million voters abstained. Of those who did go to the polls, slightly over 50 percent voted against the reforms.[131] According to longtime observer David Holiday, the negative outcome was partially the result of "well-funded attacks from rightist opinionmakers—many arousing latent racist fears and prejudices and prognosticating an eventual balkanization" that influenced the middle-class vote. Others rejected the reforms due to "the increased cost to citizens for implementation of such policies as multilingual access to justice and education."[132] The core of the reform measures entailed recognition of the rights of Guatemala's indigenous communities (of the seven million indigenous people of Central America, six million live in Guatemala). According to foreign minister Eduardo Stein, in those areas of the country most affected by the war and with a predominantly indigenous population, voters supported the referendum.[133] Stein emphasized that many of the proposed reforms could be implemented under regular laws. The failure of the referendum also indicated that the URNG lacked the power to mobilize enough voters in support of its vision of Guatemala's future. The first two years of President Alfonso Portillo, elected in 1999, indicated that such pressure would be required to force the new government to fully implement the peace accords.

In El Salvador, the FMLN's political strength permitted the new party to pressure the government to adhere to the provisions of the peace accords, which established benefits for the ex-combatants. Although the transfer of land was plagued by many difficulties, in the end the over-whelming majority of the intended beneficiaries obtained secure titles. Analysis of the various reinsertion programs reveals the special difficulties that women had to confront. While formal gender equality was achieved in most instances during the implementation of the benefits programs, the prevailing cultural norms impeded progress toward substantive equality.

The disenchantment evident among the former ex-combatants in Guatemala and El Salvador, male and female alike, was to a great degree the result of feeling abandoned by their leaders and of holding unrealistic expectations regarding the benefits to be derived from the accords.[134] While the leaders focused their energies on making sure that the peace ac-cords were implemented and on building their parties, they lost contact with their rank and file. For El Salvador, FMLN leader Francisco Jovel has affirmed that "many of the cadres of the highest leadership [focused] more on taking care of the business of San Salvador than on a dynamic of estab-lishing links between the leadership and the base."[135] The FMLN tried to rectify this situation and instituted specific programs designed to maintain and reestablish relations with its rank and file. For example, all members of the Political Commission were assigned departments that they had to visit every weekend. It was their task to communicate with the militants in those areas and explain party policies and decisions. The observation of some of these meetings leads one to conclude that the party faced a tremen-dous challenge in fostering base democracy. In one such meeting, held in San Vicente in June 1998, attendance was abysmal even though the two featured speakers, Nidia Díaz and Facundo Guardado, were eminent party leaders. Despite great efforts by Díaz to discuss the party's platform for the 1999 presidential election in a didactically appropriate fashion, there was little participation by the audience. As has been discussed, the priorities of the ex-combatants were elsewhere. They had to focus on daily survival and had little time or energy left to participate in political activities of any kind. The challenges facing the FMLN and its counterparts can best be under-stood by listening to the voices from the FMLN's grass roots.

3

Voices from the Salvadoran Grass Roots

A Case Study of San José Las Flores, Meanguera,

and San Esteban Catarina

*Today we have to make the effort to identify more with women, in order to
integrate them in all programs, those of the government as well as those of
nongovernmental organizations. So, I think that we need clear programs
with the most minimal training for the men to help them understand that women
need a place, need an opportunity, and that this is part of the respect given
in the home and that women should not only be considered
the guardians who take care of the house.*
—Mayor of San Esteban Catarina

It is impossible to fully understand the reality of the Salvadoran peace
process without listening to the voices of the grass roots. As I have argued,
statistics give us only a partial picture and, for that matter, frequently a dis-
torted one. It is essential to hear the human voices in order to grasp the difficulties people confronted in the wake of the peace accords. While I focused my research on women, I included a considerable number of men to
obtain a comprehensive view. My research assistants and I interviewed a
total of 201 beneficiaries of reintegration programs: 141 women and 60 men
between December 1995 and September 1996. The group included ex-
combatants, FMLN supporters, as well as internal and external refugees
who returned to or were settled in the towns that were studied. The study
was conducted in three towns in different areas of the country, all of which

were strongly contested during the war: San José Las Flores in the department of Chalatenango, Meanguera in Morazán, and San Esteban Catarina in San Vicente. When we conducted the interviews, FMLN mayors governed all three towns. During the conflict different FMLN groups were centered in each of the three departments. Unless otherwise noted, all the quotations that follow are taken from a questionnaire that my team of researchers and I administered to all respondents. Except for the three mayors and one FMLN official, all names have been changed to protect our respondents.

In order to put the voices of the three towns into context, I will briefly summarize the results of a 1993 FMLN study, sponsored by the United Nations Children's Fund. It assessed the overall state of the FMLN's female members a year after the signing of the accords and included 1,100 of the 3,285 women registered at that time by the United Nations Observer Mission in El Salvador.[1] The study emphasized that the accords "do not deal explicitly with the gender question" and noted that women confronted a special set of problems in the reintegration phase due to the "difficulties inherent in their condition as women and the strong influence of patriarchal ideology that permeates Salvadoran society."[2] The socioeconomic profile of the female ex-combatants highlighted the challenge of reintegrating this sector into society. Two-thirds of the women were younger than thirty, and almost 20 percent were illiterate. Many suffered from health problems. Twenty percent suffered from headaches, 12 percent had problems with their nerves, and another 20 percent had poor vision. A central problem was the psychological trauma from the war. The ex-combatants had experienced the death, disappearance, and torture of loved ones and now faced rejection from their families for having abandoned them to join the struggle. The reencounter with their children was particularly painful.

Historical and Socioeconomic Background

San José Las Flores

San José Las Flores, a small town located 85 kilometers from the capital in the department of Chalatenango, had 5,854 inhabitants before the war. Due to bad roads, the town is much more isolated than the short distance from the capital would indicate. During the conflict, San José was part of the territory controlled by the Popular Forces of Liberation. The FPL used the town as one of its strongholds. The level of fighting was particularly intense during the early 1980s, when heavy army bombardments destroyed most of the town's infrastructure. Subsequently many members of the community were forced to abandon the town. They fled to Mesa Grande in Honduras or joined the guerrilla movement. Their shared suffering forged strong bonds among them.

When the war ended ex-combatants and FMLN supporters represented the majority of the town's population. With this base of support, the FMLN succeeded in getting its candidate for mayor elected in 1994. A total of sixty-two women and twenty men were interviewed during three field visits between December 1995 and July 1996. They reported that they had had little education, and 30 percent of the men and a slightly higher percentage of the women were not able to read or write. Living conditions were poor, and the inhabitants were in dire need of the benefits available under the various reintegration programs.

Meanguera

The town of Meanguera is located almost 200 kilometers from San Salvador in the department of Morazán, which borders Honduras. The area was the scene of fierce battles between the FMLN and the Salvadoran army. During the war, the town and its surrounding areas were part of the operational territory of the Revolutionary Army of the People led by Joaquín Villalobos. At the time of the interviews in 1996, the ERP leadership had left the FMLN and started to build a new party.[3]

The town stretches out alongside a main road. Of its 10,869 inhabitants in 1988, more than 10,000 were classified as rural. Many inhabitants of the town had to flee to Honduras during the conflict or seek safe haven in areas controlled by the guerrilla movement. The civilians were frequently caught in the crossfire. When they tried to escape to Honduras, the Honduran army pursued them; and when they stayed in El Salvador, they were considered guerrilla sympathizers and faced the onslaught of the Salvadoran army. Even before the signing of the peace accords, the former inhabitants of this area started to return from Honduras. During this period they counted on the support of the renowned academic and Jesuit priest Segundo Montes. Montes, the director of the human rights institute of the Central American University in San Salvador, studied the plight of the returning refugees and became their spiritual leader. He was assassinated by Salvadoran army personnel together with five other academics, their housekeeper, and her daughter, during the November 1989 FMLN military offensive. In honor of his memory some neighborhoods in the town adopted the name Segundo Montes. Rogelio Poncel, another Catholic priest, was also active in the area. The legacy of these two priests explains the strong commitment of the town's people to the tenets of Liberation Theology.

In 1996 Meanguera was one of a handful of towns governed by a female mayor. Concepción Márquez had been elected on the FMLN ticket. My colleagues and I interviewed forty women and twenty men here. Meangueraans had a higher rate of literacy than the inhabitants of the other towns in the study. Only 15 percent of the men and 20 percent of the women interviewed did not know how to read or write. As in the rest of El Salvador, fertility rates were high. On the average, the women interviewed had four children.

San Esteban Catarina

San Esteban Catarina in the department of San Vicente is located an hour by car from the capital. The town council in San Esteban Catarina was controlled by the FMLN in 1996. Initially, its members were suspicious of our interviewing activities and sought to impede them. The mayor had to intervene before the research could proceed. Nevertheless, comments such as "Here the council is in charge not the mayor" continued to be heard. The roots of this apparent conflict over authority were to be found in the continuing rivalries between the original FMLN groups. The mayor had been affiliated with the FPL in whose ranks he had fought for thirteen years. FPL members, however, were a minority in the department of San Vicente, where the Revolutionary Party of Central American Workers had been the predominant force during the war.

The majority of the population of San Esteban Catarina consisted of ex-combatants, FMLN supporters, and resettled refugees. Most of the respondents were from an outlying community called originally Caserío Calderitas. It was subsequently renamed Napoleón Marillas in honor of a priest who was assassinated by a death squad in 1979. About seventy ex-combatants lived in this community. A substantial number of the population originated from other parts of the country, such as Santa Ana, La Libertad, and Chalatenango. These people had sought safety in the capital, San Salvador, during the conflict of the 1980s. In addition to the internal refugees there were several families who had been in Honduras during the war. Around the time of the signing of the peace accords, these internal and external refugees were sent to San Esteban Catarina, one of the areas designated to be repopulated.

A total of thirty-nine women and twenty men were interviewed. The people in the town had little formal education. More than half had never attended primary school, and only one man and one woman had more than a secondary education. All shared a humble socioeconomic background. Most lived in wooden huts without the amenities people in urban areas take for granted. The houses had electricity but no indoor plumbing. The school building was in a state of severe deterioration. Of the three villages studied, San Esteban Catarina appeared to be the poorest. With no industry of any sort, the population lived from agriculture and remittances from family members living in the United States.

Joining the Struggle

San José Las Flores

During the conflict many women and men went "to the mountains" to join the guerrilla movement. Although most were motivated by their desire to fight social injustice, some were forced recruits. As we will see in the other towns, the FMLN did indeed at times use coercion to increase its ranks. Yet the repression unleashed by the army was a much more significant reason why Salvadorans became part of the guerrilla movement. San José Las Flores and its surroundings were the site of several massacres committed by the Salvadoran army. Survivors frequently decided that their chances of survival were better fighting with the FMLN than hoping that the army would respect the lives of civilians living in the combat zone. One afternoon in December 1995, Doña Avelina recounted her own personal tragedy from the war. In 1982, on the day the army attacked, she tried to escape by hiding in a ravine at the outskirts of town. On the way there her husband was shot by a soldier and died. When she reached the ravine, she covered her eight-year-old son with her own body hoping to protect him from the hail of bullets flying around them. When the soldiers finally withdrew, she discovered that her little boy was dead, having been shot despite her efforts. Over the course of the war, four of Doña Avelina's brothers and four of her nephews were killed. Avelina herself spent the rest of the war cooking for the *muchachos*.

Doña Antonia joined the struggle because of "the repression and not having land." Doña Amparo sought change: "The people didn't have jobs, and organized we could effect change." Doña Cecilia said, "we had no other alternative than this one." Doña Carmen considered fear the most important motivator: "I joined out of fear that the armed forces were in the area persecuting people. Many people died. This made one afraid." Some women simply followed the example of their fathers, being too young to have any personal ideological convictions. Doña Rosa joined the guerrilla movement at the age of seven. "Since my father joined, so did I. If my father had been part of ORDEN [a right-wing paramilitary organization], I also would have been part of it." Others fought to avenge their loved ones. Doña Mirta took up arms "to follow my brothers. There were three of them, and all died in the war." Doña Raquel, on the other hand "was part of a massive incorporation. They said it would be only for three months but it became more." Raquel's example illustrates that at times whole villages joined the FMLN. Many did so in the mistaken belief that the war would soon conclude with an FMLN victory. While some people deluded themselves into joining the guerrilla movement, others were given no choice.

There were a number of clear instances of forced recruitment. Doña Abigail had no choice: "Well, they told us that if we didn't go voluntarily, they would take us along by force. So I joined voluntarily." Doña María said: "We organized because the FMLN told us to. We didn't know why. They told us that those who did not join—who knows what would become of them? At best, they would be killed by one group or the other." Thus people were left with little choice if they did not want to get caught in the crossfire.

At times, the FMLN gained recruits for very specific reasons. In the areas of the country that were under its control, the guerrilla movement was successful in establishing a healthcare system. These services were provided to combatants and FMLN supporters. Dental care was particularly difficult for the FMLN fighters to obtain in the mountains. Since tooth problems were common, the guerrilla movement struggled to find a solution. The PRTC was especially ingenious. It sent four cadres to Mexico to receive training in basic dental care. Francisco Jovel, the PRTC commander, told me one evening that morale had improved enormously among PRTC fighters once their dental problems were attended to. He joked that the best way for Salvadoran security forces to identify FMLN collaborators in the countryside would have been to look for the peasants with the cleanest teeth. So some Salvadorans joined the guerrilla movement to attend to their health needs. Doña Reyna, who served the FMLN as a cook, told us, "Why should I lie to you. I joined because I was pure illness. I was only bones. I joined, and I cured myself."

Meanguera

Like women elsewhere, women in Meanguera joined the FMLN to change prevailing social conditions, and almost all of them served in support roles. Doña Lucia followed the call of the FMLN: "Party members told us that they were joining forces to improve the situation and that if we won, there would be a government with the participation of all, and there would be equality." Doña Purificación wanted to "help and support the muchachos in their just war." Doña Dora also wanted to help the guerrillas. She started to feed hungry FMLN fighters in 1979 and continued to serve in this civilian support role throughout the war. Although she was not officially demobilized, her contribution was recognized, and she received land. Doña Bartola wanted to escape the army's repression, particularly "the massacres and bombardments that happened in the community." Doña Miriam had nothing left to lose: "The army killed my family, and they threw bombs. One of them fell on my house, and I was left with nothing. They burned everything."

Don Gerundio who joined the FMLN in 1982, "wanted to help to end the injustice that had engulfed the country and felt the need to participate as a combatant to stop this situation." Others had experienced suffering up close. Don Ricardo became an FMLN combatant "because the army killed my parents and my brothers. Because of this, I decided to join." A small mi-

nority regretted their decision to join. Don Eligerio thought "it was a deception, because they said that they would win the war. But, as you know,
one never knows the outcome of a war." Don Luis, who had started to collaborate in 1979, had similar thoughts: "They lied to us. They told us they
would help us, but they took advantage of us."

As in the other towns, there were a few instances when men and women
reported that they had been recruited by force. Doña Angela joined "out
of fear, because they forced us." Sometimes the pressure was subtler, and
there were no claims of outright coercion. A number of female recruits
went to the mountains to fight, "because they told us to."

San Esteban Catarina

Several of the women and men interviewed in San Esteban Catarina
also said that they joined the FMLN because they were "obligated" to do
so. Donã Flora emphasized: "We were recruited by force. And, yes, my husband stayed [with the FMLN] and he was killed." Thus, forced recruitment,
a standard method employed by the Salvadoran army was to some degree
also used by the guerrillas. The majority of the respondents, however, participated in the struggle out of their own free will.

While most men were inspired by the possibility of combating prevailing injustices, women tended to join "because family members were already
in the guerrilla movement, because their families had been assassinated, or
because they sought to escape persecution by the Salvadoran army." Doña
Felicita joined "because there was so much suffering and because they killed
my two brothers in cold blood—they hanged them." Others supported the
ideals the FMLN stood for. Doña Romilia got involved "because they were
fighting for us—the poor—and to escape the poverty, but things got worse."
Doña Fidelina, who served as a cook from the early 1970s until 1983, was
motivated by love: "I loved my people, and this is the only reason for me.
There was no clothing nor money or anything, only love for my people."
Doña Vasilia went on to become an armed combatant and was eager to
fight. She became a member of the guerrilla forces in 1977 at the age of
twelve, "because I wanted to fight and because of my mother who had been
killed by the army." The great majority of the former guerrilla members,
both male and female, joined the struggle in the 1970s and 1980s. Only

one FMLN supporter was a latecomer to the cause, getting involved with the guerrilla movement in the 1990s. Two-thirds of the men said they were armed combatants during the war, while the rest served in support functions. The four women who reported that they had been combatants were all young. Older women contributed to the war effort by becoming members of grass-roots movements or performing logistical duties.

The human cost of the war was tremendous. Doña María Teresa's story is representative: "Yes, I had one child, a girl. She died when we were in the war. She got an inflammation. I took her to a doctor who was with us in the mountains, and he told me that the girl had water in one lung. She lasted me only three more days."

Demobilization and Benefits under the Peace Accords

Under the peace accords, the Land Transfer Program was conceived to resolve disputed land claims and provide resources for ex-combatants on both sides as well as civilians who were affected by the war.[4] The government, with financing from the United States and the European Community bought land and sold it to the beneficiaries. No individual mortgage was to exceed 30,000 colones (about $3,450). In the end, beneficiaries received an average of 6.8 acres costing about $3,000. The beneficiaries were supposed to repay their loans following a five-year grace period. Spence et al. have emphasized that most international observers agreed that the lands would not be "viable under the mortgage terms if planted in traditional peasant food crops."[5] Indeed there were a lot of problems. Following a mass protest in the mid-1990s, the government chose to forgive most of the agrarian debt.

According to a study of all demobilized female FMLN members, only half of the fighters asked to be included in the Land Transfer Program while two-thirds requested credit. All potential beneficiaries who had served as combatants were eligible to receive land and could apply for credit under another program. Almost 60 percent of the women intended to use their credit to start micro-enterprises, about 20 percent wanted to improve their housing, while 24 percent planned to buy land.[6] The average age of the demobilized combatants was twenty-seven, which indicates that most female combatants had joined the FMLN while in their teens. Thus the great majority had no knowledge or experience of productive activities such as farm-ing. Further, only one-fifth of the former fighters reported having housing of their own. Female FMLN members were in great need indeed.

San José Las Flores

The needs of ex-combatants living in the town were most readily rec-ognized. With few exceptions, the combatants went through the official ONUSAL demobilization process and appeared on beneficiary lists. FMLN supporters, on the other hand, faced a more difficult situation. Returning refugees in particular had to establish that they had lost loved ones and were entitled to benefits. Since women constituted the majority of the lat-ter group, they were at a disadvantage from the outset. Doña Alicia em-phasized that women frequently experienced problems because they lacked the documentation required to qualify for benefits. The most important program benefiting the respondents was the Land Transfer Program.

Despite their great need, female beneficiaries frequently showed little knowledge of or interest in the parcel of land that had been allocated to them. Instead, they tended to defer to their male companions. Doña Al-bertina knew she had received land but complained that those in charge "have not even shown me where the land is. I know it is very far away, and people say it is a deserted area." Her complaints do not reflect any incom-petence by the official in charge but rather show the lack of interest of a number of respondents because their parcels of land were apparently not conveniently located or they had no farming experience. This became clear when respondents were questioned more closely. Doña Albertina was not very excited about her land for another reason: "My husband does not farm. He works more as a bricklayer and carpenter." Although these kinds of complaints were more representative of female beneficiaries, there were also men who cared little about the land they had received. Don Manuel admitted that he had not inspected his property: "Look, I have not gone there yet, because the other day I was going to, and then there wasn't time. That is, the officials in charge said 'not today, better another day,' and so we still haven't gone to see it." FMLN officials, who worked very hard to help the beneficiaries refused to share responsibility for these problems.

While they acknowledged some shortcomings of the program, they criticized the lack of initiative shown by some respondents.

The majority of the beneficiaries decided to farm their land collectively. Don Alfonso explained: "Here we hold the land as a cooperative. We farm and get a little out of it—mostly basic grains—but we don't produce much." Don Fabian also emphasized the benefits of communal farming: "The land here is communal, and we work all together so everything is done more easily." Yet there were also voices of dissent. Doña Amparo objected to having to share the fruits of her labor: "Here, everything is done in benefit of the community, and we have nothing of our own." To be able to farm collectively was especially helpful to single female beneficiaries since they generally had no farming experience. Doña Elena lamented, "The most important problem is that we lack technical training for women." Wounded ex-combatants faced additional hurdles. Vilma had joined the FMLN at the age of twelve. She served as an armed combatant and was wounded. Although she had received land she was not able to farm it. "It has not been possible to work the land. I can't work it, and there is no one who can. The community can't work it because the land is in Nueva Concepción."

Most beneficiaries were either producing basic grains for family consumption or were raising cattle. Those who were not producing for the market had limited possibilities of generating cash income. Although this made it difficult for them to save the capital required to repay their loans, it greatly improved the beneficiaries' food security. The families involved in cattle farming showed a greater willingness to repay their loans. They were optimistic that they would be able to acquire the necessary funds during the five-year grace period. Until they could sell their cattle, however, their daily lives were quite precarious. In the best instances, beneficiaries participated in communal farming, giving them access to their daily subsistence needs, and raised cattle individually. Doña Elena was convinced of the benefits of cattle farming: "We invested the loan in cattle and the capital is growing. We have the grace period to get the money because now we don't have to pay."

In some families, several members had been supporting the FMLN in different capacities, and all of them were entitled to land. Don Miguel recounted that his wife, his daughter, and he himself received land: "My wife received land benefits as *tenedora* [people who had occupied land generally supportive of the FMLN], my daughter for being an ex-combatant, and I got land too. The three of us received benefits." The tenedores played an important role during the war. They occupied properties in areas that were controlled by the guerrilla movement and served as a logistical support structure, supplying food and information on enemy movement.

Meanguera

Fifty percent of the men interviewed had gone through the official de-mobilization process, and two-thirds had received benefits under the rein-sertion programs. The loans they obtained had been invested in cattle and the reconstruction of their homes. Less than half of the women had been officially demobilized, yet most affirmed that they had received land. The perception prevailed among the female beneficiaries that some women had been left out of the programs because they were pregnant, lived far away from the places of registration, or had to take care of their children, which inhibited them from registering their claims. There were also mispercep-tions regarding the programs. Several ex-combatants believed that they had the right to benefit under several programs simultaneously. For exam-ple, Doña Cecilia complained that she had been left out of the Land Trans-fer Program. On closer examination, it turned out that she had been in-cluded in the Industry and Services Program and thus had no right to receive land.

Rosa Elia Argueta, the FMLN official in charge of the local land distri-bution program, confirmed that a considerable number of militants had chosen not to demobilize and exhibited no interest in obtaining land. In her view, potential beneficiaries were reluctant to get into debt or thought that the land that would be allocated to them was too far away from their town to be of interest.[7] Some of these fears were justified. The land in the Meanguera area was of such poor quality that beneficiaries needed to bor-row a great deal of money to make the land productive. Potential benefi-ciaries who had little or no experience in farming under such conditions were understandably reluctant to assume such a high debt burden. Resi-dents of the town had the option of moving to another department of the country, such as Usulután, where land was of better quality and readily available; but with their roots firmly planted in Meanguera, FMLN militants and supporters showed no interest in this solution.[8]

As in the two other towns, most female beneficiaries knew little about the land they had acquired. Doña Isidra was representative of this lack of interest. When asked whether she had seen her new property, she replied: "No, we are still in this process. We still haven't gone to inspect it." As in so many other cases it was the distant location of her land that explained her attitude. Isidra, together with several other female beneficiaries, had received land outside of the neighboring town of San Miguel, at a distance of about 30 kilometers. None of the women had seen the land. They relied on Efigenio, the local FMLN representative, to take care of everything. While Efigenio could find an available plot of land and negotiate its sale on behalf of the women, he could not farm it for them. In many instances it was clear that the beneficiaries had abdicated their individual responsibility to such an extent that they didn't even know the amount of the loan they had taken out to buy their land. Others were not fully informed regarding the total cost of the land owned by the members of their collective. In light of this detached attitude, it is not surprising that most beneficiaries felt strongly that they should not be required to repay their loans.

The ex-combatants in Meanguera had a special reason to be disappointed with the reinsertion programs. During the war, the area was controlled by the ERP. The ERP leadership reportedly told its supporters that all the occupied land was theirs and that the guerrillas would defend it at all cost. When the ERP forces demobilized, honoring the peace accords, the guerrilla army could not make good on its promise. Without its protection the occupiers had to give up their claim to the land. As a consequence many felt deceived.

San Esteban Catarina

Only six women and four men in San Esteban Catarina acknowledged having been registered by ONUSAL. Because many more claimed to have been members of the guerrilla armies and had received land and other benefits it is clear that the number of people in San Esteban Catarina who were officially demobilized was much greater. It is evident that some people had gone through the official demobilization process but did not admit it. Others should have been part of the official process but were impeded from registering. In the case of the female respondents, it was frequently their husbands who did not permit them to be registered by ONUSAL. Typically, the men decided whether "their women" would participate. As Don Jesús recounted, "My wife did not receive benefits; I did not send her. I thought the more we had to pay back, the more problems it would cause. That's why I didn't register her." Don Jesús was reluctant to accept funds under the available loan programs for fear that the family would not be able to repay them. The small number of officially demobilized beneficiaries also indicated that many of the respondents were tenedores or returned refugees.

All the men and 80 percent of the women we spoke to received land. Some women told of having been left out because they lacked proper documentation. Doña María Teresa told of the case of her own daughter: "Yes, some were left out because they had no papers. My little girl, who was going to be seventeen, was one of them. They said that since she had no papers she would not get anything." Potential beneficiaries sometimes could not establish that they were entitled to benefits because they had no proof that their companions had been killed in the conflict. Women were less likely than men to have their basic legal documents in order. For example, a 1993 study of all female FMLN combatants established that while 80 percent had a birth certificate, 40 percent had no *carnet* (the Salvadoran election ID).[9] It is clear that many women were not able to exercise their full citizen rights because they lacked proper documentation. Women were frequently confined to the private sphere of the household, while the husbands were the full citizens. Young people also experienced special problems. Ex-combatants, whether male or female, who had not reached the age of sixteen at the time of the accords were not eligible to receive land.[10]

The majority of the beneficiaries had their properties legally registered with the help of a local FMLN official in charge of the Land Transfer Program. Many, particularly women, had never visited their properties and had little information about them. Doña Sofía's response was typical: "I got land where the property of Salvador Zavala is located. I don't know it very well." Most of the beneficiaries were organized in collectives. It was not always clear whether the women we interviewed had benefited personally or whether only their husbands had received property. Even when the property title was in their names, female militants indicated that their male companions would farm the land while they would be in charge of domestic duties.

The interviews showed little evidence that traditional gender relations were changing. The mayor portrayed the current situation as follows: "The problem we have is that the man, at times, due to the tradition and custom that we have in this country, is the one that decides. And he has the control because of his practical experience in agriculture. It is he who dominates the agrarian decisions. But the women also play an important role in that they are the support in the family."

Although the great majority of the people interviewed had received land and loans, they were discouraged about their living conditions. Some beneficiaries had been able to use their loans productively, but most reported that they did not believe they would be able to repay their debts. Several had used their loans to pay for contingencies such as sickness instead of investing in their properties. Most argued that they would be incapable of repaying their loans, and several thought that "in light of so many years of struggle, the land should have been given free of charge."

According to the mayor, the lack of adequate housing was the biggest problem. He claimed that all the housing programs went to the southern parts of San Vicente, leaving the ex-combatants in San Esteban Catarina without benefits.[11] Another problem that needed to be resolved was that a number of people living in the community had been assigned properties in other locations. Yet they refused to move and continued to occupy the housing allocated to other beneficiaries.[12]

The community was creative in finding ways to help those who had not received land because they had been in hiding and were not included in any of the beneficiary lists. In some instances, several members of a family had received land. Those family members who did not need their land or were not willing or able to pay for it, ceded their properties to the latecomers in need.[13] The benefits that these "outsiders" received, however, created considerable resentment. The voices of dissent argued that this group had resettled in San Esteban Catarina only to get land, and that they had not participated in the war effort. Doña Luisa complained bitterly, "People who have not suffered have benefited the most. We have suffered bitterly because we confronted the government. This afternoon is not long enough to tell you all our suffering. And here they brought in people who have benefited and have not suffered; they don't know what war is like."

Current Participation in the FMLN

San José Las Flores

Even though this town had been a guerrilla stronghold during the war, there was great political apathy there in early 1996. The majority of the beneficiaries showed little interest in participating in FMLN activities, and only a handful had officially joined the new party. The lack of information was astounding at times. For example, few respondents were aware that the FPL, the FMLN group that had dominated life in the town for many years, had formally ceased to exist, having held its final meeting in December 1995. Doña Albertina knew about the FPL dissolution from the news, not from any local FPL cadres. Although municipal assemblies were held to give the rank and file up-to-date information on party business, they were not well attended. Doña Angelita considered that these meetings were only for former armed combatants, not for people like her who had served in a support role: "I didn't go," she said. "This was only for those that carried weapons, not for helpers." Angelita had served the FMLN as a cook for twelve years, and two of her sons were killed fighting with the guerrillas.

War-related illness also kept interested militants from attending party meetings. Doña Celina and several other women reported that they could not attend because they were ill. Doña Yolanda gave the saddest explanation for not having participated: "I didn't go. I was confined at home because my child died."

These statements indicate gender-related difficulties and an apparent lack of discussion among the rank and file concerning important developments. Party cadres failed to adequately explain key developments to the grass roots, and delegates to national meetings appear to have been selected without full participation by the base in the municipal meetings leading up to the national convention.

Similarly, the people we spoke with showed little knowledge about the events surrounding the FMLN's recent National Congress. Party officials explained that this was because FMLN supporters were having difficulty in adjusting to the postwar reality. Thus, the inability of party cadres to involve the grass roots in the decision-making process was not only a reflection of their own inadequacies but was also the result of difficult circumstances. The former combatants and supporters still held favorable views of the FMLN, but they had to give priority to the necessities of daily life over active involvement in the party. Women, in particular, stated that their daily responsibilities left them no time to engage in party activities. Doña Isabel emphasized how difficult it was to combine domestic duties with an active political life: "Only my husband went to the FPL meeting because I have small children." Doña Angelita concurred: "Only Samuel, my husband, went." Doña Vilma added: "I would have gone, but my child was ill." However, these impediments to active participation in the life of the party could not explain the limited knowledge rank-and-file members had of national party activities. For example, only a handful of militants were able to name the party's secretary general, Salvador Sánchez, who had been the main commander of FPL forces during the war.

Meanguera

In Meanguera, the FMLN leadership confronted a particularly complex task in maintaining and reestablishing ties to its supporters. As discussed in Chapter Four, the ERP, the main FMLN group present in the area during the war, broke with the FMLN in 1994. This left militants in the area in a quandary. Should they support "their" group—the ERP—and join the new Partido Demócrata (Democratic Party, or PD) being built by Joaquín Villalobos, or should they affiliate with the FMLN. Adding to the confusion, the PD dissidents claimed they represented the "true FMLN" and asked militants to join their new party. In general, local residents had little knowledge regarding the key issues that had precipitated the break. Thus they were without direction, making it difficult for either the FMLN or the PD to connect with potential supporters. A sizable minority of both men and women was alienated by the infighting and refused to be active in either party. The mayor, Concepción Márquez, was caught in the middle of this fight. She remained loyal to the FMLN and thus faced opposition from the supporters of the PD.[14] No love was lost between the former allies. One of her critics told her: "I am supporting the party of the center [the Democratic Party] and you the radical communists." To which the mayor replied: "You are not of the center, but of a corrupt party that sold out."

These special circumstances distinguished Meanguera from the two other towns in the study. Many respondents felt a need to reaffirm their militancy within the FMLN or advertise their support for Villalobos. The great majority of the men supported the FMLN and voiced disapproval of their former leader, Villalobos. Despite their acknowledged support for the FMLN, however, half of them could not name the current head of the party. Women were similarly out of touch with party affairs at the national level, although two-thirds claimed to be active in the FMLN.

The mayor had been invited to participate in the FMLN's National Congress. She did not attend, however, due to illness. The involvement of most militants in party events was obviously restricted to FMLN activities at the local level. At the time of the interviews, the FMLN held a meeting to inform the people about the state of the Land Transfer Program and the agrarian debt and the measures the party was proposing. The assembly was well attended by women and men. This suggests that FMLN militants were involved in the life of the party when it mattered to them personally, while they stayed aloof from the internal squabbles at the national level.

San Esteban Catarina

The majority of the men and women who were born in San Esteban Catarina were organized in the PRTC, whereas most of the people who were relocated there had belonged to the FPL or the ERP. By mid-1996, the partisan struggle within the FMLN had not been resolved. Doña Flora indicated that her family was not active in the party because "my companion is from the ERP, and this causes problems."

Two thirds of the males claimed to be active in the FMLN. Although 50 percent of the men were aware that the 1995 Party Congress had taken place, only one could name the party's secretary general, Salvador Sánchez. This lack of knowledge was astounding considering that several militants expressed interest in being FMLN candidates for local government positions. The picture was no different for the women. Although half of them claimed to be politically active, few had knowledge of the Party Congress, and not a single woman could name the party's leader.

It was evident that the FMLN experienced problems in its efforts to maintain and reinforce relations with its militants. Yet there were also FMLN supporters who had had little involvement with the FMLN in the first place. Doña Blanca, who had fled to the United States during the war, announced that she was not active in the party: "I never got involved, since I never understood what they wanted." When asked whether she knew about the recent Party Congress, she went on to elaborate: "They didn't tell us about the congress, but the one who knows of these things is my husband." Her lack of political involvement did not keep her from eagerly seeking to benefit from the land program. "Thanks to God they included us in the lists, and we got some land." For several women political activity was no longer a priority under the prevailing conditions. As Donã Reyna said, "Today we are not active any more, but we always give them our support." Doña María expressed similar sentiments when she said, "Today, not any more. Every one looks out for her bone. Before one had to be of one band or the other."

At the time of the interviews, an FMLN assembly took place to nominate a group of possible candidates for the 1997 elections. Several of the men from San Esteban Catarina attended, but not a single women. Women suffered from the tradition under which "the man goes and the woman stays at home preparing the food." The gender composition of this meeting confirmed the impression that men were more active in the daily life of the party than women. Even though participation in party activities was limited, this did not mean that FMLN officials were not actively involved in the life of the community. In particular, the members of the community benefited from the work of FMLN cadres who had facilitated the implementation of the reintegration programs. The beneficiaries depended especially on the member of the community council designated to solve problems related to the Land Transfer Program.

Gender Relations during and after the War

During the war, gender roles within the FMLN were not drastically different from those that prevailed in civil society. Based on a study of all demobilized female combatants, almost 30 percent had served as cooks in the guerrilla movement, and 15 percent had been engaged in health-related activities. Only 15 percent had been armed combatants, while 11 percent had been in support roles. The remaining 40 percent had exercised other functions.[15]

Women were obviously pushed to resume traditional roles once the war ended. While somewhat over 50 percent had worked in the household before the war, a year after the signing of the peace accords 95 percent reported being engaged in domestic work. However, this change was probably not quite as drastic as the figures indicate, since many women joined the war when they were still in their teens and had no primary responsibility for the household. In 1993, one-third of all women were heads of household, while another 20 percent were single. Half of the female ex-combatants had a steady companion or husband. Fifty percent of these women claimed that their partners shared all domestic tasks with them, while one-third had partners who supported them financially. Fewer than 4 percent, however, reported that their male partners helped in taking care of the children.[16]

When discussing gender relations within the FMLN it is important to keep in mind that the culture that prevailed within the guerrilla movement and the party reflected, to a great extent, the conditions of Salvadoran society. Thus a representative 1993 study found that "although there exists a level of consciousness concerning [gender] equality among FMLN members, awareness regarding the significance and implications of gender is still incipient."[17]

San José Las Flores

Both men and women in this town tended to agree that decisions during the war were made jointly. However, while men were primarily armed combatants, women served mostly in support roles. In confirmation of this, few women could be found in leadership positions at the time of demobilization. Women were frequently assigned traditional domestic tasks during the conflict, including the preparation of meals.

The majority of the women in San José Las Flores held the view that gender relations had improved since the war. Two-thirds reported that their husbands helped with domestic chores, including taking joint responsibility for childcare. Yet there were also descriptions of typically male attitudes.

Doña María felt she had a good husband, but he had his limits when it came to cooking: "Concerning meals he says he is not going to do it, thank you." Doña Vilma concurred. Her husband refused to share domestic tasks. He was in charge of their *milpa* (plot of land) and that was it. Doña Deysi reported that her husband would never participate in the kitchen. However, when necessary, he was willing to watch the children. Older men were particularly reluctant to engage in domestic chores. Don Nazario who was sixty-eight confessed that under exceptional circumstances he would be willing to lower himself to such a task: "I have done the dishes. Sure, man, I have done it. When she got sick I helped her."

Women conveyed a strong belief that their husband "worked" while they only "took care of the household." Thus, contrary to the beneficiaries' statements, traditional gender relations appeared to have changed little. The perceptions of improvement appeared to be based on how easy civilian life was compared with the harsh reality of the war. Don Manuel described his view as follows: "Before, things were pretty fucked up, primarily the suffering of walking up and down in the hills. Now things are better even though they are not good, but at least one gets a rest."

In general, family relations were greatly affected by the war. Many men and women were killed in the conflict, making traditional nuclear families the exception. Doña Alicia attested to these difficulties when asked about the relationship with her current husband: "Now we are doing fine because he loves my children even though he is not their father." In light of the difficult conditions men and women faced during their reintegration into society, it is noteworthy that there were only isolated cases of acknowledged domestic violence.

Half the women claimed to be active in the local women's movement. Those who were involved were better informed about their rights. They had received information concerning laws governing child support, paternal responsibility, and domestic violence. The other half participated more in activities sponsored by organizations, such as peasant movements, that dealt with their immediate needs. Practical concerns also dominated the agenda of the women's movement. During the period of the interviews, a women's meeting was held to plan the main activities for the year. Interestingly, the goals they arrived at concerned community needs instead of women's practical or strategic gender interests. They included rebuilding the church and the houses in the community, strengthening religious faith, presenting more projects benefiting women to potential donors, and preserving the environment.

Meanguera

Only one of the forty women interviewed reported having served as an armed combatant during the war. Almost half had served as cooks, while the others had been in various support roles. In the case of the twenty men, on the other hand, the picture was reversed. The majority had been armed combatants, and only a few were in support roles. The traditional division of labor that tended to prevail in the guerrilla movement had an obvious impact on gender relations. Although the majority of both men and women reported that decisions during the war were made jointly, men tended to make the important decisions while women carried out orders. As Doña Blanca put it: "Men made the decisions because they were in charge." The sense of joint decision-making was based more on formal equality and the climate of camaraderie in the guerrilla movement than on substantive equality. Doña María emphasized that the members of the guerrilla movement were all equal and thus made decisions jointly "because we all fought for the same goals." Both women and men did make decisions but mostly in their own realms. Doña Lucia made this point succinctly: "In the shop, where we made bombs, the person in charge was a man, and in the kitchen, I was in charge." Doña Reinalda confirmed that "the women made the decisions in the kitchen, but for the rest, it was the men."

Gender relations between former fighters and FMLN supporters in the wake of the peace accords did not differ noticeably from those in society at large. While two-thirds of the men noticed improved relations with their partners since the war, only 40 percent of the women did. While life became easier for men once the fighting ended, the situation was different for women. The perceived equality of the war days gave way to a life dominated by a traditional division of labor that favored men. This situation influenced spousal relations. The interview process itself revealed that traditional patterns were very much alive. Men continued to dominate the conversation. In many interviews conducted with female respondents they interfered, speaking for their wives or telling them what to say. Doña Martina emphasized that men "preferred to speak for their wives and won't let women talk."

The overwhelming majority of the male respondents claimed that they helped their partners with domestic chores and contributed financially to their children's living and education expenses. Not surprisingly, women had a somewhat different view. While half the women reported that their husbands helped in bringing up the children, a substantial minority (about 20%) said that their partners did not help with either the household or the children. One-third of the women refused to answer any questions dealing with current gender relations. It is reasonable to assume that they were not too pleased with the current state of affairs. Only a handful of women, however, acknowledged having been mistreated by their spouses. It was evident that this was a subject they were reluctant to talk about.

Although the town had a female mayor, it hardly meant that women enjoyed a higher status in Meanguera compared to other towns. The mayor commanded respect, not because people had a strong gender consciousness, but because she had earned it with her participation in the struggle. Almost one-third of the women in Meanguera were active in the local women's movement. The great majority, however, had little knowledge about women's rights under Salvadoran law. Almost no one had attended workshops or received instruction on domestic violence or reproductive health issues.

San Esteban Catarina

Many respondents had been widowed due to the war, and most lived in common-law marriages. Some, like Doña María, had remarried: "I found me another old man after they had killed my other one." Interestingly, the younger and older men (those under forty and over sixty) argued that during the war, only men made decisions. Several middle-aged men, on the other hand, maintained that decisions were made by both genders. Except for those over sixty, all men claimed that they participated actively in household duties, contributing financially and personally to the children's education. The older men emphasized that they spent the majority of their time farming. In their eyes, helping with household duties was of little significance, since this was "women's work." They considered gender relations to have improved compared to the war period. Considering their views, that meant they were satisfied that traditional gender roles were once again dominant. However, they believed that the tranquillity of family life was under attack from the increase in crime and violence. An indication of the prevailing insecure living conditions was the strong military presence in the village. In addition, there were patrols by the local National Civilian Police forces.

The majority of the younger women either agreed with their male cohorts that men tended to make the decisions during the war or refused to answer the question. Yet women over sixty maintained that women and men had made decisions jointly. It appears that the latter had overly rosy memories of the actual conditions women experienced during the war or simply had much lower expectations than the younger generation. Fewer than half the women thought that gender relations had improved since the war. Those who did see improvement claimed that their husbands helped with household chores and raising the children. While all the women who answered this question denied that they were mistreated by their husbands or suffered domestic violence, one-third refused to comment on this problem.

The ideological affinities of the respondents were also a factor that at times got in the way of tightly knit family relations. Although the FMLN was officially a unified party in 1996, old divisions, based on affiliation with one of the five groups, emerged whenever controversial topics were being discussed. These conflicts even played themselves out between members of the same family.

Only six of the female respondents were active in the women's movement. None of them belonged to the older generation. This was not too surprising if we take into account that no women's movement had established a local chapter in the area. Few women exhibited any kind of abstract knowledge of their rights as codified in the Family Code or knew of the existence of the Family Tribunals. Yet several women were informed regarding issues that affected their lives directly. For example, they knew about their right to alimony and that children from common-law marriages had the right to inherit. Few had benefited from workshops sponsored by the women's movement. For example, only 10 percent had received any training in health, and only one woman acknowledged having had access to information on reproductive rights.

Daily Life and Expectations of the Future
in the Three Communities

San José Las Flores

The members of this community had little confidence in 1996 that the ARENA government would fully comply with the peace accords, and many voiced disappointment that their living situation had improved so little. The sense of disillusionment was particularly evident among those who had joined the war effort in order to contribute to a new society with greater equality.

Discontent with the requirement that beneficiaries repay their loans was widespread. There was a general perception that the loans were gifts that had been earned because of the suffering inflicted on them during the war. Don Juan expressed the opinion of many: "If I have to repay the loan, I will be lost. The government has to pay it because we have suffered so much in the war. Also, they say that this is money donated by Germany." Women and men concurred that it would be impossible for them to repay the loans they had received to buy land. There was concern in the community that people would not be able to build a new life under the prevailing difficult economic circumstances. Poverty was omnipresent, and there were signs of malnourishment. In some cases, the legacy of the war complicated people's life. Don Pablo emphasized that his problems had to do with war-related illness. He was having problems making ends meet: "I am doing badly now because I got ill from the war. I have a kidney tumor. I had to spend the loan on this." Others had problems because they invested in cattle that subsequently died or were stolen. In general, beneficiaries were overwhelmed by the magnitude of their needs compared with their limited resources. Doña Liliam wondered whether she and her companion had used her loan badly: "We used up this loan; we used it badly. Well, it was necessary for us to buy some things because what they gave us [beneficiaries received a package of basic farm implements] was not sufficient."

There was also criticism of the local authorities who belonged to the FMLN. Charges of favoritism in the implementation of the benefits programs were coupled with recriminations over a perceived lack of commitment to improve the lives of the townspeople. At the same time, there were expressions of unconditional support for the FMLN. Don Cándido replied when asked whether he was politically active in any party: "Yes, in the FMLN until I die. As long as there is no political and economic justice, I will not stop fighting."

Respondents tended to have a parochial perspective on their difficulties. They did not know about the economic policies implemented by the government and how they affected their lives. Several donor agencies were pursuing development projects in the town. Alas, most were in disarray, due to misuse of funds or other problems. Reflecting conditions in the country in general, crime was on the rise. There were incidents of robbery, assault, and kidnapping. The difficult economic and social situation manifested itself in the appearance of drunks. Neither crime nor public intoxication had existed during the war. Evangelical movements were on the rise, indicating that the people were looking for new answers to their problems. All these phenomena were a sign that the social fabric, so tightly knit during the conflict, was torn. Overall, San José Las Flores presented the image of a desolate town whose inhabitants' spirits were low. The only church was in ruins, with its roof caved in; the public square lay abandoned; and the streets were dirty. These conditions made a number of ex-guerrillas question whether the struggle had made sense. With this town, which had achieved prominence as a guerrilla stronghold, in such bad shape, one also had to wonder how other, less well-known places were doing.

Yet despite these difficulties, FMLN militants and supporters hoped that the future would hold improvements for themselves and their children. Doña Miriam expressed the expectations of many: "I don't want to be a millionaire, but at least I would like decent food, good health, and work in order to support and maintain the children. I would like to see a good future so my children can have everything: a house, education, healthcare. I want them to have the best so they can make their place in the world. One gives them food but not everything they want or need."

Meanguera

The male respondents in Meanguera were quite sophisticated in their understanding of national economic policies. They knew about neoliberalism and globalization and rejected the policies of privatization implemented by the ARENA government. Their attitudes and level of information contrasted sharply with those of the respondents in the two other towns. Both men and women agreed that they were unable to repay the loans they had received. Most had no intention of even trying. They considered that they deserved these financial benefits in light of their suffering during the war.

Meanguera projected a positive image. It was less isolated than the two other towns, mainly because of its location alongside an important paved road. The town had also become a tourist attraction. The murder of the Jesuits had jolted world consciousness, and many people wanted to see the town that so strongly identified with the legacy of Segundo Montes. There was also an important FMLN museum in Perquín, a neighboring town. Because it was so well known, the town was the center of activity for a number of nongovernmental aid agencies, which implemented programs there.

In general, the townspeople presented a spirit of solidarity. This manifested itself in the number of small businesses that were jointly owned and managed by the community. Also, there was concern for the most vulnerable members of the community, exemplified by this statement by Don Carlos: "I am worried for all my compañeros in the community because there are many women who have been left alone and have many children. They don't have work to buy food. These are the ones that should get help. Also, there are people suffering from war wounds, and they have received no help."

In contrast to San José Las Flores, Meanguera showed no evidence of increased crime or other obvious signs of social deterioration. People had concrete ideas about how to improve their lives. The demobilized women in particular expressed the hope that they would be able to continue their education, which had been interrupted during the war.

San Esteban Catarina

Those interviewed in San Esteban Catarina expressed mixed evaluations of the peace accords. A typical phrase heard was the hope "to see their dreams realized, such as having land in their name, being able to sow, and having money to educate sons and daughters." They expected that in their old age they would be able to count on their children's support. As one women said: "I want to help my son to study so he can help me when I am old." Younger men were particularly critical of the ARENA government and argued that "they were poorer than ever before." In their view, the reinsertion programs were inadequate, and they felt they "had fought so hard for so little." Despite their disappointments, however, they continued to express support for the FMLN.

Several members of the community expressed solidarity with the ex-combatants of the Salvadoran army, who, in their opinion, had also been left out in the cold. On several occasions former FMLN combatants joined forces with demobilized soldiers in national demonstrations to press the government to comply with the accords. Both sides had come to realize that ex-combatants from both the FMLN and the army suffered under the injustice that some members of their respective institutions did receive benefits under the accords while others were left out.

The work of FMLN officials on behalf of the community was generally recognized. Don Cecilio emphasized: "Look, I think that those who have worked the hardest on behalf of the population have been in the Party." Doña Felipa shared his opinion: "Well, it was the Party that fought so we could realize this goal, that they would give us this little piece of land. Because before we didn't have a place to grow corn. We were renting and maybe didn't make enough to pay for the fertilizer or the rent."

In terms of gender relations, one is left with the general impression that little has changed to affect women's subordination to their partners or fathers. Some women expressed the view that they had been better off under the government of President Napoleón Duarte that had preceded the two ARENA administrations. This view prevailed even though the current mayor was strongly in favor of women's rights and fought to provide opportunities for the women in the community:

When I took office here in the municipality, there were projects, for example street building, that were financed by the Secretariat of National Reconstruction. I always sought the participation of women in those programs and saw to it that women earned the same wages as men. I incorporated 50 percent women and 50 percent men in the work of street construction. The community appreciated me. They said that it was the first time in history that a mayor gave women the opportunity to work and that no other mayor's office in the Department had taken any woman into account in the work plan. But I had problems with the Secretariat, with those who were administering the funds. The Secretariat, well there they had restrictions on women. *They even made fun of me.*

Conclusion

In all three communities we find common themes. A general problem for both genders was rising, unmet expectations. Former combatants and FMLN supporters questioned whether their sacrifices had been worth it. Although they had received benefits, particularly land, as a result of the peace accords, their standard of living continued to be abysmal. There was general agreement that the financial burden the beneficiaries assumed in order to buy land was too great and that the debt had to be forgiven. The FMLN leadership shared the concerns of its constituents. It had been aware from the beginning that the reinsertion programs would do little to improve the standard of living of its ex-combatants. In an October 1992 letter to the secretary-general of the United Nations, Boutros Boutros-Gahli, the FMLN leadership expressed its concern "that the size of the lots would leave the land-transfer programme's beneficiaries at current levels of subsistence and poverty."[18]

The FMLN leadership tried its best to rectify unforeseen problems related to the reintegration programs, and its officials worked very hard on their implementation. The early perception of widespread institutionalized discrimination against women under the peace accords was not confirmed by the study of the two hundred beneficiaries in the three villages. However, the stories that women told made it clear that the implementation of the peace accords needs to be seen through a gender lens. Such a perspective reveals the gender-specific challenges that female FMLN militants and supporters faced. Significantly, even though women did benefit from the reinsertion programs, they tended to defer to the men in all aspects of ownership, whether it concerned establishing legal property rights, knowledge of where their properties were located, or cultivating their plots. Nevertheless, one important change from prewar conditions was that women had become landowners. Don Miguel, a respondent from Meanguera, emphasized that before the war few women owned property. Those who did had either inherited land from their parents or had assumed ownership after their husbands passed away.

Based on the interviews in the three towns, the practice of forced recruitment by the FMLN, while not institutionalized, was nevertheless more widespread than commonly believed. Further, the interviews provided evidence that the FMLN faced a difficult task in maintaining and strengthening its relations with rank-and-file members after the war ended. The lack of participation by FMLN militants in local meetings is of particular concern from the perspective of internal party democracy. In general, FMLN supporters affirmed that the flow of information had been better during the war.

Although all respondents were pleased to have escaped the harsh conditions of the war, many emphasized that peace brought a host of new challenges. During the war their basic needs were taken care of. The combatants found shelter as best they could in the mountains and shared their meager supplies, or they starved together. No one had to worry about paying rent or electric bills or finding a job so that they could feed the children. Don Jesús expressed the sentiments of many: "During the war it was tough, but entering peace, entering civil life, one lacks the necessary economic resources."

4

The Vanguard in Search of a New Identity

Incipient Democratization

*Freedom only for the supporters of the government, only for the members
of one party—however numerous they may be—is not freedom at all.
Freedom is always and exclusively freedom
for the one who thinks differently.*
—Rosa Luxemburg

Political parties are key actors in the Central American transition toward
more democratic forms of government. In order to advance the process of
democratization in their countries, the former guerrilla movements have to
democratize themselves and effectively "articulate the demands and perspectives emerging from the newly-mobilized sectors."[1] For the revolutionary Left this challenge comes at a time when it has to reinvent itself
ideologically. Forrest Colburn has argued that "the shared intellectual culture of contemporary revolutions has centered on a commitment to 'socialism.'"[2] In Central America the guerrilla leadership was quite explicit
that the revolutionary war was conducted under the banner of socialism.
The demise of *Realsozialismus* in the Soviet Union and Eastern Europe,
however, led to a rethinking of socialist ideology within the revolutionary
Left of Latin America, Africa, and Asia. The socialist paradigm, the "guiding light" of revolutionary movements in the developing world, was suddenly perceived to have lost its legitimacy. Schafik Hándal, former leader
of the now dissolved Communist Party of El Salvador[3] and one of the five
FMLN military commanders during the war, affirmed recently that in light

of this postsocialist reality the FMLN started the process of formulating a new political project. Referring to the communists within the FMLN, he argued, "When we talk about the communists, we are talking about the communists at the end of this century, people who are elaborating a thinking that is not yet written."[4]

El Salvador

The FMLN officially completed the conversion from an armed guerrilla movement to a legal political party by the end of 1992. The new party consisted of the same five distinct groups that were part of the FMLN during the war: the Fuerzas Populares de Liberación, the Ejército Revolucionario del Pueblo, the Fuerzas Armadas de Liberación, the Resistencia Nacional, and the Partido Revolucionario de Trabajadores Centroamericanos. The party leadership recognized the difficulties entailed in the transformation from a hierarchical military movement into a democratic political party. According to Francisco Jovel, one of its five original commanders, the FMLN had learned several important lessons from observing the Sandinista and Cuban experiences up close. It particularly wanted to avoid the paternalism of the revolutionary leadership in Nicaragua and its failure to sufficiently democratize the Sandinista party. It also considered Cuba's dependence on the Soviet Union a shortcoming.

The FMLN conceived a long-term project that would slowly transform the authoritarian structures prevailing in El Salvador. It was foreseen that this plan would be achieved over a time period of two or three presidential elections and three to four parliamentary elections, stretching until 2005.[5] The leadership recognized that it needed to develop the capacity to govern over time. The initial priority was to gain power at the local level— the municipalities. At the grass-roots level the FMLN would be better able to attend to the needs of its constituents, in particular the ex-combatants and their families. In the wake of the 1992 peace accords, some FMLN leaders actually feared that the new party might win the 1994 elections. They argued that the new party needed time to grow into a political force capable of satisfying the demands such a victory would unleash among its supporters. In their view the FMLN's goal should be more modest and focus on gaining representation in parliament. The party could then use this platform to strengthen the parliament's power vis-à-vis the executive branch and to push for a decentralization of power in general. Before the FMLN could focus on these more realistic propositions, however, it had to evolve from a military organization into a political party.

From Guerrilla Movement to Political Party

Schafik Hándal has acknowledged that the first steps of the new party were difficult ones. The FMLN knew the rules of armed struggle quite well, but it was a novice in the political game.[6] Officials of the governing party reportedly enjoyed it when they were given an opportunity to embarrass FMLN militants who failed to observe proper protocol. In one instance, a high-ranking FMLN official went before the commission overseeing the implementation of the peace accords to denounce a number of abuses and instances of noncompliance with key provisions of the agreement. The commission chair responded to his hand-written note of protest by throwing it back to him with this comment: "Type this in triplicate, and then resubmit it for our consideration." Much more significant than these personal embarrassments was the failure of the FMLN leadership to fully grasp the complexities of the Salvadoran electoral system. Out of ignorance, the FMLN failed to insist on several reforms that would have leveled the playing field.[7]

An immediate problem that the party leadership had to confront was whether or not to preserve the FMLN's decision-making structures. During the war, the FMLN was led by a five-member *comandancia general* (General Command) made up of the commanders of the five armies. The General Command was part of a fifteen-member Political Commission, which constituted the second-highest decision-making body. Each of the five commanders selected two other members from his army to serve on the commission. The first casualty in the process of transforming the guerrilla movement was the Comandancia.[8] Thus, the fifteen-member Political Commission replaced the General Command as the highest decision-making body of the new party. The Commission was to be led by a coordinator who needed two-thirds of the fifteen members' votes to be elected. This qualified majority was very difficult to achieve, leaving the new party for several months without an elected leader.[9] Following the 1994 revision of the FMLN statutes, the coordinator needed only 60 percent of the vote to get elected. A further problem that the new party leadership had to solve concerned the composition of the FMLN's decision-making structures. Traditionally, each of the five groups incorporated into the FMLN had been given equal weight in terms of the number of seats allocated to a particular group.[10] In order to preserve unity, this system was left intact. Thus, each group had three representatives on the Political Commission. In the early 1990s, the members of the Commission were not chosen in a competitive electoral process. Rather, each FMLN group presented three candidates whose selection was ratified by the National Council.

Each FMLN group had ten guaranteed seats on the party's main deliberative body, the National Council. There were indications, however, that the quota system ensuring each FMLN group equal representation would not be maintained indefinitely. In 1992, fourteen new members who represented El Salvador's departments were added to the Council.[11] The allocation of these fourteen seats (one for each department) was based on the relative strength the five groups had in a particular department, thus favoring the three large groups, the FPL, the ERP, and the FAL.

One of the initial tasks for the emerging party was to select its candidates for the March 1994 legislative elections. While candidates were se-

Table 4.1   FMLN Legislative Assembly Candidates for the 1994 Elections by FMLN Group

Group	Candidates	Substitutes	Total	%	As % of FMLN personnel*
ERP	15	17	32	19.0	26.2
PCS	22	19	41	24.4	15.0
FPL	22	22	44	26.2	33.8
PRTC	12	11	23	13.7	8.3
RN	13	12	25	14.9	16.7
MNR	0	2	2	1.2	
Affiliation					
Unknown	0	1	1	0.6	
Total	84	84	168	100.0	100.0

Source: This distribution is based on candidate lists provided by the FMLN.

*Relative strength of FMLN groups at the time of demobilization.

Table 4.2   Party Structure of the FMLN

Level	Party Authorities
National	National Convention
	National Council
	Political Commission
Department	Department Convention
	Department Authorities
Local	Municipal Convention
	Municipal Authorities

Source: FMLN.

lected from all the five groups, the data indicate that the party was beginning to shift away from the maintenance of an artificial balance. Other factors, such as a potential candidate's political experience, began to take
precedence. The FPL's 26.2 percent share of candidates was somewhat less
than its due, based on the relative strength of the five groups at the time of
demobilization. Most noticeable, however, were the underrepresentation
of the ERP and the rise of the Communist Party and the PRTC. It is not
surprising that the Communist Party was successful in the political arena.
Its cadres constituted the second largest contingent of the FMLN's political personnel at the time of the 1992 demobilization. Even more important, the Communist Party cadres had honed their political skill over
decades, while many of the other FMLN militants had no previous experience in politics.

The nomination process for candidates to the legislative assembly involved the FMLN's national and departmental structures. In El Salvador,
the legislative assembly consists of eighty-four members. Twenty members
are elected from the countrywide national list of candidates, while the remaining sixty-four are selected by voting for candidates in individual departments.[12] In accordance with this system, the FMLN's national decision-making bodies were responsible for selecting national candidates,
while both national and departmental party structures determined the
make-up of the lists in the fourteen departments. In the case of department
lists, the Political Commission decided on the rank-order of candidates
whereas the departments selected the candidate. At the national level, the

National Council selected the candidates. The three historic FMLN leaders who decided to run in the elections occupied prominent positions on the list. Eduardo Sancho, the leader of the RN, headed the list of candidates in the department of San Salvador, while Francisco Jovel, the leader of the PRTC, occupied the top position on the national list of candidates. The Communist Party's Schafik Hándal was the FMLN's candidate for mayor of San Salvador. Only the ERP's Joaquín Villalobos and Salvador Sánchez of the FPL were not nominated. The FMLN's Political Commission decided that Villalobos could not run, because he had been found guilty of war crimes during the conflict.[13] Salvador Sánchez, on the other hand, chose not to run. He held the opinion that the government had not complied with the peace accords and questioned the wisdom of the FMLN's participation in the elections.

Another question debated by the party leadership concerned the affiliation of new party members. Should they join the party as FMLN members or did they have to affiliate first with one of the five groups? This question was not resolved until 1995 when new members were able to join the FMLN directly. The debate surrounding this issue revealed tension within the leadership and among the five groups. These disagreements, fundamental in nature, became more pronounced as the 1994 electoral campaign proceeded. A central conflict manifested itself in the controversy surrounding the choice of the FMLN's presidential candidate. The ERP, headed by Joaquín Villalobos, had its own agenda. It proposed Abraham Rodríguez, a founder of the Christian Democratic party, as the candidate of the Left, arguing that the Left needed to broaden its electoral appeal. The FMLN majority, however, united behind the candidacy of Rubén Zamora for the presidency. Although Zamora was not an FMLN militant, he shared a history of struggle with the revolutionary Left. Once it became clear that the ERP's position was not going to prevail, ERP leaders assumed a low profile in the campaign. Most observers agreed that this development weakened the FMLN's 1994 campaign.

The results of the 1994 Salvadoran elections for president, parliament, and municipal councils were mixed. The FMLN's presidential candidate, Rubén Zamora (he headed a ticket supported by the FMLN, the Democratic Convergence, and the Democratic Revolutionary Movement) was soundly defeated in the second round run-off of the 1994 elections.

ARENA's Armando Calderon Sol won with 68 percent of the vote. In the legislative elections, on the other hand, the FMLN's results were respectable. The former guerrillas obtained 287,811 votes out of a total of 1.3 million and won twenty-one out of the eighty-four seats in parliament.[14] At the municipal level, the election results were a disappointment for the FMLN. In its first electoral contest, the new party won only 15 mayoralties out of 262 towns. This raised questions regarding the FMLN's strategy for democratizing the country. While it had gained access to a platform to advocate change with its success in the legislative contest, it had failed to acquire a base to project its vision at the grass-roots level.

The Quest for Unity

Following the 1994 elections, a serious rift developed in the FMLN. The problems arose over a secret agreement concluded between leaders of two FMLN groups—the ERP and the RN—and the ARENA party. Going against an official FMLN decision, several deputies who were members of the ERP and RN lent their support to procedural changes that strengthened ARENA's control in the Salvadoran parliament. As a quid pro quo, Ana Guadalupe Martínez of the ERP became vice-president of the parliament, and Eduardo Sancho of the RN became secretary. Because of this, the FMLN suspended the ERP and RN leadership from the party.[15] Thus, problems that had been brewing within the FMLN for quite some time became public.

According to interviews with leaders of the five groups within the FMLN, the infighting that came to the surface in 1994 had historic roots going back to the days of the armed struggle.[16] Salvador Sánchez, then the FMLN coordinator, emphasized that before the peace accords, the FMLN was a military organization consisting of five armed movements. While the five groups shared a common strategy on how to conduct the war, they espoused different ideologies.[17] During the war it was possible to paper over these differences and unite behind the common goal of bringing down the government. The ideological differences, however, became more evident after the signing of the accords when the five groups announced different visions on how to rebuild, develop, and democratize the country.[18] Three groups—the FPL, the Communist Party, and the PRTC—regarded the accords "as the beginning not the institutionalization of democracy."[19] For some groups within the ERP and the RN, on the other hand, the accords represented the building of a new state. In the eyes of the dissidents, the FMLN was a part of this project, and they demanded that all confrontation with the government had to end.[20] In the opinion of the latter two groups it was possible to work within the existing institutions. *Gobernabilidad*, effective government, was to be the issue of the day, not a fundamental restructuring of Salvadoran society.[21]

Another area of conflict was the result of attempts by the two largest groups, the FPL and the ERP, to dominate the FMLN. Francisco Jovel regarded the fundamental issue "of all the problems of unity that exist among the Left and that are legendary anywhere in Latin America, particularly during periods of peace or election campaigns," to be "the tendency of the Left to atomize. This is a product of the hegemonic desires that predominate in different groups that compose the Left."[22] In the wake of the peace accords, both the ERP and FPL hoped to expand their support base and become the dominant group within the FMLN. Hegemony was considered essential in order for the group to determine the content of the FMLN's political project. The ERP considered itself well positioned because it had its own media, Radio Venceremos, its cadres were experienced in publicity, and it hoped to find support for its political positions in the urban areas. These factors failed to work to the ERP's benefit, however, because of increasing internal infighting. Militants and social movements close to the ERP rebelled against the autocratic style of the leadership. With the ERP becoming weaker and the FPL growing, the stage was set for confrontation.

The struggle over control of the FMLN resulted in frequent clashes among its leaders, culminating in the éclat over the elections of the Legislative Assembly directorate when ERP and RN deputies supported ARENA candidates. A special congress of the FMLN, held in December 1994, recognized that the differences among the five groups could not be reconciled. Amidst mutual charges of betrayal, sectors of the ERP and RN left the FMLN. Several top ERP and RN leaders, such as Eugenio Chicas, as well as a majority of the militants supporting the two groups, remained with the FMLN. The others, led by Joaquín Villalobos, Eduardo Sancho, and Ana Guadalupe Martínez set out to form a new party, the Partido Demócrata (Democratic Party, or PD). This exodus reduced the number of FMLN legislators elected in 1994, from twenty-one to fourteen, since seven joined the new "social-democratic" sector.

The division threw the FMLN into disarray. Confusion was particularly pronounced among FMLN militants and supporters in the countryside who had not been privy to the discussions among the leadership and had difficulty following the public arguments. Despite the turmoil, several FMLN leaders emphasized the positive side of the split. They argued that the power struggle over who would gain effective control of the new party had prevented the FMLN's consolidation, since it did not permit the development of a coherent postwar ideological identity. In the eyes of Norma Guevara, for example, the division permitted the initiation of a process that would transform the FMLN from an alliance consisting of distinct groups into a unified party.[23] Most importantly, the traditional arrangement that had guaranteed each FMLN group equal representation in the decision-making structures was limiting the party's internal democracy. During the height of the controversy, the FMLN's Women's Secretariat released the following statement:

> We question the viability of constructing true internal democracy in the FMLN and of fighting for our aspirations within the model of a pact of parties based on historic conditions of the Left and the established interests of each force and leadership group. These interests, however, do not correspond to the interests of the people nor of the current rank-and-file of the FMLN itself. We oppose the continuation of the practice of negotiating interests at the leadership level that takes the place of the expression of the majority interests of the FMLN's grass roots.[24]

Thus, the FMLN break-up had its positive aspects. Nevertheless, the cost of the division was considerable. During the first months of 1995, the former allies engaged in public recriminations that damaged the reputation of the Left overall. Most importantly, much energy was devoted to charges and countercharges instead of presenting credible alternatives to the neoliberal policies being pursued by the ARENA government.

The sectors remaining in the FMLN reorganized the party at the second National Convention, held December 17–18, 1994. Several crucial decisions were made on this occasion. First and most important, the FMLN continued to transform itself from a "political movement consisting of five distinct parties" to a "single party with several recognized factions." The leadership was aware of the challenges posed by the transition to a truly unified movement. As an initial step, the five groups constituting the FMLN made a commitment to dissolve their party structures.[25] Further, to emphasize the goal of unification, the old quota system that had protected the smaller FMLN groups was abandoned. In order to prevent future problems, the FMLN sought to regulate the existence of factions within the party. The convention charged the FMLN's National Council with designing rules governing the existence of factions within the FMLN.[26] Factions "were considered permanent or temporary groups that form themselves within the FMLN according to general or specific agreements of political and/or ideological nature."[27] The new statutes emphasized that "no faction could have an organic structure that would convert itself into a parallel center of decision-making."[28] Factions were also forbidden to promote the division of the FMLN or to make public statements in favor of or against FMLN decisions.

Another important outcome of the 1994 Convention was the political commitment of the leadership to establish measures of positive discrimination; the delegates agreed to support quotas for the participation of women and youth.[29] The importance given to women and young party members was also evident in the new statutes, which gave the heads of the FMLN's Women's and Youth commissions the right to participate and vote in meetings of the Political Commission.[30] Further, the party statutes were revised to reduce the size of the National Council from sixty-six to fifty-two seats. The leadership decided to end the policy of adding fourteen representatives from the country's departments to the fifty core Council members. Instead the fifty core seats were reallocated. Twenty seats were set aside for departmental representatives. Each department had the right to present a slate of candidates and have a least one representative elected by the convention delegates. The six departments with the largest number of party members had the right to two Council seats.[31] In addition to these twenty representatives, thirty members were elected directly by the convention delegates. Further, the coordinator of the FMLN's parliamentary bench and the coordinator of the Council of Mayors held ex officio Council seats.

During the course of 1995, all FMLN groups officially dissolved. PRTC militants voted on July 30 to abolish their party. Although the decision was unanimous and all PRTC assets were transferred to the FMLN, some PRTC members had reservations because they feared that the FPL would seek to dominate the other groups. These concerns were justified, since FPL cadres had exhibited such hegemonic tendencies in the past. The PRTC was skeptical about its future within the FMLN because it was the smallest of the five original groups. The Communist Party followed the PRTC's example on August 5, when it transformed itself into the Communist branch of the FMLN.

The last FMLN group to dissolve was the Popular Forces of Liberation, which held a final congress on December 9, 1995.[32] Over the course of a day filled with emotion, FPL delegates representing local party structures took a final inventory of the twenty-five years their movement had existed. Many tears were shed when the delegates remembered their comrades killed during the civil war. Symbolizing their solidarity with the fallen combatants, the participants lighted an eternal flame in their honor. Several FPL militants expressed resentment because this was their final meeting. The event started with the delegates shouting the slogan: "Long live the FPL." One militant reacted to this and remarked: "Why do they say 'Long Live!' if they are killing us?" Statements like this one indicated that sectors of the rank and file perceived the decision to dissolve as one imposed by the leadership. Schafik Hándal, the leader of the Communist Party, who was present at the beginning of the convention, aroused the suspicion of some participants. They interpreted his presence as making sure that the FPL militants were indeed disposed to join the FMLN.

The most controversial item on the agenda concerned the FPL's economic assets. The FPL had properties and businesses worth several million dollars in Nicaragua, Guatemala, Mexico, Costa Rica, and El Salvador. Dissolving the party required the FPL to put its economic affairs in order. There was considerable discussion about the money that many of the FPL businesses had lost, and several militants argued that the FPL officers responsible for overseeing the party's economic affairs should not be exonerated. Their excitement was understandable considering the amount of the losses and the miserable income of most militants. It required the intervention of Salvador Sánchez, who had commanded the FPL forces during the war, to calm the heated tempers of the delegates. He pointed out that the FPL had not been running traditional for-profit enterprises but had used these businesses to achieve its war objectives. Some FPL corporations had served as fronts for acquiring arms, while others were part of an effort to break the economic embargo that the United States had imposed on Cuba. In Sánchez's view, traditional standards of sound economic practice did not therefore apply. His argument carried the day. One FPL leader, however, shared a different assessment of these economic problems. In his opinion the FPL's economic difficulties were not unique, rather they were endemic among the revolutionary Left. He emphasized that "revolutionary movements have been a failure in managing their financial affairs." Confidential conversations with FPL leaders support this judgment. The leaders revealed that there were heated discussions inside the FPL over the mismanagement of party funds and businesses. In the end, the circumstances of the war were used to justify discrepancies for which those responsible should have been held accountable.

The convention agreed to transfer about $700,000 from the remaining FPL assets to the FMLN, to donate one property in Guatemala to the URNG, and to forgive a $100,000 debt by the Cuban Communist Party. The last measure was a sign of gratitude for the support the FPL had received from Cuba during the war and took into account the severe economic difficulties Cuba was experiencing at the time. The FPL kept almost $1 million to settle its own affairs and take care of its rank and file. As part of this, $100,000 was allocated for efforts to get FPL militants out of prisons in Nicaragua and various parts of South America. A dozen or so militants had been languishing for years in these prisons, some of them sentenced to life, for activities carried out on behalf of the guerrilla movement. Other funds were established to provide credit to FPL militants and to help FPL members who had been left out of the reinsertion programs and were in need of economic support. These funds created controversy: some delegates, arguing "We are all FMLN now," proposed that the money be used to support FMLN militants in general and not exclusively FPL members. Numerous other speakers vehemently objected to this proposal, holding that the FPL needed to take care of their own first. The delegates finally agreed to restrict the fund to FPL militants, with special emphasis on the needs of ex-combatants and those supporters whose personal suffering and losses during the war had been especially great. One delegate, in favor of this last provision, recounted the story of a female supporter who had lost six children in the war. Gerson Martínez, a member of the FPL's leadership, proposed that all members of the Political Commission including himself should be precluded from benefiting from this fund. His proposal received unanimous support.

Martínez offered another resolution intended to ensure that FMLN officials would distinguish themselves from their colleagues in other Salvadoran parties. He proposed that all FMLN deputies in parliament be obligated to give 30 percent of their salaries to the party. Martínez wanted to make sure that future candidates for public office would agree to serve out of a commitment to the people and not be motivated primarily by a desire to seek personal economic gain. This proposal passed and was later approved by the FMLN National Council. The congress concluded with the delegates taking a final vote on whether to dissolve and join the FMLN. Applause greeted the nearly unanimous vote (there was only one abstention). In a final symbolic act, the FPL flag was handed over to an FMLN representative while the participants listened to the "March of Unity."

The FMLN started to reregister its members in order to reflect its evolution toward a unified party and to consolidate the different membership registers of the individual groups. At the time of the third National Convention, held in December 1995, the FMLN had about 28,000 official members. One of the priorities of the convention was to strengthen the process of unification. FMLN leaders made the distinction between the goal of establishing a "partido único" (a single party) versus the existing reality of a "partido unificado" (unified party). Particularly at the grass-roots level, FMLN members continued to identify themselves with the old FMLN groups.[33] Seeking to ensure stability at the leadership level during this transition period, the delegates reelected Salvador Sánchez as party coordinator. The central themes at the convention included party modernization, the definition of the FMLN's political project, and the organic nature of the party.

Key figures in the FMLN leadership were convinced that it was important to begin transferring power from the established leadership figures to newer candidates. This idea was reflected in the 1995 party statutes that limited the number of consecutive terms any leader could serve. Under the new rules, no one could serve as a member of the Political Commission or the National Council for more than two consecutive terms. Party coordinators were limited to one year.[34] Equally important was a new provision that all "leadership structures have to be renovated every term and in an obligatory fashion, in a percentage no less than 30 percent of its members."[35] This meant that one-third of the membership of the Political Commission and the National Council had to be people who had not served the previous year. The goal of reform was to be strengthened further with additional revisions to the party statutes in 1997. The new measures concerned FMLN cadres who held public office. They restricted the period that any FMLN member could serve in parliament to two consecutive terms except when two-thirds of the members of the National Council approved a third-term candidacy.[36]

The FMLN failed to hold its annual party convention in December 1996 because all the party's energies were devoted to the 1997 elections. Although this violated the statutes, it was considered a minor problem by the leadership. Nevertheless, party leaders agreed that at least the mandate of the party coordinator had to be reconfirmed. This issue was solved in an ad hoc fashion. According to the 1995 statutes, the term of the party coordinator and his two deputies expired by the end of 1996. Without a Party Congress to elect the new authorities, the FMLN leadership opted to have the current coordinator and his deputies reelected to another term by the National Council. It was this leadership that led the FMLN into the 1997 elections.

The results of the March 1997 parliamentary and municipal elections were evidence that the FMLN had consolidated its political structures and that voter support for the new party was strengthening.[37] The former guerrillas almost doubled the number of their representatives in parliament. The FMLN leadership had learned from the mistakes they had made in the 1994 elections when the party failed to win several seats in parliament and the mayoralties of about forty towns by a few votes because the party chose to enter few electoral alliances.[38] A reversal of this policy allowed Hector Silva, the candidate of the Left, to gain the position of mayor of San Salvador.

The FMLN's 1997 electoral success also came with a price. Seeking to improve on the poor 1994 showing at the municipal level, the FMLN recruited "popular" candidates in 1997. These candidates were generally not party members with a long history of commitment to FMLN goals, but people who enjoyed community support. While some of them had charisma, few showed they had the skills needed to govern effectively, and most refused to accept party discipline. When the party leadership tried to correct irregularities at the local level, some mayors chose to leave the FMLN and declared themselves independent rather than accept the consequences of their actions. This was the path chosen by the mayor of Guazapa. Accused of trafficking in identification documents, he chose to quit the FMLN before the party's demands for his removal from office could succeed. Problems in the department of Usulután were particularly notorious.

The 1997 elections also proved that Joaquín Villalobos and his allies, who had formed the Democratic Party, enjoyed little support among the electorate. One year before the elections, PD leaders expressed confidence that the new party would obtain 10 percent of the vote and gain eight seats in parliament.[39] Their predictions proved to be overly optimistic. The PD suffered a devastating defeat and gained an embarrassing 13,533 votes (out of 1,119,603). Only one of its previous seven deputies was reelected to parliament, and this was only due to an electoral alliance the party had formed with the Christian Democrats.[40] The electoral defeat of the FMLN dissidents replicated the outcome of the 1996 Nicaraguan elections, when dissident Sandinistas, led by former vice-president Sergio Ramírez, failed to obtain substantial support from the voters.

Reform versus Orthodoxy

In the wake of the party's 1997 electoral success, many observers considered the FMLN to be in a position to win the 1999 presidential elections and to become the governing party. Instead the FMLN self-destructed. Having weathered the 1994 division, it failed to successfully resolve important internal disputes that had been festering for several years. These conflicts had personal and political roots. The basic disagreement concerned how to transform the FMLN into a majority party. Interestingly, the key protagonists opposing each other had belonged to the same FMLN group—the FPL. Facundo Guardado, a former FPL leader who had led the party to its electoral success as campaign manager for the 1997 elections, sought to modernize and reform the FMLN. From his point of view it was essential for the party to gain power. Only as the governing party would the FMLN be able to implement its economic and political projects. In order to achieve his objectives, Guardado was prepared to abandon and modify long-standing party positions. For example, he argued that the FMLN had to accept that neoliberalism was the predominant paradigm. Instead of fighting a battle it could not win, Guardado argued, the FMLN should abandon its support for socialist policies and find a way to administer neoliberal policies that would protect the interest of poor Salvadorans.[41] Salvador Sánchez led the opposition to Guardado. The FPL's top commander during the war, Sánchez headed the "orthodox" or "revolutionary socialist" branch of the FMLN. Sánchez and his supporters argued that the preservation of the ideological heritage of the FMLN should take priority over the urge to gain the reins of government by assuming positions considered acceptable to the majority of the electorate. The basic principles that the FMLN had fought for could not be compromised, even if this meant that the FMLN had to remain in opposition. The significant differences between these two political visions of the FMLN's future were exacerbated by clashes between individual militants who supported one group or the other. There was a tendency for the orthodox sector to demonize Guardado. His supporters, in turn, launched vehement personal attacks against Sánchez and his ally Schafik Hándal. Personal attacks were so common that several militants maintained the two FMLN factions were separated by their allegiance to different leadership figures rather than by their ideological convictions. In addition to the two main factions, there were three other dissident FMLN groups led by Raúl Mijango, Dagoberto Gutiérrez, and Francisco Jovel.

At the December 1997 Party Congress, Guardado's reform movement gained control over the party's leadership structure with Guardado himself elected party coordinator. Guardado's victory was the result of diligent preparation, or—as the opposing group saw it—manipulation by his associates. In the opinion of the opposition, the conference delegates knew little about the FMLN's internal struggles and were easily manipulated. At the convention, Guardado's followers distributed four distinct candidate lists for the National Council to the delegates, urging them to vote for those candidates whose names had been marked on the lists. A number of candidates were on several or all of these lists, a strategy that helped them to get a lot of votes. Some successful candidates, such as Violeta Menjívar, an ex-spouse of Guardado, were well-known and popular figures; but the success of several relatively unknown candidates could only be explained by this kind of election engineering. Some FMLN leaders who had enjoyed great popularity in the past but were not on the lists promoted by the reformers received relatively few votes this time. For example, Nidia Díaz, who had received the most votes in the last Council election, dropped from first to eighth place.

Guardado's strategy of packing the National Council with his supporters was a resounding success. Since the Council chooses the Political Commission, Guardado's followers could impose their will. Despite a poor personal showing in the election to the National Council (he received only 361 of the 719 valid votes cast by the convention delegates, which left him in thirteenth place), Guardado was elected to the Political Commission. With his supporters in the majority on the Commission he then managed to get elected party coordinator, defeating his main rival, Sánchez, who had been in fourth place in the Council elections with 435 votes. Menjívar, who had obtained the most votes (631), and Francisco Jovel, who had the second highest vote total (535), were elected as Guardado's deputies. Interestingly, Menjívar received unanimous support from the Council when it elected the Political Commission. Nevertheless, she decided not to run for the position of coordinator. Almost two-thirds of the old Commission members were replaced. Most significant was the failure of Schafik Hándal, one of the FMLN's historic leaders, to get reelected. Ironically, Guardado, who publicly called for the renewal of the FMLN's leadership, was himself one of the party's historic figures.

A key item on the convention's agenda was the modernization of the party. Several high-ranking leaders considered the FMLN still a "premodern" party. They advocated internal democratization; greater efficiency; and, above all, a "new ethic." The fight for a new ethic, essential for modernizing the party, was considered to be part of the FMLN's revolutionary tradition. The party required a new ethic so it could be a credible advocate for societal change.

From an organizational perspective, one of the FMLN's deficiencies was the lack of a clear division of labor between its parliamentary bench and its national decision-making structures. Further, the Political Commission tended to micromanage the party's affairs instead of leaving the administrative details to a secretariat while focusing its energies on the formulation of an alternative political platform. As part of the 1997 reforms, the administrative duties of the Political Commission were given to a newly created Executive Secretariat. The proposed term limits discussed earlier were approved, since they reduced the risk that FMLN leaders would lose touch with their constituents. They were also intended to distinguish the FMLN from the traditional parties. Positioning the party for the 1999 presidential elections, Guardado emphasized the "social-democratic" nature of the FMLN, in contrast to the predilection for "socialism" espoused by his predecessor.

The convention failed to solve the conflict between the orthodox current and the reformers who controlled the party leadership. Guardado affirmed in mid-1998 that his attempt to transform the FMLN was not yet consolidated and that the "reform movement" was more popular in the society at large than within the party.[42] Guardado considered himself a pragmatist with the task of offering the electorate concrete solutions for the many problems affecting Salvadoran society. He saw his political rivals in the party mired in traditional thought, better at denouncing prevailing paradigms, such as neoliberalism, than at offering alternatives. In turn, he was accused of moving the party to the right and selling out. Members of the orthodox faction of the party circulated an anonymous document in May 1998, in which they attempted to discredit the political plan of their ideological enemy. They argued that "it is not easy to define it or denounce it because it does not have a written platform, not internally toward the party and not toward the outside. This is not due to incompetence, but is a strategy. It is the deliberate intention [of the reformers] not to put the plan forward in a clear fashion. If it were explained openly, it would not find support within the party."[43]

A Lesson in Self-destruction: The 1999 Nominating Process

The two main FMLN factions tested their strength in the selection process for the 1999 presidential candidates. The orthodox group, led by Sánchez and Hándal, started with a preemptive strike by publicly endorsing Salvador Arias and Victoria Marina de Avilés. Arias, an economist, had most recently left his mark as an advisor to the FMLN parliamentary bench on the topic of the agrarian debt. An outspoken defender of the rights of the country's marginalized classes, he was popular with the labor and peasant constituencies. Avilés, a former human rights ombudsperson, on the other hand, was admired by a broad sector of Salvadoran society. The ticket fulfilled an important requirement established by the FMLN's National Council in May 1998—it included a man and a woman.[44] While important sectors of the women's movement supported Avilés as the candidate for the presidency, many leaders of both sexes wanted her to run for vice-president. There was great concern that Salvadoran society was not ready to support the election of a female president.

Guardado's group answered by supporting Hector Silva, the mayor of San Salvador. Silva made it clear from the beginning that he would only accept a nomination to be the presidential candidate and had no interest in being number two on any ticket. Although other nominees were under consideration, in the end only Silva, Arias, and Avilés were officially registered as candidates when the FMLN delegates convened in August 1998 to nominate the presidential ticket.

In a turbulent meeting, the convention failed to successfully complete its task.[45] According to the rules established by the FMLN's National Council, a candidate needed 50 percent plus one vote of the 1,034 registered delegates in order to be named to the ticket. In a contest between two strong candidates, it was difficult, if not impossible, for either candidate to obtain the 518 necessary votes. This was especially true in this case because only 890 votes were cast. Press accounts of the number of registered delegates who failed to attend the convention varied from 78 to 135.[46] In addition, a number of those present abstained from voting. Avilés, in particular, argued unsuccessfully that it should be enough for a candidate to obtain 50 percent plus one of the votes of the delegates present instead of a majority of the delegates who were registered. In the end, the contest was close, with Avilés obtaining 441 of the required 518 votes and Silva receiving 431 votes. Arias, who ran only for vice-president, also failed to get the minimum votes required. According to Norma Guevara, a member of the committee supervising the elections, he received fewer votes than Avilés.[47] Thus all candidates failed to clear the hurdle of obtaining the majority required by the party's rules. Avilés supporters were stunned that their candidate failed to get the required majority, since eight of the fourteen department conventions had supported her candidacy. They attributed her defeat to manipulative tactics by the reformers who supported Silva.

There were two major additional complications. One was that only Avilés was a candidate for either position on the ticket. Silva ran only for the presidential position, and Arias only for the vice-presidential spot. If Silva had been a candidate for both positions, a simple solution would have been to select the two candidates with the most votes. Also, because of the requirement that a woman had to be part of the ticket, there were only three possible outcomes: Avilés-Arias, Silva-Avilés, and Avilés-Silva. Since the Avilés-Arias ticket did not enjoy majority support and since neither Avilés nor Silva were prepared to consider the number two spot on a ticket headed by their nemesis, there was no obvious solution. The meeting ended with as much tumult as it had begun, with Avilés supporters calling on Silva to withdraw his candidacy, something he refused to do.

The FMLN leadership was concerned with its public image. In light of its guerrilla past, it was vulnerable to charges of undemocratic behavior. Thus the leaders wanted to make sure that no procedural rules were violated. This limited their ability to find a way out of the dilemma by devising pragmatic procedures that would have ended the crisis. Following several hours of negotiation on how to solve the impasse, candidate Arias expressed the sentiments of the FMLN leadership: "What is advisable is that a second round takes place. Otherwise, it will create the impression that we have not been faithful to the democratic principle embodied in the rules governing the candidate selection, and it will seem that we cut a deal."[48] It was decided to reconvene the convention within fourteen days.

All three candidates wanted to change the selection rules for the second round. According to the proposed change, the candidate with a simple majority of those voting would win. During the following days, advocates for the different candidates attempted to secure the votes of the delegates who had not attended the first round. On August 25 Hector Silva made the surprise announcement that he was withdrawing his candidacy in order to support party unity. His supporters argued that with Silva out of the picture other nominees should be permitted into the contest. In the end, however, only Avilés and Arias ran in the second round. The reformers argued successfully that because Avilés was running unopposed, the FMLN should keep the original requirement of a qualified majority of the registered delegates. Once again Avilés failed to clear this hurdle. She obtained 435 votes. There were 31 invalid votes, and the rest of the delegates abstained. Reportedly, this result reflected the position of the FMLN leadership. In the second round most FMLN leaders failed to support Avilés. This threw the race wide open. It forced the FMLN to call a new convention, requiring the election of new delegates and inviting the entry of new candidates.

Days of heavy politicking followed. In the end, Facundo Guardado, the FMLN's coordinator, emerged as the competition to Avilés and Arias. The candidacy of Guardado was not a great surprise. For several months he had made it clear that he considered himself to be among three potential FMLN candidates who had a chance of winning the presidency. Nidia Díaz, another member of the FMLN's Political Commission, joined Guardado on the ticket.[49] Seeking to prevent a recurrence of the difficulties of the first two rounds, the rules for the third round were changed. Winning candidates required only a simple majority, and delegates voted for a particular ticket instead of for individual candidates. The Guardado-Díaz ticket received 33 more votes (463 to 430) than the ticket of Avilés and Arias. The FMLN finally had its official candidates for the presidential race. The cost, however, was high. Guardado's victory was Pyrrhic indeed. He received only a few more votes than Avilés. Guardado's failure to unify the opposing camps behind his candidacy left the FMLN as divided as ever. Avilés supporters were disgusted with the final outcome of the selection process. In their opinion, Avilés had been defeated by foul play. They argued that Guardado's followers had manipulated the process. Further, both Guardado and Díaz had served as FMLN commanders during the war, and this was seen as a major drawback. It restricted the appeal of the ticket to the faction of hardcore FMLN militants who supported the reformers instead of broadening the ticket's appeal to members of the electorate who were sympathetic to the goals of the reformers but resented the war records of his two nominees. Further, many Avilés sympathizers in the revolutionary socialist faction, particularly women, failed to support the final ticket. This hurt the FMLN in the election, since the members of this group were considered to be the most active militants in the party.

The fallout from the convention affected the FMLN in numerous ways.

Internal divisions became more profound, many FMLN activists and supporters no longer saw the FMLN as a viable political option, and society at large reevaluated its opinion of the FMLN. The damage was severe. The FMLN presented to the Salvadoran electorate the picture of a party that was deeply divided and unable to solve its disagreements in a civil fashion. Ironically, the FMLN's openness had backfired. Holding a public convention covered by the media and adhering strictly to the established selection rules paid no dividends. Instead of being praised for demonstrating internal democracy, the FMLN was perceived as a divided party that could not be entrusted with running the country. This benefited the governing party, which had selected its candidate in the traditional fashion, hidden from public scrutiny. ARENA leaders were quick to denounce the FMLN as being too immature to govern. Some FMLN leaders publicly explained the party's difficulty in the selection of the presidential ticket as the price the FMLN had to pay for observing internal democracy. Unfortunately for the new party, this argument was not well received by the voters—the FMLN was soundly defeated in the first round of the March 1999 election. A few days after the election, Facundo Guardado assumed responsibility for his party's poor showing and resigned from his positions as party coordinator and member of the Political Commission. He left, accusing the orthodox sector of being "a minority, fanaticized and anxious to gain power."[50]

Following its electoral defeat, the FMLN decided to hold a party convention to rally the party faithful and to resolve the disputes between the reformers and the revolutionary socialists. The FMLN's fourth convention took place May 9, 1999. The convention was closed to the public except for the formal opening and closing ceremonies. This was an apparent attempt to avoid another spectacle. The public display of infighting and turmoil that had engulfed the three nominating conventions had to be avoided at any price. FMLN leaders were convinced that many potential voters had been turned away by this public display of immaturity among the ranks of the FMLN. The May meeting resolved little. Finding no consensus, the showdown between the two main FMLN currents was postponed until the convention could be reconvened at the end of July. In an apparent victory for the revolutionary socialists, the delegates decided to move up the date for the election of new party authorities (then dominated by reformers) from December to July. Further, reforms to the party statutes adopted by the convention defined the character of the FMLN as "a democratic, pluralist, *revolutionary and socialist* party."[51]

The delegates approved new provisional rules for the election of party authorities. These rules, to be approved at the July meeting, established that candidates running for one of the thirty national seats on the National Council could do so as individuals or as part of a list. Candidates were to be elected by direct, secret vote. In the case of the twenty seats allocated by department, each department delegation had the right to present a list of three candidates. The convention would than elect one representative from each list by majority vote. In a further move to democratize the party, it was decided that the candidates for parliament at the national level should be elected by the convention delegates and not by the National Council.

The July 1999 convention saw the victory of the orthodox faction of the party. The revolutionary socialists gained control of over half the seats in the National Council. This put them in position to get their candidates into the Political Commission and to elect Fabio Castillo, a proponent of their ideology, party coordinator. Castillo, considered one of the most brilliant lawyers in the country, was a legitimate candidate for the coordinator position, having obtained the most votes in the election for National Council. He had two deputies, Raúl Mijango and Irma Amaya. Mijango was the key candidate of the reformers. The July elections brought the most significant change in the composition of the FMLN's national decision-making structures since the signing of the peace accords. For the first time the coordinator position was not held by one of the historic FMLN figures, and none of the original five guerrilla commanders held a seat on the Political Commission. Furthermore, only Fabio Castillo, Raúl Mijango, and Ileana Rogel were reelected to their seats on the Political Commission. In addition to those three, only seven members of the National Council secured consecutive mandates. This was true change. It remained to be seen, however, whether the extensive renewal of the FMLN leadership would benefit the party's development.

Nicaragua

The development of the Sandinista party occurred in a fundamentally different context from that of its Salvadoran counterpart. The FSLN came to power as a result of the revolution and remained in power for over a decade. This created important opportunities and, at the same time, hindered the party's development. Following their 1990 electoral defeat, many FSLN militants "realized that the FSLN was not prepared to function as a political party. It had not developed this partisan political experience because all its efforts were always channeled into trying to govern while defending the revolution from North American aggression; and all this was in the context of a confusion of state and party."[52] Because the FSLN went directly from being a guerrilla movement to assuming the role of governing party, the crucial process of transformation from an authoritarian, hierarchical, elitist organization into a democratic mass party was delayed. This led to an interesting contradiction. The Sandinista leadership could rightly lay claim to having institutionalized electoral democracy in Nicaragua.[53] Yet at the same time that the FSLN was successful in democratizing society, it failed to strengthen the internal democracy of the party.

When the FSLN gained control of Nicaragua in July 1979, all power was concentrated in the nine-member Sandinista National Directorate. Each of the three Sandinista factions controlled three seats. The FSLN was a vanguard party with an estimated 1,500 members in 1979.[54] The membership increased during the first years of the revolution, but the party still had only 12,000 members in 1985.[55] Membership expanded further during the late 1980s, leaving the FSLN with a reported membership of 30,000 in 1988.[56] This was still a low figure compared to traditional mass-based parties. Apparently the FSLN leadership had made a conscious decision to rely on "an elite party of limited membership, systematically incorporating only the most committed revolutionary individuals."[57] The FSLN could not be considered a mass-based party since "it maintained its military structure from the days of the insurrection and . . . [failed] to implement the principles of democratic centralism envisioned by V. I. Lenin as the path to follow upon taking power."[58]

Below the Directorate was the Sandinista Assembly, a body appointed by the FSLN leadership that lacked decision-making power. Although its members held important party and government positions and were "influential in their own areas of responsibility, the authority of the Assembly [was] quite circumscribed."[59] It convened only a few days every year and lacked independence from the Directorate. The first Sandinista Assembly was constituted in September 1980, during the Third National Assembly of Sandinista Militants, held September 13–15, 1980. It consisted of sixty-six members whose selection was based on evaluations made by the party leadership.[60] This Assembly included fifteen women, representing 23 percent of the membership. An analysis of the First Assembly provides clear evidence that the majority of the initial members earned their appointments based on their contributions during the guerrilla struggle. The Assembly was later expanded to over one hundred members and changed its composition on an irregular basis. For example, the Directorate replaced some members before and after the 1984 elections. Between 1984 and 1991, however, the Sandinista Assembly remained basically unchanged. Membership came to be recognized as being "a permanent status."[61] In 1994, the membership composition of the party's structures was significantly affected by the decision of the Party Congress to establish a 30 percent quota for women and a 10 percent quota for youth.[62] Also, the terms for members of the Sandinista Assembly and the Directorate were limited to three years.[63] The party, however, subsequently failed to enforce this provision.

Daniel Ortega's faction assumed greater and greater control within the Directorate. Ortega's status had evidently been greatly strengthened during his years as Nicaragua's president—he was now the *primus inter pares*. In 1991, his "de facto leadership of the party was codified by his election to the newly created position of secretary-general."[64] After the Directorate was enlarged from nine to fifteen members in 1994, the status of individual members changed substantially. Knowledgeable sources affirmed that there were different categories of members—those who had real power and those in support roles. Following the 1996 general elections, in which the FSLN suffered its second defeat in a row, the Directorate became immobilized, and Daniel Ortega basically made decisions alone. Several members ceased to attend the regular meetings, and divisions within the Directorate over the future course of the FSLN became increasingly public. Henry Ruiz, for example, one of the original nine Commanders of the Revolution, was outraged over the party's lack of support for the poor majority, the FSLN's core supporters. He was particularly incensed over the fact that the FSLN leadership had cut a deal with the newly elected Alemán government over the highly sensitive property issue. The agreement protected the property rights of high-ranking Sandinista officials while leaving poor peasants and urban dwellers open to possible expropriation. As a consequence of his belief that the party leadership had abandoned the rank and file, Ruiz announced in November 1997: "I don't want to continue in the FSLN."[65]

Efforts of Internal Democratization

The FSLN's 1990 electoral defeat ushered in a period of self-reflection within the party. At a historic meeting in June 1990, the majority of the party notables agreed to abandon violent struggle as an option to regain power and recognized that the FSLN was deficient in its democratic development. A document acknowledged "authoritarianism, lack of sensitivity to rank-and-file concerns, imposition of leaders and organizational structures without democratic discussion . . . and arrogant behavior and abuse of power on the part of Sandinistas with civilian and military responsibilities."[66] Although the Sandinista leaders recognized their past errors publicly, they failed to relinquish any real measure of control to the grass roots.[67]

The first signs of an incipient internal democratization could be detected in 1991 when the FSLN convened a National Congress. At this point, the party finally institutionalized formal democratic procedures in the election of its national authorities. The 581 delegates, who represented all departments of the country, elected the members of the National Directorate in a secret ballot. The choices of candidates given to the delegates for election to this body were limited, however. The Directorate "decreed that election to the new body would be by slate only, with no voting for individual members."[68] Thus, the seven old and two suggested new members (Sergio Ramírez and René Núñez) ran on an unopposed slate. This procedure was adopted in an effort to avoid the defeat of any of the seven remaining original Directorate members. Several of them had become very unpopular and were certain to suffer defeat in an open contest. The old Directorate also sought to prevent individuals who lacked the approval of the old guard from gaining seats in the inner sanctum of power. The imposed election procedure, which in effect eliminated the candidacy of Dora María Téllez who enjoyed the support of many rank-and-file members, engendered considerable controversy. Female militants were furious over the exclusion of Téllez and intensified their efforts to change the FSLN's gender composition.[69]

Efforts to democratize the party were most evident at the level of the Sandinista Assembly. It finally ceased to be an appointed body. For the first time the delegates of the Party Congress elected its ninety-eight members. Interestingly, less than 50 percent of the previously appointed members obtained the support necessary to be reconfirmed in their positions.[70] According to the revised party statutes, the Assembly was to be "dominant over the National Directorate."[71] This reversal of roles was first evident at the 1994 Congress. The delegates first elected the members of the Assembly, which then proceeded to choose the new Directorate.[72]

The FSLN's efforts were not limited to the national level. Departmental and municipal party officials, who used to be appointed, also became subject to election. While this was an important development, there were important limitations from a formal democratic perspective. Candidates were not allowed to campaign for their positions, which tended to benefit those who had charismatic personalities and a proven work record.[73] In general, however, the FSLN began to move away from its position as a party made up of only the vanguard of the revolution. A few months after the 1990 national elections, the FSLN relaxed its membership criteria and established the category of party affiliate. By August 1990, the FSLN reported 60,398 affiliates in addition to 35,349 traditional members.[74]

In an effort to reach out to the grass roots and to strengthen the internal democracy of the party, the Sandinista Assembly decided to select the FSLN candidate for the 1996 presidential elections through an open primary, a *consulta popular* (people's consultation). Party militants were enthusiastic, thinking that this would be a real opportunity for the people to have input in the candidate-selection process. The Women's Commission of the Sandinista Assembly decided to support Vilma Núñez as a nominee. Núñez enjoyed an excellent reputation among the party faithful. She had served the party as the president of the FSLN's Ethics Commission (1991–94) and the revolutionary government as the vice-president of the Supreme Court. Since 1991 she had been a member of the Sandinista Assembly. Widely popular, she had received the most votes of any female candidate (coming in fourth overall after Tomás Borge, Daniel Ortega, and Lumberto Campbell) in the 1994 Sandinista Assembly elections. Núñez was an attractive candidate because she could make a legitimate claim that her electoral appeal extended beyond core FSLN supporters. As the president of the Centro Nicaragüense de Derechos Humanos (Nicaraguan Human Rights Center), she had acquired prominence in Nicaraguan society for her excellent work on behalf of human rights.

According to Núñez, she accepted the nomination out of the conviction that a contest among several candidates would strengthen the party's democratization. At the same time she was "completely clear and convinced that she had no possibility of winning."[75] While Núñez harbored no illusions and was certain that Daniel Ortega would be the FSLN's candidate, she became disenchanted with the way the party leadership was handling the selection process. Initially persuaded of the leadership's desire to democratize the party she "soon started to realize that the democracy that was being promoted, was not a genuine effort." Ortega's allies apparently were threatened by her candidacy and took steps to make sure Núñez would not succeed. "The whole party machinery began to function to dismantle my candidacy. In no way can I say that they stole my candidacy. I am convinced that Daniel did win. What they did, however, was to undertake this campaign to keep me from gaining more votes." In spite of these efforts, Núñez obtained 26 percent of the vote. Backed by this substantial show of support, Núñez challenged Ortega at the party's nomination convention. Although many female militants who had initially supported her had been persuaded to abandon their efforts to get her nominated, she received 30 percent of the votes.

In Núñez's opinion, her gender was not a factor in this contest. "I don't think that we had [an instance of] gender consciousness here to say: Let's support this woman that has fought, that has a track record . . . I don't think either, that one has to." Núñez emphasized that she wanted to be supported because of her proven record, not because she was a woman. Interestingly, the women's movement that had organized itself into the Women's Coalition in order to support female candidates was lackluster in its support of Núñez.[76] "At no time did I sense that the Women's Coalition was supporting me," reported a hurt Núñez. Some overly suspicious feminist leaders even thought that Núñez's candidacy was "only a maneuver on my part to lend legitimacy to the candidacy of Daniel." In hindsight, Núñez offered a pessimistic view of her effort: "Examining it already from a distance, I think it accomplished nothing." It appears that Núñez's defeat is better understood in the context of the desire of the Ortega faction to maintain control of the party than from a gender perspective. Yet if her analysis is correct, female militants lost an excellent opportunity to strengthen gender awareness within the FSLN.

Orthodoxy versus Reform

The key debate within the party as it evolved after 1990, concerned the future nature of the FSLN. Should it transform itself into a modern social-democratic party or remain true to its roots as a "party of cadres involved chiefly in day-to-day struggles in the unions, the neighborhood, and the countryside."[77] These opposing perspectives manifested themselves in the position the two camps took vis-à-vis the Chamorro government. The orthodox or radical faction sought a confrontation with the new government to protect the rights of the Sandinista base, whereas the pragmatist reform wing argued that a tactical alliance with the Chamorro administration was necessary to defend revolutionary achievements.[78] While the rhetoric of Sandinista leaders, in particular Daniel Ortega, was very critical of government policies, the FSLN bench in the National Assembly did in fact support the administration's agenda. In Ortega's case, it appears that his position reflected his need to cater to the needs of different constituencies and his own ambivalence about deciding on the right strategy.

For two years the Sandinistas cooperated with the Chamorro government so fully that many spoke of a "cogovernment." The pendulum started to swing in 1993, when a group of prominent Sandinistas—the Group of 29—criticized the party's course in an open letter. "Fearing a challenge from the left . . . Ortega began to identify more closely with the popular factions and to distance himself, at least in rhetoric, from Chamorro."[79] Because the leadership was divided, an Extraordinary Party Congress was convened for May 1994 to decide on the FSLN's course of action.[80] In the weeks before the scheduled congress, two main groups emerged: Daniel Ortega headed the Democratic Left and Sergio Ramírez led a reform movement that advocated for a return to a Sandinista majority. The Democratic Left emphasized the importance of socialism, whereas Ramírez's movement focused on democracy. Beneath the rhetoric, the differences distinguishing the orthodox group from the reformers were "between commitment to the popular classes and openness to multiclass compromise and between more democratic versus more verticalist methods of work."[81]

The 1994 Congress failed to unify the two camps behind a common platform and strategy. Instead the different ideological factions fought openly. The results of the elections to the national governing bodies of the party indicated majority support for Daniel Ortega's orthodox faction. His group won 53 percent of the seats in the National Directorate and 65 percent of the seats in the Sandinista Assembly.[82] Significantly, Sergio Ramírez was not reelected to the Directorate. Although the existence of opposing factions within the FSLN was public knowledge, the party—unlike the FMLN in El Salvador—was not in favor of institutionalizing them. This decision, however, did little to impede groups with opposing visions from emerging within the party.

Many Sandinista militants had grown disenchanted with the orthodox party leadership and supported Sergio Ramírez's reform movement. Ramírez maintained that party unity had been corrupted by money. He opposed the view of those within the FSLN who argued that "in order to have political power one has to have money."[83] In Ramírez's view this mindset had led to the *piñata* (the appropriation of government resources by high-ranking Sandinistas following the 1990 election defeat) which, in turn, discredited the FSLN in the eyes of many supporters.

A crucial issue for reform-minded militants was whether to try to reform the party or to create a new movement. Even among those party members who supported Ramírez's ideas, many opposed splitting the party. Vilma Núñez, courted by both factions to run for a seat on the National Directorate, was one of them: "I considered that Sergio's choice, to form another party, to separate himself, was not the correct one. I thought then that the right thing for him to do was to stay within and to try to change the party from the inside, because I thought that he as well as Dora María Téllez had a lot of power within the Front. Sergio Ramírez was the intellectual brain of the military leadership and guerrilleros. These were people with a lot of power, with a lot of experience . . . Thus the choice to break up never convinced me."

Despite the misgivings of Núñez and many other militants, the FSLN split in January 1995, when three members of the Directorate, Dora María Téllez, Luis Carrión, and Mirna Cunningham, together with Ramírez and other renowned Sandinista intellectuals left the FSLN. Subsequently Ramírez created the Movimiento de Renovación Sandinista (Sandinista Reform Movement, or MRS). The new party was most influential in the Nicaraguan parliament. Of the thirty-eight Sandinista deputies only seven publicly supported Ortega's FSLN.[84] The deputies paid a high price for supporting the MRS, however. In the 1996 elections, the FSLN dissidents were, for obvious reasons, not nominated as FSLN candidates; and those that ran on the MRS ticket failed to get elected.

Interestingly, both the FMLN in El Salvador and the FSLN broke up around the same time. The MRS suffered a fate similar to the Democratic Party in El Salvador, which was formed by FMLN dissidents following the 1994 division. Both new parties failed to gain significant support from the electorate. In the opinion of Victor Hugo Tinoco, the FSLN dissidents made a fundamental political misjudgment in thinking that they could successfully compete with the FSLN.[85] The experience of the MRS and the Democratic Party demonstrated that there was no room for two viable parties on the revolutionary Left.

The apparent similarities in the divisions affecting the FSLN and FMLN should not obscure the fundamental difference in the evolution of the two parties. The problems in the Nicaraguan case had their roots in the FSLN's time as the governing party. The three FSLN factions that existed before 1979 merged into the FSLN that ruled the country for more than ten years. Divisions in the FSLN began to emerge after the 1990 electoral defeat. Dora María Téllez, one of the key FSLN dissidents, emphasized the important contrast between the two former guerrilla movements. She pointed out that the FMLN was not a unified party but a coalition of five distinct groups at the time of its break-up. Her interpretation of the events in El Salvador was that two of the five FMLN constituent groups "decided not to go forward with the formation of a unified party."[86] Thus, in the Salvadoran case militants divided over the proper strategy on how to get into government while in Nicaragua the FSLN struggled with defining its role as the main opposition party.

Zoilamérica and the 1998 Party Congress

The May 1998 FSLN Congress brought the party's weaknesses to public light. The Congress convened following the FSLN's second general election defeat in a row. It was clear that the Congress needed to reform the party program, strengthen the FSLN's organizational structure, and elect new party authorities that would lead the FSLN back into power. When Zoilamérica Ortega Murillo, Daniel Ortega's stepdaughter, accused him in February 1998 of having sexually abused her, the focus of the Congress changed dramatically.[87] Her charges brought the internal discussion over party reform to a halt. Ironically, Zoilamérica had been invited in January 1997 by the National Directorate to become a member of the Commission of Design of the FSLN, charged with elaborating a proposal for the transformation of the party.[88] Now, in the eyes of many militants, any recommendation coming out of this commission was inevitably tainted by what was seen as Zoilamérica's effort to destroy the leader of the party.

With the reform efforts stalled and the Congress "converted into a place where the discussion focused on who would remain in the [party] positions," a number of Sandinista leaders expressed their outrage that their hopes for reform had been destroyed.[89] Vilma Núñez, for example, voiced her disapproval in an open letter to the FSLN that included strong criticism from a gender perspective:

> The fight to get positions, the efforts allotted to further concentrate power, and the system of representation by various factions . . . has weakened the possibilities of this Congress . . . [I have decided] not to continue to be part of party structures that have transformed themselves into entities void of content that neither decide nor lead; that do not perform the function that the party statutes assign to them; and that only serve to hide a system that is increasingly less democratic and, because of this, less revolutionary . . . My experience [as a presidential nominee] has served to reaffirm my conviction that *there will be no transformation in the FSLN if women are not listened to, if our sentiments are not respected, if we are used or abused, if we have ever less power to make decisions and to act, if our contribution continues to be underestimated and if we are denied the right to full participation.*[90]

In her letter, Núñez reaffirmed her commitment to the Sandinista cause while strongly criticizing the party leadership.

At the Congress, the Ortega supporters closed ranks behind their embattled leader. Like Núñez, many key Sandinista figures, including several present and former members of the National Directorate, chose not to legitimize the Congress and did not attend. In the absence of Henry Ruíz, Humberto Ortega, Luís Carrión, Jaime Wheelock, Dora María Téllez, and Sergio Ramírez, the nature of the Congress was considered by some observers to be more "Danielista than Sandinista." The leadership crisis revealed that the FSLN remained a captive of its past. Loyalty to the historic leadership tended to prevail despite the opinion of many militants that change in the leadership was in the best interest of the party. Despite expressions of dissent, the tradition of an elite party with its members following the directions of a charismatic leader imposed itself over the FSLN's incipient internal democratization. Daniel Ortega was reelected to the position of Secretary General even though he was under the cloud of the charges raised against him and had very low approval ratings. According to a poll conducted before Zoilamérica went public with her allegations, 55.4 percent of respondents gave Daniel Ortega's work as Secretary General an unfavorable rating, while only 32.2 percent approved of his conduct as party leader.[91] His poll numbers were similar to those of President Alemán who had equally low approval ratings. These numbers indicated that the country's two main political figures had difficulty in gaining support beyond their hardcore constituencies.

Ortega's reelection raised few eyebrows. It was expected that party loyalists would support their embattled leader, who was the sole candidate for the party leadership. The election of Tomás Borge to the position of deputy secretary, however, was controversial. Borge, one of the cofounders of the FSLN, who had held this post since 1994, claimed the right to be reelected without opposition. He based his claim on his distinguished record as a Sandinista leader. It was not to be the case. Víctor Hugo Tinoco, a leadership figure of the next generation and the FSLN's parliamentary whip, challenged him. Tinoco said that he chose to run for party deputy because a broad sector of the membership urged him to do so.[92] This was the first time in the FSLN's history that one of the original leaders was being challenged by a member of the new leadership generation.

In the election of members of the National Directorate, Tinoco obtained more votes than Borge. Indeed, he received the second highest number of votes after Ortega. Nevertheless, in the race to become Ortega's deputy, it was Borge's turn to be victorious. He succeeded in defeating Tinoco (224 votes to 199) because he campaigned astutely for the deputy position. Tinoco appeared ambivalent about his challenge to Borge, campaigning only half-heartedly. This left his supporters in doubt as to his seriousness. Borge, on the other hand, brought his mattress to the conference center for a sleepover with the out-of-town delegates and effectively evoked the FSLN's guerrilla past in his favor.[93] The most important factor ensuring Borge's victory, however, was the endorsement he received from Daniel Ortega. Borge justified his struggle to remain in a key leadership position in *machista* terms, reflecting the adverse climate for gender equality at the Congress: "Youth is not in the years, it is in other things. If it concerns youthful energy, I can swim across the Xiloá Lagoon. If it concerns sexual energies, I just had two children. So why should I retire."[94] Borge's boastful remarks were disturbing in a context where women were under attack.[95] Tinoco argued that many militants perceived the charges brought by Zoilamérica "as an aggression against Sandinismo." The controversy fostered the anti-women factions in the party and resulted in a backlash for the struggle to achieve greater gender equality.[96]

The central battle was between those who sought to bring about change in the FSLN and those who were clinging to the status quo. Formally there appeared to be important changes in the composition of the National Directorate, with eleven new members entering the leadership. The Directorate now included Catholic and Protestant priests, a businessman, and two leaders of the Sandinista youth. The new faces obscured the fact that several of the new leaders had served the FSLN in one capacity or another for a long time. What bound the new members together was their shared loyalty toward Ortega. In addition, the new leaders were considered "pliable" by most observers. For example, female militants who did not have a record of assuming independent positions replaced the outspoken women of the outgoing Directorate.

On the surface the Congress was an exercise in democratic decision-making. For example, the elections to the Directorate and the Sandinista Assembly were conducted by secret ballot. Also, in order to decentralize the party, the delegates elected only 30 percent of the new Assembly members. An additional 30 percent of the membership was to be determined by the various interest groups in the party, which had yet to be defined.[97] The rest were to be selected in meetings held at the town and department level.[98] Yet the real power struggles went on behind the scene, with the Ortega faction controlling the nomination process. Mónica Baltodano, an outgoing Directorate member, expressed the outrage many militants felt over these machinations: "It is shameful what is going on inside of Sandinismo. There are political and economic deals being made behind the scenes and at the margins of the Congress's rank and file."[99] Baltodano, who had been in charge of party organization, chose to leave the leadership out of the conviction that she could fight better for the transformation of the FSLN "outside of the National Directorate than inside of it." She preferred, she said, "to be a dreamer than to be the killer of dreams."[100]

Sandinista dissidents viewed the FSLN's evolution toward a democratic party with skepticism. Dora María Téllez maintained:

> From a formal perspective, there is progress but from the point of view of substance there is none. A process of democratization within a party should tend to shape the party's leadership, to strengthen the party as an organization, not to deplete it . . . If one reads the statutes from a formal perspective, one sees them much improved. But at the same time one sees a diminished leadership, the absence of a program, of a political vision, a political strategy—in short, conservatism.[101]

Following the 1998 Party Congress, there was profound disappointment among those who had hoped the FSLN would use this opportunity to reform itself. Victor Hugo Tinoco affirmed that the party had "serious problems in organization." In his view the Congress did not bring about the "changes necessary to prepare the FSLN for the future."[102] Although there had been an influx of new people into the decision-making structures, there had been "no structural change in the party." Tinoco was particularly concerned with the party's weakness at the intermediate level. Thousands of committed militants, including all the *comandantes guerrilleros* (Guerrilla Commanders, a rank just below the Commanders of the Revolution), who had been part of a "generational cohort of the 1970s" had left the party in frustration in the early 1990s. These cadres had a wealth of experience and were the backbone of the FSLN's organizational structure. Their absence left a hole that the FSLN was unable to fill. In the wake of the 1998 Congress, the FSLN was left with some of its historic leaders and new party members who had joined in the 1980s and 1990s. For the moment, Daniel Ortega and his supporters were firmly in charge and could impose their decisions on the party. In the eyes of several high-ranking party members, the Sandinista Assembly had "not the most minimal influence over party decisions." Although the period of openness and self-reflection that had characterized the FSLN in the early 1990s appeared to be at its end, one should note that most analysts concurred that Tinoco, despite his unsuccessful challenge to Borge, had positioned himself as the eventual successor to Daniel Ortega.

Guatemala

The original nucleus of what became the URNG emerged in 1960, when a group of army officers started to form a guerrilla movement. They protested corruption in the military and the government and were incensed over the Guatemalan government's decision to permit the use of its territory for the training of Cuban exiles who later participated in the Bay of Pigs invasion. These reformist officers attempted a coup on November 13, 1960. It failed, but it gave birth to the first guerrilla activities in the country. Yon Sosa and Turcios Lima, joined by students, workers, and peasants, led the effort to establish the first guerrilla *foco*.[103] This foco in the mountains of Concuá, Baja Verapaz, only two hours from Guatemala City, was destroyed by the army in March 1962, and more than half of the twenty-three insurgents there were killed in combat.[104] By 1963, the surviving guerrillas formed a movement that became known as the Fuerzas Armadas Revolucionarias. FAR militants were subsequently involved in the creation of several other armed groups. The first one, the Ejército Guerrillero de los Pobres announced its existence in 1972. At the same time, another group of disgruntled FAR militants started to build the Organización Revolucionaria del Pueblo en Armas. ORPA went public officially in 1978. Both the EGP and ORPA organized primarily within the indigenous community. The three groups, together with a faction of the Partido Guatemalteco de Trabajo, which had existed since 1949, officially formed the URNG on February 7, 1982.

The divisions and infighting that had plagued the Salvadoran and Nicaraguan guerrilla movements also affected the Guatemalan revolutionary Left. A key issue in all three cases was the difficulty the leadership of the Communist Party had deciding whether to join the armed struggle or to continue to work within the system. In all three countries, this conflict resulted in a division of the Communist Party and led to conflict between the "traditionalists" and those who took up arms. In Guatemala, this situation was the basis for the long-standing animosity between sectors of the PGT and the FAR. Over the years many conflicts rooted in personal rivalries and disagreements over the most effective war strategy developed between the various guerrilla groups. Dissidents were often punished by the withdrawing of material support. One militant who chose the option of the armed struggle recounted: "Since the disagreements were very intense, the PGT, to exert pressure, left me without a cent."[105] The problems between the various groups did not always manifest themselves in such a relatively benign fashion. In some instances, these differences were settled by force, resulting in the death of cadres who had played significant roles in the struggle. This legacy complicated tremendously any attempt to unify the four groups.

According to Comandante Jorge Soto, the leader of the FAR, the process of unifying the various guerrilla groups into the URNG was long and complex.[106] In 1978–79, at a time when the ORPA was still consolidating its organization, the EGP and the FAR initiated the first efforts to join forces. Ricardo Ramírez, the historic EGP leader who was elected the first president of the URNG in April 1997, affirmed that this attempt mostly took the form of coordinating the activities of those sectors of Guatemala's social movement with ties to the two groups.[107] In mid-1980, conversations were initiated with the ORPA, which subsequently joined the unification effort. It is evident that the Guatemalan guerrillas benefited from the Salvadoran experience. "When the FMLN was formed—the first voluntary attempt of the FMLN," said Jorge Soto, "we were invited to attend, to be something like witnesses of this process. This influenced us and accelerated a little the process of our unification."[108] In the final months of 1980, an attempt was made to form a *dirección unitaria* (a single leadership body). This attempt did not succeed "due to the internal problems that the unification process generated in some organizations."[109] Comandante Ramírez acknowledged that early unification attempts failed because the leadership, without sufficient consultation with the grass roots, imposed them.[110] Later attempts saw the guerrilla movements debilitated from counterinsurgency offensives launched by the Guatemalan army in the early 1980s. With their organizations in disarray neither the leadership nor the rank and file found it easy to overcome long-standing animosities among the various groups.[111]

Unification efforts intensified because the four guerrilla groups considered that the triumph of the July 1979 Sandinista revolution and the increased activities of the Salvadoran guerrillas showed that the situation in the region favored advances by the Guatemalan revolutionary organizations.[112] Alas, this turned out to be an illusion. The Guatemalan military launched its offenses of 1980 and 1981, which led to a fragmentation of the guerrilla forces and their strategic retreat. In the early 1980s, "the guerrilla movement lost contact with its broad support bases. It saw itself forced to retreat and moved into a defensive phase during which the most important objective was to preserve what it had in order to advance later."[113] It was under these difficult circumstances that the unification project finally made progress.

The URNG was constituted during 1982 in Managua, Nicaragua, amidst infighting among the leaders and the rank and file of the four organizations. Officials of the Department of the Americas of the Cuban Communist Party who mediated the unification process finally suppressed the mutual recriminations.[114] Ramiro Abreu, an official of the Central Committee of the Cuban Communist Party in charge of Central America, acknowledged that Cuba "served as a channel, as an intermediary between the different factions."[115] When the dirección unitaria was finally established, it had limited decision-making power. It was not until 1985, with the creation of the *comandancia general* that the URNG had an executive national structure, whose members had the authority to make decisions on behalf of their respective organizations. The three leaders in the Comandancia were Rodrigo Asturias for the ORPA, Jorge Soto for the FAR, and Ricardo Ramírez for the EGP. Ricardo Rosales, the leader of the PGT, joined the Comandancia first in 1986. Before 1986, Mario Sánchez, who headed a PGT splinter group, represented the PGT. The URNG did not want to get involved in the internal squabbles of the PGT and asked the two PGT factions to nominate a representative who could speak for the whole Communist Party. When the two factions were unable to reach an agreement, the URNG decided to choose Ricardo Rosales, the Secretary General of the traditional party. Rosales had legitimacy because the Soviet Union and its allies recognized his party. Approval by the Cuban Communist Party was particularly helpful. This process took so long that the participation of the PGT in the URNG was not made public until 1990.[116]

In August 1996, as the end of the peace negotiations came in sight, the URNG leadership agreed to take this unification process to its logical conclusion and dissolve the historic structures of the four constituent groups.[117] This move was an effort to initiate the difficult transition from a secretive, hierarchical, political-military movement to a democratic party. In neighboring El Salvador, the FMLN had suffered from intense infighting among its five groups after having signed the peace accords. These problems eventually led to the 1994 exodus of militants belonging to two of its constituent groups. The FMLN finally decided in 1995—three years after the accords—to dissolve its five original organizations. The URNG learned from this experience. It started the dissolution process even before the Guatemalan accords were signed.

In October 1996, the FAR was the first URNG group to officially dissolve. Its example was followed in February 1997 by the EGP. The ORPA and the Communist Party held their final meetings in El Salvador in March 1997.[118] The dissolution process was difficult for the members, since many shared a strong identification with the political-military goals of their respective organizations. One reason for the dissention among the rank and file was that the grass roots had little to no say in the decision to abolish the individual groups. In the case of the ORPA, it was reportedly left to Comandante Santiago to inform the combatants of Rodrigo Asturias's decision to dissolve."[119] Some militants chose not to obey their leadership's instructions. In the opinion of the dissenters they "were not prepared to enter this new phase of the struggle." While many objected in private, some militants took a public stance. For example, two high-ranking members of the Communist Party (where the decision to dissolve had been made by the party's Political Commission) refused to join the URNG and preferred to remain outside the evolving URNG structures.

During the war, the two key URNG structures had been the Comandancia, consisting of the commanders of the four groups and the National

Table 4.3   Party Structure of the URNG

Level	Party Authorities
National	National Assembly
	Executive Committee
Department	Department Assembly
	Department Executive Committee
Local	Municipal Assembly
	Municipal Executive Committee

Source: URNG.

Directorate made up of seven representatives from each group. Like the FMLN, the URNG ensured equal representation for each group regardless of its troop strength. In 1996, this body of twenty-eight was enlarged to forty-four. The four comandantes, who held their positions on the Directorate ex officio, each had the right to name ten representatives. It was this Directorate that in April 1997 elected the Provisional Executive Committee. This body represented the highest decision-making authority of the emerging party and had as its main task guiding the URNG through the legalization process. Table 4.3 shows the URNG party structure.

In the elections for the new party authorities, the group quotas were no longer observed. In addition to the seats reserved for the four comandantes, the EGP had five representatives, the FAR had three, the ORPA had two, and the PGT had one. This outcome, which reflected the relative military strength of the four groups, is interesting because the elections were supposed to be secret. Ricardo Ramírez, the EGP leader, was elected party president, while Jorge Soto became vice-president.[120] The new party leadership faced the challenging task of building a viable political movement. The dissolution of the original group structures had left a vacuum, and the leadership struggled to reconnect with its base while at the same time seeking to recruit new members.

On September 11, 1998, URNG president Ricardo Ramírez died from heart failure. This untimely death added another complication to the URNG's transition toward a political party. While there was immediate speculation that the death of the EGP comandante would lead to a power struggle within the URNG, the leadership effectively presented a united front. Arnoldo Noriega was chosen to take the place of Ramírez on the Executive Committee, and Soto assumed the leadership of the party in formation.

The URNG confronted an enormous challenge in shedding its image as an authoritarian movement. Even some longtime supporters held the view that "one of the fundamental problems of the Guatemalan movement is that it does not accept criticism. It is a movement in which space for dialogue, for discussion, is just beginning to open up. But, in general, the leader's monologue dominates. He rejects the slightest hint of criticism and in reality expects submission." These critics characterized the URNG as sectarian and dogmatic and accused it of having "a lack of respect for diversity" and of using authoritarian, Stalinist methods to destroy "those who think differently."[121]

Some disgruntled former URNG supporters who did not believe in the capacity of the URNG to transform itself even advocated its dissolution. In their opinion, other movements to the left of the political spectrum "should unite not with, but against the URNG. It should disappear because it renounced the political program of the Left by agreeing to the contents of the peace accords and because by doing so it openly became part of the Right." The URNG was further accused of having carried out kidnappings during the final stage of the peace negotiations in order "to assure the retirement of its leadership" and having eliminated "its own people who have ceased to be useful to the group in power."[122] While these polemical positions represented a minority opinion, they manifested the deep divisions among the Guatemalan Left and reflected a political reality that saw a loss of popular support for the URNG because of a number of high-profile scandals involving URNG leaders.

The URNG understood that it needed to broaden its base of support if it wanted to play a significant role in Guatemalan politics. Evidence of this was the party leadership's decision to join an electoral coalition to compete in the November 1999 elections. This electoral alliance, the Alianza Nueva Nación (New Nation Alliance, or ANN) consisted of the Desarrollo Integral Auténtico (Authentic Integral Development, or DIA), the Unidad de Izquierda Democrática (Democratic Left Unity, or Unid), the Frente Democrático Nueva Guatemala (New Guatemala Democratic Front, or FDNG), and the URNG. The alliance's candidate for the presidency was Alvaro Colom, the former director of the Fondo Nacional para la Paz (National Fund for Peace, or Fonapaz). Significantly, he was not a URNG militant. Rosalina Tuyuc, a FDNG representative in the Guatemalan parliament, was supported by many female militants as the alliance's candidate for vice-president. When the FDNG pulled out of the alliance, however, citing disagreements with the URNG leadership, Vitalino Similox was nominated as the ANN's candidate for the vice-presidency.

On May 9, 1999, the URNG fulfilled the last requirement to become a legal political party. It held a National Assembly to elect the party leadership. Anticipation was high in the weeks leading up to the Assembly. In the end, the result was anticlimactic. The 110 delegates who represented 55 municipalities, reelected the Provisional Executive Committee without making any changes. Jorge Soto was confirmed in his position as party president. Only a few weeks earlier, the URNG leadership had planned to elect a new National Political Council at the Assembly and to determine the candidates for the November elections. But the new party was clearly overwhelmed by this task. Instead, it ratified the status quo while postponing all difficult decisions to a later date. URNG leaders claimed that their failure to produce candidate lists was not entirely the party's fault. In determining the lists, the URNG had to reconcile the preferences of the other members of the electoral alliance with its own. With the other members of the alliance behind in their selection process, the URNG apparently preferred not to act unilaterally. As one leader emphasized, shortcomings were to be expected, since "this is the first time that we have gotten involved in this mess."

The URNG's failure to elect a National Political Council, however, clearly indicated that the emerging party structures were still quite fragile. Electing this national decision-making body would have demonstrated that the consolidation of the party structures was proceeding as planned. The postponement indicated that the URNG had not yet matured to the point where it could guarantee that all the commitments by its leadership regarding quotas for women and indigenous groups would be observed. It could also be interpreted as a sign that the URNG leadership was afraid to risk party unity by instituting measures that many members considered controversial. In this context, even the reconfirmation of the Executive Committee was problematic since it violated the URNG's commitment to strengthen the role of women and indigenous groups within the party. Comandante Lola remained the only woman who was a full member on the Committee. Among the five substitute members, there was also only one female representative, Fermina López.

Postponing the election to the National Political Council until after the November 1999 elections left decision-making in the URNG highly centralized, raising concerns over its future leadership style. Comandante Lola acknowledged the difficulties ahead: "We legalized a skeleton. Now we have to put muscles and meat on it." Ricardo Rosales, the URNG's secretary of organization, acknowledged that the URNG was not able to adhere to its original time plan for the construction of the party. In his view it was preferable to accept delays and build the party democratically with the participation of rank-and-file members who showed a true commitment to the URNG. He argued that by doing so the URNG distinguished itself from Guatemala's traditional parties whose membership base was established primarily with legal requirements in mind.[123] Not withstanding these affirmations, it remained to be seen how committed the URNG's members were to the new party's political program.

As we discussed previously, the URNG leadership had problems in maintaining close ties with its wartime supporters, since it had to dissolve its wartime military structures before the new party structures were operational. The disillusionment of many URNG ex-combatants coupled with their problems in obtaining the legal documents required to officially join a political party further complicated the situation and left many of URNG's original supporters outside the new party. They were replaced by an influx of new people who frequently lacked the commitment to the political principles that had originally given rise to the guerrilla movement.

For these reasons, newcomers dominated the URNG's constituent assemblies in some townships and thus came to control the newly elected municipal party authorities. The URNG leadership tried to rectify these problems by giving greater attention to incorporating their historic supporters.[124] In this task the URNG faced the challenge of explaining to their longtime cadres the difference between the "formal party structure," which included those legally registered as party members, and "real party structures," which consisted of the traditional base.[125] An additional problem was that civilian supporters who had operated in clandestine structures during the war were often not even known to those party bureaucrats who were supposed to establish contact with them.[126] In short, the URNG faced a complex situation, seeking to maintain and strengthen its ties with its core supporters while reaching out to new converts. The party leaders were overwhelmed by the demands of building a popular democratic party in a societal context that lacked a democratic culture.

Contrasting Left and Right: The Nicaraguan Resistance

The armed movements in Central America that attempted conversion into political parties included the Nicaraguan Contras, a counterrevolutionary force. It is instructive to compare the problems faced by the revolutionary Left with those encountered by a movement built to overthrow a revolutionary government.

Following the 1990 electoral defeat of the Sandinista government, the Contra leadership believed it could finally realize its ambition of playing an important role in postrevolutionary Nicaragua. The commanders of the Nicaraguan Resistance were convinced that it was their right to take control of army and police structures. A sense of betrayal was widespread once it was clear that Sandinista officers would continue to hold high-ranking positions in these institutions. The harshest criticism was reserved for President Violeta Chamorro's decision to retain Humberto Ortega as head of the armed forces.[127] The president actually had little choice, since the Sandinistas had passed Military Organization Law Number 75 two days before the 1990 election. This law "broke the link between the FSLN and the army but did not subordinate the military to executive authority. For all practical purposes, it declared the EPS [Sandinista People's Army] an autonomous body by creating a military council with the authority to name the army chief, determine promotions, and make virtually all important decisions affecting the armed forces."[128]

Upon demobilization, several leaders of the Nicaraguan Resistance did obtain important government positions. Israel Galeano became director of Interinstitutional Coordination in the Ministry of Government, while Oscar Sobalvarro was given a position as vice-minister of the Repatriation Institute. Azucena Ferrey and Alfredo César, who had served as civilian members of the Contra directorate, joined parliament when they were elected to the National Assembly in February 1990. Carlos Hurtado and his successor, Alfredo Mendieta, who were Ministers of Government (in charge of the police), as well as José Boanerges Matus, the Minister of Agrarian Reform, were also affiliated with the Nicaraguan Resistance. Although some individuals associated with the Resistance held important political positions, the Contras failed to become a central political force in post-Sandinista Nicaragua.

A key handicap was that the February 1990 elections took place before the Contras had demobilized. Thus they were not given the opportunity to participate in the electoral process as an organized political movement. Initially, the great majority of the Resistance viewed Chamorro's victory as their own. It soon became evident, however, that the Contras lacked effective advocates in the new government. This was not surprising, since "both in terms of social class (elites vs. medium-to-poor peasants) and regional base (Pacific Coast vs. Interior), government officials had few links with the contra base."[129] Most of the fighters and their families were part of the poor majority that had traditionally been marginalized. Not surprisingly, the new administration, faced with a host of competing demands, tended to give low priority to the needs of the poor, since they had little bargaining power.

The Resistance also encountered great problems in speaking with a unified voice. Interviews with several Contra commanders revealed that a particular leader could, at best, count on the loyalty of the group of fighters he had previously commanded. This made it impossible for any leader to speak on behalf of the entire Resistance. Azucena Ferrey emphasized that the members of the Resistance never represented a cohesive force. People joined for multiple reasons, and "the Resistance was always an expression of people who had a defined political ideology and those who did not. I think this was one of the factors that impeded greater control. In addition, the hierarchical structure based on military rank did not help the Resistance."[130]

The most visible Contra group in the early 1990s was a hard-line sector, led by Sobalvarro and Rodolfo Ampié, two former commanders. They headed the Asociación Cívica de la Resistencia Nicaragüense (Civic Association of the Nicaraguan Resistance), a nongovernmental organization created to assist with the reinsertion of the Contras into civil society. This group controlled considerable assets, which made it a player in the Contra community. Most of their funds came from CIAV-OEA, the institution entrusted with verifying the demobilization process. CIAV-OEA had been allocated about US $50 million from USAID to help with the difficult task of demobilization and reintegration into society.[131] Sobalvarro and Ampié considered any Contra leader who was willing to enter into dialogue with the Sandinistas a traitor. In their view, efforts to build alliances between Contra and Sandinista supporters were political projects intended to coopt the Resistance. They were also suspicious of attempts to create an official party that would represent the Nicaraguan Resistance.[132]

By 1993, several political parties had formed that explicitly claimed to represent the demobilized Resistance. In May of that year, the Partido Resistencia Nicaragüense (Nicaraguan Resistance Party, or PRN) obtained legal status. Luis Angel López, the party's president, argued that the Contras should no longer wait for other parties to represent their interests but needed their own political organization.[133] He acknowledged that sectors of the Resistance opposed the new party, yet he claimed an improbable membership of 80,000. The PRN distinguished itself from the established parties by calling for the abolition of the army and the creation of a national police to guarantee public order.[134] In addition to the PRN, there were other attempts to organize the ex-combatants politically.

The same year, Edén Pastora, a Sandinista commander who betrayed the FSLN and became the head of the Contra Southern Front, formed the Movimiento de Acción Democrática (Democratic Action Movement). Pastora claimed to have the peasantry behind him and to be the only former Contra leader with the charisma and credibility to successfully compete in the 1996 elections. His ideological views were quite distinct from other commanders who had waged war against the revolutionary government during the 1980s. With his roots in the Sandinista struggle to overthrow the Somoza dictatorship, he despised those Contra commanders with connections to Somoza's National Guard. Opposed to the conservative views espoused by the former leaders of the Northern Front, Pastora considered himself a Social Democrat. He argued that the other leaders of the Resistance lacked "political skill and moral authority."[135] With these divergent positions and historic animosities, the main figures who had led the military opposition to the Sandinista government never managed to

formulate a political program that was supported by a majority of their followers. While the emergence of these parties indicated efforts by different
factions of the Resistance to gain political representation, their political
clout was limited at best.

How minimal was the political support these parties enjoyed became evident in the October 1996 elections. The Nicaraguan Resistance Party received 21,068 votes, gaining one seat in parliament, while a mere 5,272
voters supported Pastora's Democratic Action Party.[136] The weak performance of the two parties claiming to represent the Resistance had several
roots. Infighting continued to plague the PRN, culminating in a "takeover
of the PRN nominating convention by a group of outsiders."[137] Pastora's
party, on the other hand, suffered when its founder was barred from running as a presidential candidate because he had renounced his Nicaraguan
citizenship during the days of the Contra war. In light of these problems it
was not surprising that the demobilized fighters of the Resistance found
"their" parties so unappealing that some even supported the FSLN in the
1996 elections.[138]

Conclusion

The Nicaraguan Resistance had been a creation of the United States,
which had financed and directed the counterrevolution, and this came
back to haunt it. The United States abandoned its former allies once the
Sandinistas were out of power. Suddenly, the Contras had lost their raison
d'être. The Contras did not succeed in building a viable political movement following their demobilization. Bad timing of the 1990s elections
contributed to this failure, but the most significant reason was that the
Contra membership and their supporters did not have a coherent ideological agenda or a universally recognized leadership. In the end, there was no
organic movement that could be transformed into a political party, only a
group of Nicaraguan peasants who had been used as pawns to advance
agendas that were foreign to their interests.

The record of the Salvadoran guerrillas compares favorably with the experience of the Nicaraguan Contras. The former guerrillas enjoyed a crucial advantage over the Nicaraguan Resistance, because the FMLN entered
the postwar era as an organized political force. The timing of the peace ac-

cords permitted the FMLN to build a viable political party in time for the 1994 elections. Although the conversion from a hierarchical, secretive, military force into a democratic political party posed considerable challenges for the FMLN leadership, by 1994 the Salvadoran guerrillas were beginning to learn to navigate these hurdles successfully.

Lack of a common political vision and personal rivalries among the five groups that originally were part of the FMLN resulted in its 1994 division; but these events, which could have destroyed the revolutionary Left, instead led to its consolidation. The split occurred early on in the history of the new party and involved mostly a small group at the leadership level. The March 1997 elections demonstrated that the FMLN had an effective political structure. The FMLN increased its level of electoral support so that it equaled the governing party in strength. This electoral success had its own price. It exacerbated the power struggle within the FMLN between the revolutionary socialists and Facundo Guardado's reform movement. The controversy surrounding the nomination process for the 1999 presidential election showed how this internal struggle over control of the FMLN impeded the party's progress toward internal democratization and damaged its reputation in the eyes of the electorate.

The fight between the revolutionary socialists and those seeking to reform the FMLN was not the only ideological struggle within the revolutionary Left. The competition for votes between the FMLN and those FMLN members who had left the party following the 1994 elections continued into the new millennium. Juan Ramón Medrano, the only representative of the Democratic Party in parliament, acknowledged in December 1999 that his party had committed a strategic error when it sought an alliance with the Right. Three months before the March 2000 elections, the PD reconstituted itself as the Partido Social Demócrata (Social Democratic Party, or PSD) to emphasize its social-democratic ideology and to distance itself from its past failures. At the refounding convention, Medrano argued: "We will overcome the errors of the past such as the closeness we had with the Right in which we were deceived and never obtained anything positive."[139] Medrano was referring in particular to the San Andrés pact that the PD had concluded with ARENA following the 1994 elections. At that time, the PD leadership was convinced that a strategic alliance with the governing party would convert the PD into an important player in Salvadoran politics. Instead the voters punished the PD for its opportunism.

For the March 2000 election the newly formed PSD allied itself with Rubén Zamora's Convergencia Democrática (Democratic Convergence) and formed a coalition named Centro Democrático Unido. This coalition competed with the FMLN for the votes of the moderate Left. The March 2000 elections were a great disappointment for the alliance. It failed to obtain the 6 percent of the vote required for the partners in an electoral alliance to maintain their legal status. The FMLN, on the other hand, became the strongest party in parliament.

Changing the culture of a party formed over decades is necessarily a slow process. New attitudes and beliefs held by the leadership take time to filter down to the grass roots. In the case of the FSLN in Nicaragua, many militants at the local level continue to hold the principle *"dirección nacional ordene"* (National Directorate give us the order) dear. Víctor Hugo Tinoco maintained that the grass roots were accustomed to carrying out the orders of the leadership and continue to demand to be given instructions.[140] In the case of the Sandinistas, the legacy of the guerrilla war and its decade as the governing party have influenced the evolution of the FSLN toward greater internal democracy.

The 1990 electoral defeat presented the Sandinista leadership with a historic opportunity to strengthen internal democracy. Instead, the leaders focused their energies on resolving the conflict between two opposing groups with different visions of the FSLN's role as an opposition party. When the reformists led by Sergio Ramírez left the party in 1995, the FSLN lost many of its best cadres, who could have played an important role in democratizing the FSLN. The 1998 charges of sexual abuse leveled against Daniel Ortega once again diverted attention from the task of party reform. The FSLN membership decided to close ranks behind its leader, and the voices of dissent were silenced.

The FSLN emerged from the 1998 Party Congress in a weakened position. Instead of assuming the role of strong opposition to the Alemán government, the FSLN leadership sought accommodation. There had been numerous signs of an impending deal between the Sandinistas and the governing party. For example, before the 1998 Congress, President Alemán endorsed Ortega's reelection as party leader and publicly urged the Congress delegates to vote for him. The pact between Nicaragua's two major parties was finalized in December 1999. The Liberal party and the Sandinistas joined forces to reform the Nicaraguan constitution with the support of 72 of the 93 deputies in parliament. Of the seventeen articles that were reformed, one concerned the future of President Arnoldo Alemán, who was guaranteed a seat in parliament following the end of his presidential mandate. Knowledgeable observers interpreted the guaranteed seat as a way for the president to escape potential corruption charges after leaving office. In an apparent quid pro quo the Nicaraguan parliament refused to lift Daniel Ortega's parliamentary immunity, making it impossible for Zoilamérica to proceed with the court case against her stepfather.

Dissenters within the Sandinista party considered the pact between former political enemies a sellout of the revolutionary principles the Sandinistas claimed to support, while party leader Daniel Ortega praised the reforms as "a way to abandon the weapons . . . We have to give up resorting to war in order to change governments. We paid a high price to learn that this was essential."[141] The reaction of several important donor countries in Western Europe to the implications of the pact between the Sandinistas and the government were not favorable. The pact was seen as a sign that the two major parties were weak and were cutting deals in order to insulate themselves from challenges to their hegemony. There was great concern that Nicaragua was taking a step back from democratizing its governmental structures and was reverting to the days of two-party rule. Indeed, concerns over events in Nicaragua were so great that donor countries froze their aid programs and the International Monetary Fund delayed Nicaragua's entry into the Most Indebted Countries Initiative. Being part of this initiative was essential for Nicaragua to effectively deal with its enormous foreign debt problem. Thus, the Sandinistas who had started the decade contributing to the democratization of Nicaragua were now assuming positions they had previously criticized. It appeared that the ambitions of individuals were given priority over the best interests of party or state.

The URNG in Guatemala appeared simply overwhelmed by the task of building a new party, exerting pressure on the government so the agreements of the peace accords would be fully implemented, taking care of its demobilized combatants, and fighting an election campaign. A key problem was the lack of capable cadres to attend to all of these different tasks.

For example, many of the most capable URNG officials went to work for the foundation created to facilitate the reintegration of the ex-combatants into society. This created a shortage of party leaders who could engage in the vital task of party building. Concerns by funding agencies over the potential misuse of their funds further complicated the situation. These concerns resulted in a strict separation between the party and the foundation and restricted the possibility of URNG officials working for both organizations even further.

The slow development of the URNG into a democratic mass party resulted in criticism from inside and outside the party. The party leadership chose to focus on the 1999 elections and neglected to consolidate the incipient party structures. Female militants were particularly concerned that the commitments to strengthen their role in the party continued to await implementation. The slow progress in building a viable party made the URNG vulnerable to criticism from those who proclaimed that the URNG was incapable of evolving into a democratic party.

In addition to the many institutional and societal hurdles and the serious internal problems that both the FMLN and the URNG faced, they also experienced enormous constraints in their struggle to transform into political parties because of a severe shortage of economic resources. In no case was this more evident than for Guatemala's URNG. URNG leaders were unified in their complaints about the lack of funds, which represented a significant disadvantage vis-à-vis the political Right. The evidence that resources were tight was everywhere. For example, in November 1997, almost one year after the signing of the peace accords, a visit to the party headquarters showed a dilapidated building with mostly empty offices that lacked the most basic furniture. Packages were everywhere, indicating that the emerging party's operational base was still under construction. In March 1999, a big sign on the entrance advertised various food products sold by URNG members. In El Salvador, the national FMLN party office exhibited signs of a similar lack of financial resources. Even key party figures had economic problems. FMLN leaders shared a modest living standard, as anyone visiting the residences of Schafik Hándal, Gerson Martínez, or Nidia Díaz could confirm. The advantage of this relative lack of economic resources was that FMLN leaders remained in touch with the economic reality of the average citizen.

5

Transforming the Party

Gender Equality in the Revolutionary Left

The construction of a true democracy entails the full realization of women and their creative participation in all spheres of national life. This is a fundamental principle in the societal program for which the FMLN fights. We have a commitment to win equal rights for women, [and] to overcome their marginalization and oppression in Salvadoran society.
—FMLN, *Carta de principios y objetivos*

The Sandinista Popular Revolution will abolish the detestable discrimination that women have suffered with regard to the men [and] establish economic, political and cultural equality between women and men.
—FSLN, *Programa histórico del FSLN*

The Guatemalan woman must be guaranteed, under conditions of equality, her full participation in political, civil, economic, social, and cultural life, and the eradication of every form of gender and sex discrimination that constitutes an obstacle for the full display of her talents and potential in support of the development and progress of the country.
—URNG, Posición de URNG sobre la mujer guatemalteca

Women are at the core of the newly mobilized sectors that the revolutionary Left seeks to represent in Central America. Their increased importance is evidenced by the proliferation of strong women's movements throughout the region. Women's movements have been effective advocates for the realization of women's rights that have traditionally been neglected by a male-dominated party system. Starting in the late 1980s, women's movements publicly challenged the political parties to incorporate their demands into their political programs. The question is to what extent the former guerrilla movements have responded to this challenge from their female members.

Margaret Randall maintains that revolutionary movements have too often neglected to fight for women's rights upon assuming power. In her view "socialism's failure to make room for a feminist agenda . . . is one of the reasons why socialism as a system could not survive."[1] Indeed, she considers the lack of a feminist agenda "a fundamental error of twentieth century revolutions."[2] Richard Harris supports this position. He emphasizes that "the historical evidence indicates that Marxism must be refocused to encompass the feminist perspective, and socialist regimes must take the appropriate steps to create the ideological context and material conditions for the genuine emancipation of women and the elimination of gender inequality in all its forms."[3] If we accept this premise, it will be of great significance for the political future of the Central American revolutionary Left—whether in opposition or in power—to embrace gender equality as a central goal.

In order to provide a context for the Central American data, I will present some figures on women's representation in the Cuban Communist Party. In the early years of the Cuban revolution, women were a distinct minority within the party. For example, in 1967 women constituted 10 percent of the membership. Their numbers grew to 15 percent by 1974.[4] From 1985 to 1993, female membership increased from 21.6 percent to 26.3 percent.[5] As of 1996, women represented 29.4 percent of the 767,944 party members. The relative strength of women at the rank-and-file level, however, did not translate into significant representation in the leadership structures. For a long time, Vilma Espín, the head of the Cuban Women's Federation and one-time spouse of Raúl Castro, was the only female who held full membership on the Politburo. Between 1985 and 1991, three women were represented in the Politburo. Yet at the Fifth Party Congress in 1997, only two women were elected to the twenty-four-member Politburo. At the level of the Central Committee female representation decreased from 18.2 percent in 1985 to 16.9 percent in 1991. In that year, 38 women were elected to a Central Committee consisting of 225 members.[6] In 1997, the Central Committee was reduced to 150 members. Of these only 20 (13.3%) were female.[7] At the regional level, one could observe a similar decline. Female participation in the provincial committees was reduced from 24.5 percent in 1988 to 20.6 in 1991. Only at the municipal level did women make strides, increasing their strength from 21 percent to 25.5 percent over the same time period.[8] The Cuban experience indicates that female participation in a party of the revolutionary Left does not necessarily translate into strong representation in national decision-making structures. Interestingly, as the number of female party members increased, their numbers in leadership structures declined.

The evidence shows that women have started to play a significant role within the revolutionary Left in El Salvador, Nicaragua, and Guatemala. The record of the major revolutionary parties in the three countries, however, is mixed. Although one can find significant similarities, there are also great differences. For example, FMLN women successfully strengthened their role within the party, sometimes with the support of a women's movement that was nevertheless conflicted in its position vis-à-vis the party. On the other hand, their Nicaraguan counterparts in the FSLN were rather isolated in their struggle for gender equality. There, a vocal, well-organized women's movement had historic reasons to stay aloof from developments inside the FSLN. The challenges in Guatemala were particularly complex, with the added complication of the ethnic question. I argue that several key factors account for the different development of the three parties: (1) the role women played in their respective guerrilla movements during the war, (2) the strength of the international climate in favor of increased women's participation, (3) the effectiveness of the strategies pursued by female militants, and (4) the relationship between the party and the women's movement in each country.

The data on Guatemala are limited because the URNG transformed itself into a political party so recently. For this reason my analysis includes the Frente Democrático Nueva Guatemala, a party on the Left that shared ideological affinities with the former guerrillas.

Gender Equality in the FMLN

The initial efforts of female FMLN activists and their supporters to change gender relations in the party led to several public announcements by the party in support of gender equality. Following the signing of the peace accords, the party leadership had apparently started to rethink its position regarding its female constituents. This was quite a contrast to the FMLN's record during the war, when references to women's emancipation were conspicuously absent from official FMLN documents. The 1993 party program contained an explicit statement in support of women's rights: "The construction of a true democracy entails the full realization of women and their creative participation in all spheres of national life. This is a fundamental principle in the societal program for which the FMLN fights. We have a commitment to win equal rights for women, [and] to overcome their marginalization and oppression in Salvadoran society."[9]

At the time this statement was made public, the situation for women in the party was difficult to say the least. FMLN women who held their first national meeting in August 1993 criticized the party for its lack of support: "We consider that in the FMLN our problems have not been incorporated in an adequate fashion into revolutionary thought and practice. By not having a consciousness that is able to see the inequality between the genders, cultural schemes are reproduced, discriminatory practices manifest themselves, and the great potential of women is not recognized and promoted. Our leadership and our militants have been tolerant of this situation, because of their conscious or subconscious sexist ideology."[10]

The peace accords had certainly changed reality. Female militants would have never challenged the FMLN leadership publicly during the war. Now, however, they vented their increasing frustration with a party that seemed incapable of living up to its promises. Although their criticism was ostensibly directed against the FMLN, it really addressed problems prevailing in the five constituent groups. As discussed earlier, in 1993 the FMLN was far from being a unified party. Thus, the struggle for gender equality took place on two fronts. Women who had been subordinated within their respective groups during the war tried to free themselves from their old shackles. At the same time they fought to make sure that the new party they were building would be different.

The Party and the Women's Movement: From Subordination to Autonomy

Female FMLN members who had started to organize during the war renewed their efforts in the wake of the peace accords. One example of this drive was the emergence of the Movimiento de Mujeres "Mélida Anaya Montes" (Mélida Anaya Montes Women's Movement, or MAM). MAM had been founded by militants in the Popular Forces of Liberation in July 1992 and was initially closely associated with the FPL. However, as a reaction to the FPL's lack of support for women's rights and the efforts by party members to exercise control over the movement, the MAM leadership declared its autonomy from the FPL. Nevertheless, the great majority of MAM members continued to be active in FPL structures.

Women affiliated with other FMLN groups experienced similar problems. The key issue always concerned autonomy. According to interviews with several high-ranking female party members, the women's groups created by the FMLN were often used to secure funds from development agencies eager to support women's organizing. The leadership viewed its affiliated women's groups as perfect vehicles to raise funds for the party. Moneys contributed by development agencies for the purpose of strengthening women's organizing were frequently spent for general party purposes instead. Following the peace accords female militants resented being treated as pawns to raise funds for the party coffers, a role they had acquiesced in during the war. FMLN militants affirmed that "The [organizing] efforts before the peace accords had as their principal objective the collection of funds and the mobilization of women in support tasks for the war, since the work of women had considerable support from international groups."[11] Although FMLN women realized that they were, in essence, being used, they rationalized their participation in this deception in the hope that these "efforts would open the space for more authentic women's work." However, as soon as the female militants "wanted to make small shifts in how they conceived their work," they were confronted with "jokes, total marginalization, disparagement before the grass roots, and intervention by the leadership to correct these deviations."[12]

The discrimination women suffered in their respective FMLN groups made them realize that they had to seek their independence from the party. Female FMLN members were conscious of the importance of avoiding a repetition of the Nicaraguan experience. During the revolutionary experiment of the 1980s, the women's movement in Nicaragua had remained subordinated to the Sandinista party.[13] While the great majority of FMLN women agreed on the importance of achieving and maintaining autonomy from the party, they had important differences over how to achieve this in-dependence.

In one instance, a women's organization became so infuriated with the manipulation of women by its party's leadership that it broke completely with its group. This was the case of Mujeres por la Dignidad y la Vida (Women for Dignity and Life, or Las Dignas), founded by militants of the National Resistance. The Dignas's experience led its members to conclude that their autonomy was incompatible with party militancy. On the other hand, the majority of women who had been active in guerrilla structures were open to continued dialogue within their movements. They argued that activism in a women's movement did not preclude continued work in a party. Indeed, these roles could be combined. For example, in El Salvador, the Instituto de Investigación, Capacitación y Desarrollo de la Mujer (Institute for Women's Research, Training, and Development), originally closely associated with the Communist Party, also sought (and eventually achieved) greater independence.[14] Unlike the Dignas, however, the ac-tivists in the Institute concurred with the MAM and considered it impor-tant to remain active in the FMLN. These female leaders took the position that the most effective strategy was to change the FMLN from within.[15] In their view, women's pressure inside the FMLN had made the leadership more aware of women's issues.[16] At times these opposing viewpoints led to internal fights that weakened the movement.

These different positions became the basis of severe conflicts between FMLN activists. The issue came to public light during the 1994 election campaign. In 1994, the central dividing issue among the women who par-ticipated in Mujeres '94 (Women '94), a women's coalition formed for the elections, concerned the question of *doble militancia*: Were active partici-pation in both the women's movement and a political party compatible? The conflict concerned women who served as representatives of their women's group in Women '94 and were simultaneously active party mili-tants. To no one's surprise, the main opponents in this debate were the MAM and the Dignas. The Dignas considered party militancy incompati-ble with membership in a women's movement, while the Mélidas argued that these roles could be combined.[17]

The dilemma of autonomy versus integration that the female FMLN members faced was an issue confronting women in many Latin American societies in transition from authoritarian rule toward more democratic politics. Throughout the region, female activists argued that they were being used by their political parties, and many broke off all contact. By the mid-1990s, however, many women came to see the issue "not as a choice between either autonomy or integration, but as the necessity of both."[18]

The female activists who attempted to contribute to the building of the FMLN were affected by these debates. Fighting for gender equality within a political party isolated them from those sectors of the women's movement who frowned upon trying to change political parties from within. In order to strengthen their position within the party, these women demanded the creation of an institutional mechanism—a Women's Secretariat.

The Women's Secretariat

In August 1993, the FMLN created a Women's Secretariat. One should not infer from this that the party leadership was fully supportive of women's rights. Evidence indicates that it agreed to the creation of such an institution to appease female activists who demanded a Secretariat and to present the picture of a progressive movement to its many international supporters. This explains the criticism voiced by the Secretariat's leadership against the party. Specifically, female activists complained that the Secretariat was not given any program funds and that the disorganization within the party made it impossible for it to obtain vital statistics. For example, despite numerous requests, the party would (or could) not reveal the number of female members at the municipal level.[19] In addition, the Secretariat lacked a clear mandate and identity. Indeed, it took several years for the Secretariat to become a recognized institution within the party. This situation made it difficult for the Secretariat to develop into an effective force.

The turmoil engulfing the FMLN during 1993–94, particularly the infighting among the five FMLN groups, also affected the Secretariat. Until 1995, the Secretariat had to balance the interests of the five distinct groups. Each group had its own representatives on the Secretariat. Not all of them shared the same vision, and there was frequent turnover.[20] When female leaders did have a clear objective, they realized that the Secretariat did not have the clout to make it a reality. For example, its members failed to per-

suade the party leadership to agree to a 30 percent female quota in the selection of candidates for the 1994 parliamentary elections

In its early years, the Secretariat appeared ill equipped to take on the
challenge of changing gender relations within the FMLN. Senior female
FMLN leaders considered the Secretariat to be subordinated to the FMLN's
Political Commission.[21] The Secretariat's leadership acknowledged this
lack of autonomy. It affirmed that "At the organizational level we have difficulty finding a structure that provides democratic and participatory ori-
entation to the program from the perspective of *our interests as women and
not as party members.*"[22] The Women's Secretariat confronted an experience similar to the one faced by female militants in the Sandinista party.
In Nicaragua, the revolutionary leadership had acted on the belief that the
survival of the revolution required the subordination of the struggle for
women's emancipation. In El Salvador, one noticed a comparable tendency. In many instances the Women's Secretariat appeared to work on behalf of the overall goals of the party instead of focusing its energy on representing the interests of the female membership.

Judging from the main activities it sponsored between August 1993 and
April 1995, the Secretariat limited itself to fighting for practical as opposed
to strategic gender interests. Its effectiveness was further curtailed by its extreme lack of resources. In the opinion of Norma Guevara, this reflected
the poor financial state of the FMLN and should not be interpreted as lack
of support for the female members.[23] Regardless of the reasons behind the
lack of funding, the financial straits had an adverse impact on the Secretariat's effectiveness. This could be observed during the Third National Assembly of FMLN Women, which was organized by the Secretariat and held
on April 30, 1995, in San Salvador.

While plagued by organizational difficulties, this meeting constituted
encouraging evidence that grass-roots democracy was in the process of being strengthened. Three hundred delegates, representing all fourteen departments, met to elect the Secretariat's new leadership.[24] Overcoming a
defective sound system and poor logistics, the women participated in an
electoral process that indicated effective grass-roots democracy. The Secretariat's leadership, seeking to control the outcome of the elections, presented a slate of candidates that would have ensured the representation of

all five FMLN groups.[25] Yet its proposal was rejected in a heated debate, with the resistance being organized by María Ofelia Navarrete, a charismatic leader who enjoyed particular influence because of her long involvement in the revolutionary struggle and her prestige as a member of the FMLN's Political Commission.

As a result of these open elections, no representative of the Communist Party or the National Resistance obtained a seat on the seven-member Secretariat. The Popular Forces of Liberation gained four seats, one went to a woman formerly affiliated with the Tendencia Democrática, and PRTC members obtained two positions. The outcome reflected the number of FPL members among the delegates and how little known the candidates of the Communist Party and the RN were among the assembled women. The FPL was more effective in getting its delegates to the meeting and thus "packed" the convention. Violeta Menjívar, an FPL member elected to the Secretariat, lamented that the two groups were not represented and argued that "the elections were so democratic as to be antidemocratic."[26] While it is easy to see her point of view, true grass-roots democracy has its own dynamics. The leadership, however, evidently feared the consequences of excluding the two groups. In order to rectify the election result, the newly elected leadership invited the Communist Party and the RN to nominate a representative to the Secretariat's executive board.[27] While the Communist Party responded positively to this offer (the RN remained silent), it never sent a representative.

There were signs that the militants were seeking to leave the conflict among the various FMLN groups behind. As a strong indicator that the unification of the FMLN was considered an important goal, the delegates chose Ana Gertrudis Méndez as the new coordinator even though she was opposed by members of her own Tendencia Democrática. This group resented her announcement that she would no longer be beholden to any FMLN group. Declaring her independence Méndez argued that it was time to put partisan bickering aside and be loyal only to the FMLN.[28] Under her leadership, the Secretariat played a central role in getting the party to adopt a gender perspective.

It had taken two years (1993–95) for the leadership to define its mission and develop clear goals. Initially, the Secretariat was established as a "movement" representing the broadly conceived interests of women, instead of an institutionalized party structure with a specific mandate. Once its identity was secure, the Secretariat could move forward on its goal of transforming the party in the direction of greater gender equality. The leadership formulated three specific objectives it sought to achieve:

1. That the political rights of women in the party and in society be recognized and made to count.

2. That the party analyze the situation of women from a gender perspective that permits recognition of the existing inequalities between men and women. These need to be corrected as a fundamental step toward achieving democracy in the party as well as in society.

3. That the party adopt a gender perspective in establishing its identity, strategic and operational plan, party principles, statutes, internal rules, and organic structure.[29]

The most serious challenge facing the Secretariat was the continued resistance by powerful sectors within the FMLN to moving the party toward gender equality. In an important symbolic gesture, the party leadership refused to grant the same level of monetary compensation to the head of the Secretariat as was given to the leaders of other party bodies with the same institutional rank. Female leaders often felt that they were taking one step forward and two steps back. Shortly after the Secretariat had succeeded in getting the party leadership to incorporate a women's-rights agenda into the FMLN's 1997 Socio-economic Proposal and to adopt a gender perspective in the daily functioning of the party, the Secretariat's vocal leadership was replaced with more docile figures. At the 1997 party convention, Méndez, a tireless advocate for gender equality within the party, failed to get reelected to the powerful Political Commission and lost her position as the Secretariat's leader to Mercedes Peña. In Méndez's view she had paid the price for having pushed too hard for gender equality, thereby antagonizing influential male and female colleagues. The new FMLN leadership under Facundo Guardado that controlled the party's policies during 1997–99 was considered less supportive of gender equality than the orthodox faction that had been in charge before. Thus, the fight between the reform and the orthodox factions within the party also had repercussions for the construction of gender equality.

Measures of Positive Discrimination: The Impact of Quotas

By 1996, the FMLN's Women's Secretariat was starting to play a central role in the effort to raise the consciousness of the male leadership regarding women's rights. The Secretariat maintained that the position of female militants within the party could only be strengthened if the gender composition of the party structures were changed fundamentally. Women's underrepresentation in leadership positions was "the most discussed topic" after the war ended. Already in 1993, FPL militants demanded that their group adopt a 30 percent quota to increase female participation in decision-making structures. Once the FPL congress had approved the quota, however, "the topic took on a lower profile, which contributed to the nonimplementation of the agreement."[30] With this precedent in mind, the Women's Secretariat renewed the fight.

Female leaders argued that the strong participation of women during the war had earned them the right to have significant representation in party structures. The female militants certainly had a case. Of the 15,009 FMLN members who were officially demobilized, 4,492, or 29.9 percent, were female.[31] In order to achieve acceptable levels of representation for women, the Secretariat fought for the introduction of measures of positive discrimination. It maintained that "the democratization of the FMLN has to include and guarantee special measures so we women can achieve full participation at all levels of decision-making."[32] The Secretariat argued that gender equality in the party could be achieved only if "initial disadvantages were compared. This would assure the creation of mechanisms that would specify the participation and leadership roles of women and the establishment of goals and indicators to measure progress objectively."[33]

The initial demand focused on the introduction of quotas. FMLN militants could point to the experience of other progressive parties, particularly in Argentina and Chile, where the introduction of quotas had changed the gender composition of leadership structures. In the case of the Chilean Partido Humanista and other parties on the Left, support for measures of positive discrimination had resulted in a great influx of women into the party and the fielding of a significant number of female candidates for public office.[34] Mark Jones has emphasized the significance of increased female representation in a country's legislature and demonstrated the effectiveness of quotas in achieving this objective in the Argentine parliament.[35] A number of recent studies have concluded that "Quotas are proven to be the most effective means of achieving gender parity in leadership [positions] in the short term."[36] Using these experiences and arguments to bolster their case, female activists advocated the adoption of quotas.

Eventually, the party leadership agreed to guarantee women representation in party structures based on the number of female party members. The basis of this agreement was a political commitment made by the party leadership. The Secretariat would have preferred a change in the statutes instead. According to deputy party leader Francisco Jovel, the leadership opposed a revision of the statutes because they believed that the Supreme Election Council would not approve such a change, since it was considered to violate the equality clause of the Salvadoran constitution.[37] The Secretariat's leadership was savvy enough to realize that the commitment itself would not guarantee greater representation for women. Thus it developed effective strategies, such as separate candidate lists for elections to the party's decision-making bodies and public office positions, to ensure women's representation.

The establishment of a quota system for women was controversial. There were technical problems and substantive disagreements. The quota was supposed to be based on the number of women affiliated with the FMLN. This was not a feasible proposition because in the early 1990s no one knew the exact number of female members.[38] On the basis of estimates of the party's gender distribution, a commitment was made to aim for a female participation rate in all party structures of *at least* 30 percent. By the 1995 party convention, FMLN records had become better. They showed about 28,000 current members, one-third of them female. Precise FMLN membership figures were impossible to obtain due to the ongoing campaign to reaffiliate the membership from the five member groups to the FMLN.

The relative influence of women in the party remained fairly stable during this process. By March 1996, FMLN records showed a total of 33,000 members. Of those, 10,890, or 33 percent, were women. As the 1997 election campaign started to heat up, the membership drive received less attention and proceeded at a slower pace. In March 1997, FMLN sources claimed a membership of 40,000 to 80,000.[39] The higher estimates appeared to be based on inflated figures, however. According to a high-ranking FMLN source, the number was below 50,000, one-third of them women. Based on these estimates, the FMLN women fought for a quota of 35 percent, as opposed to the 30 percent they had conquered previously. The 35 percent quota was approved by the party leadership and became part of the internal rules governing the candidate selection process.

In addition to these technical difficulties, some female leaders were against quotas in principle. Catalina Rodríguez de Merino, a senior party official with a long history in the movement, voiced the opinion of a number of female ex-combatants who opposed the quota system: "This is an insult," she argued. "We have fought in the war. We earned our leadership positions."[40] Most senior FMLN leaders, however, including Norma Guevara and Lorena Peña, argued that the quota system was a necessity. Aída Herrera, then the coordinator for the Revolutionary Party of Central American Workers, emphasized that the quota system was not a panacea. Quite frequently not enough women volunteered to be nominated for the positions that the quotas made available.[41]

Particularly in the countryside, female militants argued, the prevailing division of labor raised the cost for women to assume the burden of party office to prohibitive levels. FMLN women recognized this problem at their first National Convention in August 1993: "A great obstacle to an increased political participation of women is the domestic workload. The 'rules of the game' are determined by the hours and the lifestyles of men and objectively exclude women who have to assume domestic responsibilities."[42] This view was asserted in interviews with female FMLN militants conducted in three rural municipalities. The majority of the respondents maintained that their household responsibilities precluded any consideration of running for public office or seeking leadership positions within the party.[43] Women had to take care of the children, secure food for their families under difficult conditions, and share in agricultural activities. Those who nevertheless wanted to be politically active had to face jealous husbands. Their companions felt threatened if their spouses participated in activities where they would encounter male colleagues. These conditions, particularly male chauvinism, held women back.

A historical analysis of the evolution of the gender composition of the FMLN's national decision-making structures indicates clearly that measures of positive discrimination strengthened women's participation in the party structures. For comparative purposes it is interesting to note that during the war three women held positions in the Dirección Revolucionaria Unificada (Unified Revolutionary Directorate), the highest decision-making structure of the Salvadoran guerrilla movement, apart from the five commanders. The Directorate consisted of fifteen members. Thus women represented 20 percent of the commanders during the war.[44]

Following the transformation of the FMLN into a political party in 1992, the FMLN elected its new party authorities. As discussed earlier, they consisted of a Political Commission with fifteen members and the sixty-six-member National Council. The first Political Commission had three female members while the party's National Council was made up of nine women and fifty-seven men. At the December 1994 party convention, when the commitment to implement a female quota was not yet in force, four women, Nidia Díaz, Angela Zamora, María Ofelia Navarrete, and Mirna Perla (the wife of murdered human rights advocate Herbert Anaya), were elected to the FMLN's Political Commission.[45] Further, women increased their participation in the National Council from 13.6 to 18.2 percent when twelve female militants were elected. The Council also included a specific women's delegate who had a voice but no vote.[46] Thus, following the 1994 convention, women held about 20 percent of the votes in the two most important political structures of the new party. Salvador Sánchez, the FMLN's coordinator, acknowledged in 1995 that "the levels of female participation are still pretty low, as are also their levels of representation in the different party structures."[47]

The political commitment to guarantee a minimum level of female representation was first implemented at the party's December 1995 National Convention. As discussed, the quota was based on the number of female party members. Party records at the time indicated 28,000 members, one-third of them female. In order to ensure that women would indeed gain the seats allotted to them, separate slates were used for male and female candidates in the elections to the National Council. This was an efficient mechanism that led to the election of 17 women (32.7%) to the fifty-two-member body.[48] The council members, in turn, honored the political accord guaranteeing women's representation and voted for five women to join the Political Commission. In the elections for municipal and departmental party structures, however, female candidates were not as successful,

Table 5.1   Gender Composition of the FMLN's National Structures, 1992–2001

	Political Commission				National Council			
Year	Women	%	Men	%	Women	%	Men	%
1992–94	3	20.0	12	80.0	9	13.6	57	86.4
1994–95	4	26.7	11	73.3	12	18.2	54	81.8
1995–97	5	33.3	10	66.7	17	32.7	35	67.3
1997–99	5	33.3	10	66.7	20	38.5	32	61.5
1999–2001	6	40.0	9	60.0	19	36.5	33	63.5

Source: Internal data provided by an FMLN official.

demonstrating the need to universalize the voting procedures used at the national level.

The results of the December 1997 FMLN party convention were encouraging for women. They made progress toward achieving formal equality, and the convention added a new objective to its Document of Principles. The new objective emphasized that the FMLN needed "to strengthen [its] left-wing profile for [building] a socialist society from a gender perspective."[49] This was an important acknowledgement that the FMLN leadership now conceived the fight for gender equality as part of its identity as a leftist movement. In addition, there were quantitative advances for women. Violeta Menjívar obtained the most votes from the delegates and was elected to the position of vice-coordinator of the party. Female militants succeeded in maintaining one-third of the seats on the party's Political Commission and increased their representation on the National Council from 33 to 38.5 percent. This progress continued at the 1999 convention when women raised their representation on the party's executive committee to 40 percent. Their numbers in the National Council, however, declined from twenty to nineteen (36.5%) of the fifty-two seats.

The advances female militants made within the FMLN were largely limited to the national level. In the country's fourteen departments, the FMLN had only one female coordinator in mid-1998. María del Carmen Córdova headed the party structures in the department of La Paz. The picture was not much brighter for women at the local level. In the 244 towns where the FMLN had municipal structures, only forty-four women occupied the positions of coordinator or vice-coordinator.

There were also some women who occupied leadership positions in the party or held public office who did not live up to expectations. These officials were easy targets of criticism. A number of female representatives on the FMLN's parliamentary bench failed to earn the respect of their colleagues because of poor job performance. Even male leaders who supported gender equality in the party argued that these women damaged the party's image and cautioned the party not to go too far with measures of positive discrimination. Although there was an obvious double standard at work—several male leaders had equally bad work records—this situation led to a critical reexamination of the benefits of quotas.

Quality of Participation

While it is important to establish the formal participation of women in FMLN political structures, it is the quality of this participation that is crucial. This quality is a function of the social construction of gender and authority prevailing in Salvadoran society and the FMLN. Formal equality can be legislated, but societal norms are very difficult to change. The advances women made within the FMLN threatened many male militants. Men feared the loss of power that would result from women's advancement as well as being held accountable for their acts of sexual harassment or irresponsible fatherhood. As a consequence, women frequently encountered hostility from some groups within their party. In 1995, Eugenio Chicas, then the FMLN's vice-coordinator, criticized that "the party still suffers from a male-dominated structure [estructura machista]." In his view "many women feel alienated from the FMLN."[50]

In order to change this male-dominated culture, the Women's Secretariat advocated the adoption of an official gender policy by the FMLN leadership. Female leaders argued that "internal democratization, including the democratization of gender relations, is essential if the party is to play its revolutionary role in society . . . [and] break with the double standard that permits the male to be a revolutionary in one area of life and an oppressor in another."[51] These arguments persuaded the members of the FMLN's National Council to approve the proposed gender policy in April 1996. It set the parameters for a fundamental rethinking of party theory and practice. After years of lobbying and education by the Women's Secretariat, the FMLN leadership had reached the conclusion that it was necessary to apply a "gender perspective" to the daily functioning of the party in order to increase the membership's awareness of the difficulties women were facing within the party and in society at large.[52] The members of the FMLN's Political Commission even agreed that they themselves had to become more familiar with gender theory and accepted training sessions offered by the Women's Secretariat. The international climate was an important factor in the leadership's decision. The Fourth World Conference on Women, held in Beijing, in particular highlighted the importance of instituting specific policies to achieve greater gender equality.

Despite the leadership's apparent good will, the party's culture vis-à-vis women was slow to change. Men and women had difficulty changing their thinking. It is interesting to look at the example of key female leaders and how they fared within the party. A number of female leaders enjoyed tremendous prestige and had occupied positions of power for many years. Nevertheless, they faced real hurdles in their daily work within the FMLN. Although some structural problems had been eliminated, psychological barriers remained. These psychological hurdles reflected the gender-specific societal conditions women in leadership positions had to face.

The political career of Nidia Díaz is a good example. Her personal record had contributed greatly to strengthening women's image within the FMLN and Salvadoran society. A high-ranking commander during the war, Díaz played a key role in the peace negotiations, starting with the meeting between the government and the guerrillas in La Palma. Following the peace accords, she became a highly visible member of the Salvadoran legislature, being elected to two consecutive terms. When she had to leave due to term limits, she was elected to the Central American parliament. At the 1994 party convention, Díaz received the most votes in the National Council elections and could have been a serious contender for the position of party coordinator had she decided to run. Since she did not, Salvador Sánchez ran unopposed. He was reelected in 1995, when Díaz—who once again received the largest number of votes—again took the position that it was not the opportune moment for her to seek the party leadership. However, she did agree to be a candidate for deputy coordinator, a position to which she was easily elected. Díaz's level of support in the party was not unique. In the 1997 party convention, another woman, Violeta Menjívar, received the most votes of any candidate. She received 631 out of 719 votes in the National Council elections. She then received unanimous support from the newly elected Council to become a member of the Political Commission. However, like Díaz before her, she elected not to run for the position of coordinator.

The reluctance of both women to vie for the position of coordinator was based on their conviction that they could not be effective party leaders while simultaneously serving in parliament. Díaz, in particular, considered herself already overcommitted and was pessimistic concerning the level of support she could expect were she to assume this important post. Díaz pointed out that she had been burned in the past when she was urged to accept new duties. Generally she did accede to these calls to serve with the understanding that significant institutional support would be provided. Invariably, the promised support failed to materialize. This left Díaz trying to find ways to incorporate new duties into an already heavy schedule. In addition, she had some reservations about whether the time had come for a woman to assume the leadership of the party. At a time when the party was still struggling to overcome past divisions, it was not the right moment for a potentially divisive leadership struggle with female militants confronting traditional male stereotypes.[53]

Psychological barriers in the form of societal norms and attitudes against women's advancement in the party were particularly evident in the controversy surrounding the nomination process of the 1999 presidential candidate. This process clearly demonstrated to Díaz and other female leaders that the FMLN was a long way from reaching gender equality. The 1999 election campaign was overshadowed by the conflict emanating from the party's nomination process. As described earlier, the candidate of the women's movement, Victoria de Avilés, did not obtain the support necessary to win the nomination. Instead, Facundo Guardado and Nidia Díaz were the choice of the delegates. Guardado's followers played on machista sentiments in promoting their candidate, arguing that a woman would not be an effective president. With Avilés defeated, support for the FMLN's electoral ticket from the women's movement vanished. Not even the inclusion of Díaz, who was greatly respected by female leaders, could change this. Díaz received little to no support from Salvadoran feminists. Although not an outspoken feminist herself, she was supportive of the feminist agenda. Under the circumstances, however, her solid record was not enough to obtain the support of the women's movement. Its leaders felt betrayed when Avilés could not secure majority support from the party.

The women's movement and sectors of other social movements who generally supported the FMLN were in a quandary. Should they support the FMLN ticket despite its rejection of "their candidate" or should they punish the FMLN by abstaining. The FMLN tried to convince these groups that it constituted the lesser evil, an argument that had worked in the past. This time, however, the FMLN failed to persuade its longtime supporters. For the first time in Salvadoran history the "social left" maintained its independence from the "political left."[54] While their position was a key factor in the FMLN's election defeat, leaders of the women's movement viewed it as positive since it ended their emotional dependence on the FMLN.

Avilés herself was furious and disappointed. Being an outsider, she knew next to nothing about the FMLN's internal divisions before she was drafted as a candidate. Originally, she had thought that her candidacy was supported by the FMLN as a whole. Only after she had become a member of the FMLN and the selection process started to heat up did she realize that there were two main factions. Suddenly she had to come to terms with her identification with the orthodox faction.[55] After the second convention, Avilés faced a lot of pressure to withdraw her candidacy. The women's movement left this difficult decision up to her. Out of respect for her many supporters, the former human rights ombudsperson decided to carry on.[56] She considered it important to take her chances despite the mounting odds. What if she were successful in the end?

Díaz's decision was also a very personal one. She decided to accept her party's nomination for vice-presidential candidate in the March 1999 election despite strong personal reservations. Her judgment was based on the conviction that she could heal the rift that had divided her party. Too much was at stake—the FMLN could not afford to squander the historic opportunity to take power. Her own future was not the issue. Until the very end, Díaz was willing to sacrifice herself.[57] In a meeting with Avilés before the final showdown, Díaz offered to withdraw her candidacy if Avilés would be willing to accept the vice-presidential spot. Avilés, however, was not about to join a ticket headed by the main representative of the FMLN faction that opposed her. She also viewed the offer as a personal and not a formal one.[58] From the perspective of the women's movement, Díaz was not sincere and had lent her prestige to the effort to get rid of Avilés.

Nidia Díaz's decision to become a candidate had been a difficult one. During the months of the campaign, she came to realize the high price she had to pay for trying to do what she considered best for her party. As a former leader of the PRTC, the FMLN's smallest constituent group, Díaz was marginalized from the outset. Lacking a significant core constituency she had to rely on a close circle of friends and advisors to survive in the campaign. In these circumstances, the hostility she faced from the women's movement was even more hurtful.

Díaz also had to confront a male-oriented campaign designed by North American public relations specialists. The campaign's focus was on Guardado, the male presidential candidate, while little attention was paid to promoting the ticket's female candidate for vice-president. For example, for every three pictures taken of Guardado, Díaz managed barely one. The FMLN leadership chose to downplay the inclusion of a charismatic woman on its ticket. In Díaz's opinion, personal jealousies also played a role. Guardado resented Díaz's apparent popularity on the campaign trail and tried to isolate her when he could. This reality limited her chances of adding her strength to the ticket.

The Women's Secretariat tried to heal the rift between the social movement and the party. It invited female leaders to breakfast meetings to promote the candidacy of Nidia Díaz. Alas, no one showed up.[59] Several members of the Secretariat were conflicted about lending support to Díaz, since the Secretariat had officially supported the candidacy of Avilés. In the end, loyalty to their party won out. Yet the Secretariat's support for the FMLN ticket alienated some sectors of the women's movement and weakened the alliance for gender equality. The aftereffect of this episode was a debilitated Secretariat.

From a feminist perspective, the 1999 fiasco constituted further evidence that obtaining formal gender equality could be an empty victory. More significant than the gender of an office holder was his or her position in support of women's rights. In the final analysis, female legislators were hardly more supportive of a feminist agenda than male parliamentarians. This insight became broadly accepted following the FMLN's 1997 success in getting its female candidates elected to parliament. Salvadoran feminists naturally expected that these women would support an agenda of women's rights. Instead, the feminists were bitterly disappointed. On key issues, such as legalized abortion, female FMLN parliamentarians failed to join forces with the women's movement.

In 1998, conservative legislators tried to preempt any effort by the women's movement to successfully advocate the legalization of abortion. They accomplished their objective with an amendment to Article One of the Salvadoran constitution that protects the sanctity of life. Members of the governing party ARENA proposed incorporating a passage stating that life would be protected from its inception. This passage completely eliminated a woman's right to choose, which was already extremely restricted. Until 1998, abortion was legal only if a physician recommended it for health reasons. After the amendment was adopted, danger to the life of the mother was no longer a valid reason for a doctor to perform an abortion.

The amendment passed with overwhelming majority. Seventy-nine of the eighty-four legislators voted in favor. Lorena Peña, the most outspoken FMLN legislator in favor of women's rights, did not participate in the vote, having returned from Japan the night before. The FMLN, afraid of a backlash from the Catholic Church, argued that its deputies should vote their consciences. Eugenio Chicas, an FMLN deputy, was the only member of parliament who openly opposed the reform. The passage of this amendment by such an overwhelming margin indicated that the feminist position had little support. Female militants were furious and argued that they had the right to expect support for their view from the female legislators they had helped to elect. Key leaders argued that had the FMLN supported their position, the feminists would have supported the revolutionary Left's presidential ticket even though Victoria de Avilés was not on it. The reproductive choice issue was just one of many where leaders of the women's movement felt they had fought in vain to get women elected.

After years of struggle to get women into positions of power there was great disillusionment. A new debate started, and the fight for gender equality went from a formal to a substantive focus: did the participation of women in decision-making structures make a difference? Knowledgeable insiders considered that the FMLN was far from reaching the goal of meaningful female participation. One female activist summarized it this way:

I think what is happening is that the same women who have filled the spaces of this formal percentage [the quota] need to be more convinced of the specific demands of the moment. I have the impression that they are not convinced and that this impedes them from having an impact on the party structures. If they were convinced that the fight for women's rights takes precedence over the struggle of the party, they would make their voices and their demands felt. I think that at this point women continue to have little impact on the party.

Based on this realization, the Women's Secretariat changed its strategy and became more sophisticated in its struggle for gender equality. It now focused on tactics that would contribute to "the quantitative *and qualitative* inclusion of women into the party."[60] Equally important, female militants realized the necessity of gaining the support of their male colleagues if they wanted to transform the party. This led the Secretariat to advocate the consideration of "*women and men with gender consciousness* for internal party positions and for public office."[61]

Gender Equality in the FSLN

The Sandinista commitment to women's emancipation in Nicaragua was already expressed in the 1969 *Historic Program of the FSLN*. According to this document, the Sandinista revolution "will abolish the detestable discrimination that women have suffered with regard to men [and] establish economic, political, and cultural equality between women and men."[62] The progressive position regarding women's rights taken by the FSLN early on—quite in contrast to the guerrilla movements of El Salvador and Guatemala—raises some interesting questions. Who wrote the section on women's rights, and what relevance did the program have in the daily life of Sandinista militants? The authorship of the program has been attributed to Carlos Fonseca, the cofounder and charismatic leader of the FSLN. Yet high-ranking FSLN officials now admit that Fonseca might not be the real author. There is well-founded speculation that an international FSLN collaborator conceived the section on women. Further, Dora María Téllez, one of the top female commanders, has affirmed that the program was not discussed during the conflict since "it was a program to be executed after the

Revolution . . . I never recall that we have had an ample debate about the participation of women, nor about anything on gender."[63] Thus, during the war, the progressive content of the Sandinista program had little to no impact on gender relations within the FSLN.

Once in power, the revolutionary government reaffirmed its commitment to fight for the full equality of men and women. The 1979 *Statute of Rights and Guarantees of Nicaraguans* and the 1987 Constitution stated the Sandinista position. Yet despite the official support for gender equality and the strong participation of women in the revolution—they constituted an estimated 30 percent of the combatants and held several key combat positions—women were underrepresented in the decision-making bodies of the revolutionary government.[64]

Several former field commanders did obtain important government portfolios. Mónica Baltodano became vice-president of the Council of State, Doris Tijerino headed the police, and Lea Guido became minister of health. Yet these women were the exception to the rule. The gender composition of the Sandinista army, created after the successful insurrection, clearly indicated that the female combatants, who had contributed greatly to the success of the insurrection, were no longer appreciated in a traditionally male domain. The military leadership actively encouraged "women to assume nonmilitary duties."[65] In 1980, women represented less than 10 percent of army personnel; and out of 231 top army officials, only 13 women (6%) held command positions of any significance.[66] Revolutionary Nicaragua was no exception to the rule that women are welcome to assume counter-traditional roles only when there is a perceived need. Once the crisis has ended they are supposed to return to the private sphere of the household.

In some instances the career path of female militants changed over night. Vilma Núñez, who had worked as a lawyer for the FSLN during the insurrection and had been imprisoned by the Somoza regime, was nominated to the vice-presidency of the Supreme Court. She received word of this honor while still in prison. Despite her personal success story, Núñez was not blind to the lack of correspondence between the positions of authority women obtained in the revolutionary government and party structures and the significant participation of women in the revolutionary struggle. She did "not agree with those compañeras who didn't recognize this reality because they personally had the opportunity to assume positions of importance."[67]

Revolutionary Nicaragua (1979–90) presented a good example of the challenges the revolutionary Left faces in the struggle for women's rights when it is in power. The Sandinista experience reflects the complex reality a leadership confronts when it attempts to build a new society. On the one hand, the Sandinista commitment to women's emancipation translated into "legal reforms intended to eliminate discriminatory laws; improvements in living conditions; an increase in the public presence of females; [and] the opening of opportunities for women to organize and start to question their subordination."[68] On the other hand, there was only limited progress toward substantive gender equality.

In the view of Paola Pérez Alemán, the Sandinista record was mixed. Improvements for women, such as access to education and health care, coexisted with continuing "oppressive gender relations" in the private sphere.[69] In general, progress in the area of practical gender interests was not repeated in the area of strategic gender interests.[70] Two key factors contributed to this situation—the traditional gender views espoused by the Sandinista leadership and the limited capacity of the women's movement to fight for radical change in gender relations. In another assessment of Sandinista policies toward women, Ana Criquillon maintains that "the specific demands of particular sectors or social groups, particularly women, . . . were for much of these ten years considered diversionary or—in the best of cases—secondary, relative to the strategic interests of the Revolution."[71] It was this subordination of women's interests to the survival of the revolution as defined by men, that led many feminists to criticize the Sandinista record. Margaret Randall maintains that "the FSLN's inability to confront feminism . . . had contributed to its defeat" in the 1990 elections.[72] It is only fair, however, to point out that the views of the FSLN leadership were representative of the sentiments held by society at large. Even after a decade of revolutionary rule, Helen Collinson reached the conclusion that "Feminism remains a dirty word for large sectors of the Nicaraguan revolution. Seen as an anti-male doctrine, it is commonly defined as the opposite of machismo—in other words, extreme and unacceptable."[73] For the purpose of our discussion it is important to emphasize that Sandinista policies vis-à-vis women while the party was in power had significant impact on the situation of FSLN militants, once the party was in opposition.

Female Participation during and after the Revolution

Considering that women represented 38 percent of the FSLN's membership in 1979, a large number of leadership positions should have been occupied by female militants.[74] Indeed, in the days following the Sandinista victory, women occupied a number of important positions in the party. For example, female militants headed the party structures in five of the country's departments where they held the post of FSLN political secretary.[75] This early success story changed rapidly. Female militants were soon replaced in many of the positions they had held initially. Dorotea Wilson maintained that these positions were lost due to a lack of gender consciousness. "These positions disappeared because they were not occupied from a gender perspective. These were positions, indeed, because we had earned them with our capacity, with our responsibility, and for having demonstrated that we were capable."[76] According to Wilson, the reality of the war days favored greater equality in gender relations. The normal rules of society did not apply, since there were no children or households to take care of. But with the return to the norms of public life, "*machismo* and male chauvinism blossomed" and men secured their positions first. In addition to those women who were pushed out, many others who had been active in the FSLN during the war assumed traditional gender roles and limited their activities to the private sphere of the household. Dora María Téllez affirmed that many female combatants "returned to the exact roles that they had had before, without any variations" as soon as the "specific combat circumstances had ceased to exist."[77] This development was reflected in a decline of female membership in the FSLN to 22 percent in 1984.[78] In general, women participated in greater numbers in the guerrilla movement than in the Sandinista party, and female leaders tended to experience more equality in gender relations during the days in the mountains than following the taking of power.

Women were excluded from the center of power—the nine-member National Directorate—while the FSLN governed Nicaragua. They were, however, represented in the Sandinista Assembly. While the Assembly was a body appointed by the Directorate and lacked decision-making power, membership was only awarded to militants with distinguished records. In the beginning the Directorate consisted of sixty-six members whose selection was based on evaluations made by the party leadership. The first Assembly, constituted in 1980, included fifteen women, representing 23 percent of the membership. The level of female participation in this body remained stable during the 1980s.

Dora María Téllez has emphasized that the low levels of female participation in the party's decision-making structures became a hot topic at the end of the 1980s. Interestingly, the focus on women's role in the party coincided with "the atomization of AMNLAE."[79] The Asociación de Mujeres Nicaragüenses, Luisa Amanda Espinoza (Association of Nicaraguan Women) was formed by the Sandinista leadership to represent women's interests. AMNLAE grew into an important mass movement claiming to represent eighty-five thousand members in 1985.[80] However, the organization suffered from a fatal flaw. It was completely subordinated to the party leadership.[81] Evaluating AMNLAE's development in 1998, Téllez characterized it as "an organization that the FSLN created to organize women. It is not a women's organization. This is how it was born, how it grew, how it developed, and this is how it continues to be. It was impossible to change it."[82] This lack of autonomy prevented AMNLAE from evolving into an effective advocate for women's strategic gender interests. When AMNLAE disintegrated following the Sandinista election defeat, it gave birth to a number of autonomous women's groups. These organizations became the driving force behind the push to realize an agenda for gender equality in the 1990s. Their efforts to transform Nicaraguan society also translated into important changes within the FSLN. The Nicaraguan women's movement consisted basically of former FSLN militants. Changing the FSLN continued to be a goal close to their hearts.

It took women a long time to break into the party leadership. It was not until 1994 that women were elected to the FSLN's National Directorate. Since the Sandinistas were in opposition by then, the significance of the Directorate in the country's political process was much reduced. Dorotea Wilson, a key advocate for gender equality within the party and one of the five women elected to the fifteen-member National Directorate in 1994, recalled that a concerted effort to increase women's representation within the FSLN had started at the 1991 Party Congress. Women thought that their time to gain access to the Directorate had finally arrived when Dora María Téllez was proposed for a seat. In the eyes of many, Téllez was assured a seat. She had been a high-ranking commander during the insurrection and had occupied key positions in the revolutionary government, including Minister of Health. She had also demonstrated her capacity within the party, particularly as Political Secretary for Managua. A charismatic leader, she enjoyed the support of many rank-and-file members.

Yet the FSLN leadership had other ideas. In order to preserve the prevailing balance of power, the Directorate engineered voting procedures that were effective in keeping Téllez from being elected.[83] Female leaders were furious that the male leadership had designed exclusionary procedures and had exerted strong pressure on Téllez to withdraw her candidacy. They were convinced that the exclusion of Téllez was related to her gender. Téllez herself described her exclusion this way: "It had to do with my personality, it had to do with my gender, it had to do with my political positions, and it had to do with my generation."[84] This incident was not the only time Téllez was to suffer discrimination at the hands of the party. In one of the darker moments in the history of the Sandinista party, Téllez was subjected to a terrible smear campaign. In 1995, Téllez and her supporters left the FSLN. In an outpouring of homophobia by Sandinista party members, her sexual preference—Téllez had the reputation of being a lesbian—was linked to her political "deviancy."

In the opinion of Mónica Baltodano, Téllez's problems were the result of her ideological positions (she favored a faction within the party that later evolved into the MRS) rather than a manifestation of gender discrimination.[85] Her potential integration into the Directorate was perceived as reinforcing a group within the leadership that did not have majority support. Sergio Ramírez, who shared Téllez's views, did manage to join the Directorate on the same occasion. He was perceived to have greater clout, having served as vice-president and being the leader of the Sandinista parliamentary bench. The other male who joined in 1991 was René Núñez. In the eyes of many party militants, he had always been a member of the Directorate, albeit not an official one so as not to upset the delicate balance between the three factions. Núñez participated in the meetings of the Directorate from the beginning and served as its secretary. Considered "the man of all secrets" he knew more about the party's dirty linen that any of his colleagues.[86] Whatever the main rationale for excluding Téllez was, the perception that gender discrimination was the cause prevailed.

The Fight for a Quota

In the wake of Téllez's defeat, female militants redoubled their efforts to break into the exclusively male leadership club. In light of the positive experience with quotas for female participation in El Salvador, many FSLN women argued that the party needed to institute measures of positive discrimination. Even though some leaders expressed reservations, most recognized the advantage of quotas. Vilma Núñez expressed the majority opinion: "I don't think that quotas are ideal, but they are a mechanism that serves to help women to succeed, to break through this discrimination."[87] The discussion of how to implement a quota was similar to the one we analyzed in the case of the Salvadoran Left. One issue was whether to base the quota on the number of female FSLN militants or on the gender distribution of Nicaraguan society.

According to the FSLN, women constituted 24 percent of the party membership in the late 1980s and held about 20 percent of the seats on the Sandinista Assembly.[88] Male party leaders favored basing the quota on women's relative strength in the party, while female leaders advocated taking the country's gender statistics as the norm, which would have led to a quota of 50 percent. Looking at the gender makeup of leadership of the country's political parties, it was easy to make the case that something needed to be done to change male-dominated party structures. One study found that of the 272 people in the national executive bodies of the twenty-four legally recognized parties in 1993, only 24 (less than 1%) were women.[89]

At the 1994 National Convention, female militants demanded that 50 percent of all positions in the party structures be allocated to women. This admittedly unrealistic demand was part of a conscious strategy to counter the leadership offer of 25 percent representation.[90] The women's strategy proved successful when the party statutes were revised to allocate a minimum of 30 percent of all positions in the party's decision-making structures to women. As a result of the new quota, five women, Dora María Téllez,

Table 5.2   Gender Composition of the FSLN's National Directorate,
1979–2001

Year	Women	%	Men	%
1979–91	0	0.0	9	100.0
1991–94	0	0.0	9	100.0
1994–95	5	33.3	10	66.7
1995–98	3	23.1	10	76.9
1998–2001	5	33.3	10	66.7

Source: Internal data provided by an FSLN official.

Mirna Cunningham, Mónica Baltodano, Benigna Mendiola, and Dorotea Wilson, were elected to the Directorate which was enlarged from nine to fifteen members.

The statistics presented in Table 5.2 clearly demonstrate that the introduction of quotas changed the gender composition of the FSLN's decision-making structures. The decline in female representation between 1995 and 1998 has the following background: In January 1995, after the split of the FSLN discussed in Chapter Four, three members of the Directorate, Dora María Téllez, Mirna Cunningham, and Luis Carrión resigned their seats. Since the statutes did not provide guidelines for such a scenario, the leadership decided to offer the three vacant positions to the three candidates who received the highest number of votes after the top fifteen in the 1994 Directorate elections. Edgardo Garcia, who had obtained the sixteenth-highest vote total, came to substitute for Carrión. The case was more complex when Doris Tijerino and Leticia Herrera, who were next in line, were asked to assume the two female positions that had been abandoned. Considerable controversy prevailed concerning this proposed substitution. Herrera maintained that she was never officially invited to become part of the Directorate, although she acknowledged that there were unofficial soundings.[91] In the end, neither of the two women joined. High-ranking female FSLN leaders speculated that both these potential candidates for seats on the Directorate disagreed with the political position of the current authorities or did not want to become part of a leadership that was being criticized by important sectors of the party. Until 1998 the Directorate functioned with only thirteen members, leaving the party in noncompliance with its own statutes. To put the Sandinista record in perspective, it is interesting to note that President Alemán's Partido Liberal Constitucionalista (Liberal Constitutionalist Party) included only one woman in its leadership body.[92]

The FSLN finally was in compliance with its own quota on female representation following its National Congress in May 1998. Five new women assumed positions on the Directorate. Yet complying with the 30 percent quota did not fulfill the expectations of many militants. In the weeks leading up to the Congress, several female leaders were advocating an increase in the female quota to 50 percent. They based their demand on women's 50 percent representation in the party's membership. The majority of male and female party leaders, however, claimed they had no knowledge of either the exact level of party membership or its gender composition.[93]

According to reliable sources, the party leadership apparently had already prepared a document to be presented at the Congress, recommending that the FSLN adopt a female quota of 40 percent. Female leaders speculated that this was done in an effort to appease female party activists and to curry favor with a delegation of women from the Socialist International who were in Nicaragua to attend the Congress. Once the meeting was in session, however, the quota remained at 30 percent. The adverse climate vis-à-vis an agenda for women's rights was evident when not a single female member of the old Directorate was reelected. Two of the three women who were replaced were strong independent-minded figures. As discussed in Chapter Four, the Congress was under the cloud of the allegations against party leader Daniel Ortega for having sexually abused his stepdaughter. In this context the Ortega supporters wanted to make sure that every member of the new Directorate would be supportive of the longtime leader.

The allegations by Ortega's stepdaughter had led to a series of controversies within the FSLN in the preceding months. Several important female leaders decided to distance themselves from the party under these circumstances and chose not to run for reelection. Others paid the price of being perceived as lacking in support for the embattled party leader. Dorotea Wilson and Mónica Baltodano, strong advocates for gender equality within the party, chose not to run, while Benigna Mendiola failed to receive the support necessary to get elected. Of the five new female members on the Directorate, only Marta Heriberta Valle was considered a strong advocate for women's rights. Gladys Baez and Doris Tijerino had long track records as Sandinista militants but had not distinguished themselves as defenders of women's rights. Leaders of the women's movement considered them submissive to the wishes of the male leadership. Emilia Torres also lacked a background of taking independent positions as did María Esther Solís, who completed this quintet. Solís had obtained her position due to the quota for Sandinista youth and was considered a lightweight. In the eyes of key Sandinista militants as well as leaders of the women's movement, the struggle for gender equality within the FSLN had suffered a setback.

Female party members also sought to increase women's participation in the Sandinista Assembly, which had been around 20 percent in the 1980s. In the 1994 elections, women fell three seats short of the 30 percent quota based on the number of votes received by male and female candidates. Thus, the new statutes were applied, and three women were allocated seats, bypassing male candidates who had received more votes.[94] While the quota was implemented at the national level, a similar commitment to execute official party policy could not be found in the departments. Ironically, the FSLN's progress toward internal democracy was hurting women. In the mid-1980s, when leaders at the intermediate level were selected and imposed by the National Directorate, female leaders occupied 56 percent of the positions, a level that corresponded to the relative strength of women in the party. By 1996, when candidates for intermediate positions were elected by duly constituted local assemblies, female participation declined to 29.2 percent. What concerned female leaders the most, however, was that in almost 80 percent of the intermediate leadership structures not a single woman occupied one of the important positions, including secretary of organization or finance.[95] Formal adherence to the quota could not prevent the exclusion of women from positions of power.

Many male party members viewed the enforcement of measures of positive discrimination unfavorably. There were indications of mounting resistance to the enforcement of the party's gender policy. Men and women grew further apart in their views about the role of women in the party. While men started to object to efforts to secure the limited goal of formal equality, female activists argued that it was time to move toward substantive equality.

Paying for Past Sins: The Lack of a Women's Secretariat

Mónica Baltodano, in charge of the FSLN's Organizational Secretariat (1994–98), argued that the quota should be seen as an initial tool in the struggle to increase women's participation. In her view, female party members and activists in the women's movement needed to move beyond their focus on formal compliance with the quota and demand increased allocations of those party positions where the real decision-making power was located. For example, in 1998 not a single woman held the position of political secretary in any of the nine departments and autonomous regions. It was particularly evident at the departmental and local levels that a quota mandated from above accomplished relatively little. Women entered the party structures, yet they remained excluded from the important positions. Women are not given "the principal responsibilities, when it comes to the election of the secretary of the organization or the treasurer," Baltodano noted. In those positions, "their presence is very low . . . It is proven that women do not rush to get elected to important posts. There is much greater shyness. The cost is very high to stand for election and to assume the challenge."[96] Similar problems rooted in a mere emphasis on formal adherence to the quota were manifest in the candidate selection process for the 1996 parliamentary elections.[97]

This situation led female leaders to rethink the strategy and advocate election for specific positions. They argued that "it didn't do much good to have women in these structures if they were not in leadership positions." Under the procedures they proposed, the quota would be applied not only overall, but for every specific position. Thus, if it were implemented, women would be guaranteed 30 percent of all positions, including those of political secretary. Not surprisingly, this initiative met stiff resistance from male leaders and failed to receive sufficient support at the 1998 Congress.

The FSLN lacked a viable organizational structure that allowed women to organize effectively in support of an agenda of women's rights. Although the Sandinista Assembly did have a Comisión de la Mujer (Women's Commission), it lacked the institutional support and resources available to the established party secretariats. Nevertheless, the Commission was used as a platform to advance the struggle for gender equality. Because of its limitations, however, female leaders advocated the creation of a Women's Secretariat that would be part of the FSLN's national structure and would be given the same support and recognition as the other secretariats, such as party finances or organization. According to Mónica Baltodano, the feminists within the party, supported by leaders in the Nicaraguan women's movement, opposed the creation of a Secretariat for fear that it would be used to control the women's movement.[98] In her view, such a Secretariat "was indispensable, in order for a permanent mechanism to exist that would . . . permit us to obtain the resources to train women, to make our own propaganda, and to develop a campaign of consciousness raising . . . directed also toward men."[99]

The controversy surrounding the creation of a Women's Secretariat had its roots in Sandinista policies toward women while the party was in government. As discussed above, the women's movement was created and controlled by a Sandinista leadership that maintained that the defense of the revolution required the subordination of women's interests. The shortcomings in Sandinista policies were officially recognized in March 1987. The FSLN Directorate acknowledged in the *Proclama Sobre la Mujer* (Pronouncement about Women) that "discriminatory laws and social practices, the subordination of women in society and the family, paternal irresponsibility, physical and moral mistreatment, and machismo" continued to prevail in Nicaraguan society.[100] The document emphasized that the struggle for women's emancipation should no longer be subordinated to the revolution's priorities.[101] This acknowledgment only confirmed what women had been arguing all along. It provided FSLN militants with the justification needed to start to build an independent women's movement. In light of this legacy, it is easy to understand why leaders of the women's movement rejected the idea of creating an institution that could potentially be used to revert to the old days of party control. Another factor that complicated the already difficult situation between the women's movement and the Sandinista party was the 1995 split of the FSLN. Mónica Baltodano, an advocate of women's rights within the FSLN, explains:

The feminist movement was strongly affected by the breakup that took place. Here the reform movement, the groups allied with Sergio Ramírez demonstrated greater ability to exchange ideas with these women's groups . . . The majority of the feminist organizations and the feminist leadership supported Sergio . . . They didn't support me. They felt that Dora María Téllez represented feminist interests better than I. I was considered more a woman of the party structure, of the organization. They never supported me strongly. My support came from the FSLN party members.[102]

Thus, in contrast to the FMLN in El Salvador, the Sandinista party did not have a Women's Secretariat to oversee and advocate the implementation of the FSLN's gender policy. It lacked an institution that could serve as a bridge between the party militants and the women's movement. The lack of such a coordinating structure had a negative effect on relations between the party and the feminist movement. Even more important, the work of female militants to advance an agenda of women's rights within the party had to be conducted under unnecessarily difficult circumstances. The May 1998 Party Congress finally remedied this situation. During its course, the FSLN established a Women's Secretariat.

The creation of a Secretariat did not show increased support for gender equality within the party. On the contrary, in the eyes of many, the 1998 Congress was a severe setback for those militants seeking to establish more equal gender relations. Vilma Núñez held the view that "we have seen a setback . . . If we look at how the party has developed in terms of recent results culminating in the current [1998] Congress, the setback is evident." Her view was not surprising considering the fallout from the charges leveled by Ortega's stepdaughter.

Quality of Participation: The Zoilamérica Factor

The Zoilamérica case raised crucial questions concerning gender equality within the FSLN. Her charges created a firestorm that engulfed Nicaraguan society, the Sandinista party, and the women's movement and led to seemingly irreparable rifts. In a document introduced in court, Zoilamérica charged that she had been "sexually abused by Daniel Ortega Saavedra, since she was eleven years old, with these acts being maintained for almost twenty years."[103] What made this case so explosive was not only that the charges involved the most eminent Sandinista leader but that they threatened the past, current, and future credibility of the Sandinista revolutionary program itself. Ortega's stepdaughter exposed the double moral standard prevailing in the party and emphasized that there could be no "polit-ical discourse that is inconsistent with a personal, individual practice." She further alleged that high-ranking Sandinista officials, including her own mother, had been aware of her predicament but had chosen to remain silent. In addition, Zoilamérica explicitly argued her case from a gender perspective. "I have to reiterate that *those injuries to my gender are the most severe to my integrity and human rights*. It was from the characteristics of my sexuality, from the exploitation of my position of disadvantaged inferiority that the essence of the domination and incarnation of the patriarchal sys-tem mixed."[104]

Whereas the majority of the Sandinista leadership, male and female alike, closed ranks behind Ortega and rejected the charges, an important minority saw its worst possible scenario confirmed. When feminist leaders formed a Committee in Support of Zoilamérica, a witch-hunt started. Death threats against those women who supported Zoilamérica were com-mon, and the whole case was treated as an aberration of radical feminism. Some of Ortega's defenders maintained that radical feminists had invented the whole case in order to destroy the Sandinista party. This view was par-ticularly repugnant to women in light of the high incidence of sexual abuse in Nicaraguan society. Yet this argument served to convince party militants to support their leader in the interest of the party's survival. In the eyes of female militants, however, the "survival of the revolution" argument had reared its ugly head.

Ortega was not the only leader engulfed in controversy. Tomás Borge, one of the most outspoken defenders of the former president, was under a cloud himself. In March 1998, Cornelia Marshall, a German who had worked as a translator for Borge in 1990, accused him of sexual harassment. Borge, who vigorously defended Ortega, denied the charges. His credibil-ity, however, was severely damaged. Yet other Ortega supporters were above suspicion. Several supportive high-ranking women could point to impec-cable records of having advocated gender equality in the party. Not sur-prisingly, the case destroyed many long-standing friendships and greatly af-fected the climate for women in the party.

In the eyes of female leaders, the party's retreat regarding gender equal-ity was particularly hurtful because women had been optimistic in light of earlier indications that male attitudes in the leadership had started to change. In the mid-1990s, the Sandinista National Directorate had participated in a seminar on gender theory, listening for four hours to a specialist on the subject. At its conclusion, several members of the Directorate expressed their astonishment that their behavior toward women had its roots in machismo, maintaining that they were acting in this way "because they considered it to be natural."[105] While one might question the effectiveness of such an exercise in changing hearts and minds, it was the openness of the male leadership to engage in a dialogue on the party's gender policy that was important. A few years later this openness was nowhere to be detected. In contrast to his previous commitment to gender equality, Daniel Ortega addressed the delegates at the 1998 Congress and criticized measures of positive discrimination. He pointed to the party's quota system as an obstacle to men's assumption of leadership positions although they were better qualified than the women. This criticism was perceived as "an effort to discredit women."[106] Ortega's hostility toward women was obviously rooted in the Zoilamérica case.

Nicaraguan feminists were particularly concerned that the strong women who had served on the Directorate between 1994 and 1998 had been replaced. They maintained that the female cadres who now were in power were likely to give priority to the official party line rather than lend support to women's rights. They had little confidence that the new leadership would be capable or willing to resolve the case against the party leader. Female militants warned that the FSLN's "internal democracy is perceived in a traditional way, without a gender perspective."[107] In their view, the party needed "to adopt the gender policy as a global theme, train women, and promote them to leadership positions." Instead men "continued to believe that the issues of women should be resolved by women."[108] Without a drastic shift in prevailing attitudes, high-ranking officials were justified in their fear that the party had ceased to make progress toward formal, much less substantive, gender equality.

Gender Equality in the URNG

In order to understand the position of women within the URNG, it helps to examine the role women played in the FDNG. This party was formed in 1995 with the clandestine support of URNG militants. Competing in the 1995 elections, the FDNG gained 10 percent of the vote and subsequently had six deputies in parliament, three of them women. The high incidence of women on the FDNG's parliamentary bench should not be interpreted as the result of the party's commitment to gender equality. Instead it reflected the strength of the female deputies who had gained a national reputation on their own merits. Mariela Aguilar, the head of the Women's Secretariat, confirmed that 50 percent of the FDNG's deputies being women "has to do with other reasons that are not exactly related to the gender struggle. It is because they are natural leaders—more than natural—historic leaders."[109] For example, Nineth Montenegro, a key FDNG leader, had emerged on the national scene as the leader of the Grupo de Apoyo Mutuo (Group for Mutual Support), an organization of women that pressured the government to account for their husbands, who had been disappeared or detained. The other two female deputies, Rosalina Tuyuc and Manuela Alvarado, were prominent figures in the struggle for indigenous rights.

According to Montenegro, discussions about gender equality within the FDNG were not initiated until 1997. Then, one of the first goals was to increase the number of women in the party's decision-making structures. For example, until 1997, the party's executive committee consisted of ten members and included only one woman. To rectify this situation, female members proposed the introduction of a 30 percent female quota. In this fight, the FDNG women were not able to count on the support of the women's movement, since relations between the party and the movement were not close.[110] Manuela Alvarado, who headed the Women's Commission in parliament, favored the creation of a Women's Secretariat within the FDNG to better organize female militants in their struggle for gender equality.[111]

When the FDNG held its National Assembly in June 1997, the delegates approved the creation of a Women's Secretariat, officially named Secretaría de Asuntos Políticos de la Mujer (Secretariat of Women's Political Matters), as well as the 30 percent quota. It speaks for the persuasive powers of the female national leaders that they were able to push for a 30 percent quota when only 9 percent of the party's affiliates in 1997 were female.[112] By the time of the November 1999 elections, women's participation had increased. The FDNG officially had 13,566 members, 21 percent of them female.

The leadership's commitment to increase women's participation within the party proved limited. Although the newly elected Executive Committee had five women among its fifteen members, only 10 percent of the seats on the FDNG's Political Council were held by women.[113] The explanation given by Mariela Aguilar was that while the Executive Committee's role was mainly to implement policies, "the Political Council is to define policies and party lines at a macro level, and there are few women with that experience, or maybe they do exist but they are not in a position to get involved at this moment."[114] Thus the FDNG was confronted with a situation similar to the one we encountered in Nicaragua and El Salvador where many women were reluctant to assume the burden of party or public office or felt they were not prepared for such an important position. The party leadership also rationalized their noncompliance with the quota by noting that Guatemala's Supreme Electoral Commission had refused to approve the modified statutes, claiming such a provision violated the constitution. The difficulties female FDNG militants faced in their struggle for gender equality were similar to those facing female combatants in the URNG.

The struggle for gender equality in Guatemala clearly has its roots in the era of the reformist governments led by Juan José Arévalo and Jacobo Arbenz. Particularly during the Arbenz government, women became active in the public sphere. One of the first manifestations of women's organizing was the creation of the Alianza Feminina Guatemalteca (Guatemalan Feminine Alliance) which fought for the right to vote, just salaries, and other demands raised at that time. The March and April 1962 protests against the government of Ydígoras Fuentes were another catalyst for women's organizing. In the wake of these events, the first women committed to seeking social change "went to the Sierra de Las Minas in the east of the country . . . [and] rose up in arms," joining the guerrillas.[115]

During the thirty-six years of conflict, specific statements on women's rights were notably absent from the manifestos and programs of the four groups integrating the URNG. Women's issues were part of URNG platforms only in the most general fashion. Comandante Lola has claimed this was because different priorities prevailed during the conflict. "I believe there were errors, justified in their great majority. It wasn't that we didn't consider gender issues important, but that our life was very hard, full of activity directly related to combat, to military activities, to the recruitment for military units. Thus it was not a priority at that moment."[116] It is also important to point out that the Guatemalan guerrilla movement was part of the first wave of Latin American guerrilla movements (1956–70). Gender equality was hardly on the agenda then, and few women participated in combat. The traditional views espoused by the URNG leadership during the 1960s and early 1970s were difficult to overcome. URNG officials have acknowledged that "the gender theme was rejected" by many male leaders before the signing of the peace accords. The dialogue and discussions with various sectors of civil society, especially the Women's Forum, during the peace negotiations led to greater acceptance of the importance of focusing on gender equality.[117]

The four URNG groups differed somewhat in the opportunities they provided to female constituents. Comandante Lola has confirmed that the EGP was late in taking up gender issues: "I couldn't say it was in the last years, rather in the last months, that an effort was made to have discussions among ourselves [the women]. . . . This is one of the lacunae that we have, but I think that all organizations were in the same situation, because we didn't consider it necessary. It was a lack of vision."[118] In the case of the FAR, however, women succeeded somewhat earlier in getting their views incorporated into official documents. In 1991, an FAR meeting ended with the resolution that "In Guatemala, women's liberation is an inseparable part of society's liberation." One can even find specific references to gender equality. The resolution went on, "It is our fundamental goal to promote the effective and efficient incorporation, participation and representation of the Guatemalan woman in the political, social and economic process; as part of the integral development of Guatemalan society, in the context of the search for democracy, peace, and the construction of a New Guatemala, where gender equality will be one of the elements that define the democratic character of society."[119]

The views expressed in the resolution of the 1991 FAR Congress became the basis of a September 1996 FAR document that elaborated the group's position on the gender dimension in revolutionary thought. The document uses Molyneux's concepts of strategic versus practical gender interests to discuss the challenges confronting women in Guatemala. It emphasizes that only a focus on the realization of women's rights can lead to a fundamental restructuring of society, one that would guarantee gender equity.[120] Thus, of the four constituent groups, the FAR appears to have played the key role in formulating an agenda on women's rights. The URNG as a whole only recently started to emphasize women's rights. According to high-ranking leaders, it was only in 1994 that a section on women's rights was incorporated into an official URNG document.

Female URNG militants differed in their views on how to advance an agenda of women's rights most effectively within the emerging political party. In January 1997, following the signing of the peace agreement, women organized the first meeting of female militants and formed the Espacio de Mujeres (Women's Space) in the URNG. Several key protagonists in the struggle for women's rights held the position that one should not advocate the creation of a Women's Secretariat within the party. Having observed the fight for gender equality within the FMLN and FSLN, they were concerned that such a Secretariat would stifle women's autonomy and allow the party to control the agenda. Most women who held this position eventually changed their point of view and agreed to the necessity of creating an institutional forum to fight for women's rights.[121] Thus, when the initial structures of the new party were created, a Secretaría de Asuntos Políticos de la Mujer (Secretariat for Women's Political Matters) was set up, headed by Comandante Lola.[122]

The Secretariat for Women's Political Matters

The Secretariat's work focused on achieving two main objectives: "To strengthen the participation and the integral contribution of the women who are part of the URNG in the construction of the party and in the struggle that it promotes for the effective fulfillment of the peace accords, democracy, economic development, and social justice," and "To contribute to the fight for the eradication of discrimination toward women in Guatemalan society, for the equality of rights between men and women, and for the construction of relations between the two genders based on equality."[123] Even though the party leadership agreed that "these two objectives should be promoted simultaneously, without postponing or subordinating either one of the two,"[124] it became soon evident that the first objective was prioritized. Thus, the URNG followed the path established by its Nicaraguan counterpart during the Sandinista revolution, when women's emancipation was subordinated to the overall goals of the revolution.

A key issue for the newly formed Secretariat was the fight to implement measures of positive discrimination to strengthen female representation in the party structures. Female leaders, following the initial standard employed by the FMLN in El Salvador, argued for a 30 percent quota. After considerable discussion, the URNG leadership made a political commitment that neither gender should have more than 70 or less than 30 percent representation in the new party structures. This commitment "was supposed to be implemented in the election process for the leadership bodies at the municipal, departmental, and national levels."[125] Such a commitment was indeed important, especially in light of the composition of the provisional executive committee of the URNG; Comandante Lola was the only woman among fourteen men. With biting criticism, members of the women's movement characterized this situation as "Lola y los catorce" (Lola and the fourteen guys).

When asked why only one woman had been elected to the executive committee, male leaders argued that women simply did not have sufficient support to get elected and that one had to accept the outcome of a secret, democratic election. Women's participation was hardly more significant in the URNG's National Council. Only four women were among its forty-four members. Female leaders recognized that much work lay ahead of them for the new quota to be adhered to in the elections for permanent party authorities. Comandante Lola admitted that, given the low historic level of female representation, increasing women's representation was a

Table 5.3   Gender Composition of the URNG's National Structure, 1997 and 1999

	Executive Committee				National Council			
Year	Women	%	Men	%	Women	%	Men	%
1997	1	6.7	14	93.3	4	9.1	40	90.9
1999	1	6.7	14	93.3	election to Council postponed			

Source: Internal data provided by a URNG official.

long-term project; one could not expect to reach a 30 percent base immediately.[126]

Her realistic appraisal of the future for women's rights within the URNG proved accurate when the party held its first National Congress in May 1999 to elect permanent party authorities. As discussed earlier, the URNG leadership chose to postpone the election of its Political Council and simply ratified the existing Provisional Executive Committee on which Comandante Lola was the sole female representative. With this act, the URNG violated its commitment to guarantee women 30 percent of the seats on its highest decision-making body.

The November 1999 legislative elections were further proof that female militants had a long way to go in their efforts to increase female participation in key positions. Only one of the nine URNG deputies elected to parliament that year was a woman. Female candidates experienced great difficulties in their efforts to be ranked high on candidate lists, a requirement to have a reasonable chance of getting elected.[127] In general women were underrepresented, considering that female militants represented 25 percent of the 5,202 party members. There were some indications that the URNG leadership realized the importance of preparing women for leadership positions in order to strengthen women's participation within the party. For example, female militants were allocated one third of all spaces in leadership training courses held in Spain. These courses were supposed to train 700 cadres who could fill party positions at all levels.

The challenges confronting women in the URNG were even greater than in El Salvador because of the complex ethnic composition of the female constituency (a number of female militants did not speak Spanish) and its high incidence of illiteracy. Fermina López, a Maya Quiché, noted that very few indigenous women were participating in the URNG. She attributed her own selection as deputy head of the Women's Secretariat to the leadership's need to have some members with her ethnic background in leadership positions.[128] The agreed-upon strategy was for female party activists to assess their current strengths and weaknesses and to train and educate women to fill the available positions of leadership. The URNG was still some time away from using mechanisms, such as separate ballots, to guarantee the established female quota. The Secretariat also needed to expand its organizational structures to have an organizational base for its work. By Spring 1999, the Secretariat had municipal structures in less than 40 percent of the eighty towns where the URNG had established offices. Representatives of the National Secretariat participated in the municipal assemblies and exerted pressure on the local party members to vote for the establishment of a Women's Secretariat. Even when they were successful, however, the new bodies were weak. The women elected to head the local structures were often not qualified for the job or simply did not carry out the tasks they were meant to do.[129] The weakest link in the Secretariat's structure was at the level of the country's departments, where it had no representation of any kind.[130] The daily operations of these local structures were severely limited by their lack of funds. The priority of the National Secretariat was to consolidate the existing bodies before trying to establish new ones.[131]

Relations with the Women's Movement

While the URNG leadership created the Secretaría with the intention of giving women increased representation within the party, it also sought to reach out to Guatemalan women in general. This was an important decision because the URNG had come under increasingly vocal criticism from female leaders who were disenchanted with the URNG's policies following the peace accords. One bridge, connecting the URNG to those sectors of Guatemala's social movement that were sympathetic to the URNG's social and political agenda, was the Unión Nacional de Mujeres Guatemaltecas (National Union of Guatemalan Women, or UNAMG).[132] The UNAMG had originally emerged in 1980. It was the result of several years of organizing by women close to the guerrilla movement. The organization suffered greatly from the repression unleashed by the Guatemalan government in the 1980s. For example, in 1985, Silvia Gálvez, a cofounder and general secretary of the UNAMG was disappeared. In these difficult circumstances, the organization became defunct. It was resurrected in 1997, under the leadership of Luz Méndez. Méndez, a key URNG leader with a recognized record of fighting for women's rights, emphasized that the UNAMG was autonomous from the party. Some sectors of the women's movement, however, which rejected the notion of *doble militancia* (active participation in both the women's movement and a political party) considered the UNAMG to be subordinate to the URNG. Whereas only time could clarify the degree to which the UNAMG was independent, it represented an important link between women sympathetic to the political project of the URNG and the women's movement at large. In 1999, Comandante Lola acknowledged that the URNG's Women's Secretariat had not developed a relationship with the women's movement and was not participating in activities sponsored by women's groups outside of the URNG. She attributed this fact to the priority the Secretariat had given to party building and planned to address this situation in the near future.[133]

Conclusion

Here are the key factors that shape the struggle for gender equality in the three countries under discussion: Female FMLN militants played the most significant role in the guerrilla movement during the war, providing them with a strong argument in favor of women's participation in the party. Sandinista women also contributed greatly, whereas female URNG militants were a distant third. The international climate favoring increased women's participation in decision-making bodies was strongest at the time of the Guatemalan peace accords. While it translated into strong provisions in favor of women's rights in the accords themselves, it had little significance in the early development of the URNG. FMLN women, on the other hand, did benefit from international pressure for gender equality. In the case of Nicaragua, Sandinista women were first able to take advantage of a favorable international climate when the FSLN was out of power. For reasons discussed above, it was the women's movement that grew strong while party activists faced a difficult struggle in the Sandinista party. FMLN members were clearly most effective in pursuing shrewd strategies to strengthen formal equality in the party. They did so with the support of the women's movement. FSLN women had good ideas but ultimately lacked the clout to get them adopted, while URNG priorities worked against its female party members.

The analysis of the revolutionary Left's record on gender equality reveals that the fight for gender equality is complex. Although the three countries have much in common, there are important differences. Idiosyncratic developments make it impossible to adhere to universal recipes. For historic reasons, the strength of the Nicaraguan women's movement is a key factor in the lack of progress of female militants within the Sandinista party. On the other hand, FMLN women in El Salvador have made considerable advances, although effective support from the women's movement alternated with lost opportunities due to infighting.

The Nicaraguan situation clearly demonstrates that measures of positive discrimination and strong organizational structures are necessary but by no means sufficient conditions to advance the struggle for women's emancipation. Without a fundamental change in the consciousness of women and men, advances in women's rights will remain limited. The Zoilamérica case indicated that the progress women achieved in the party had not yet been consolidated. Only the future will show whether these precarious achievements will be able to weather the storm of the strong backlash brewing within the party. Recent events in Nicaragua have strengthened the conviction of key feminists that the FSLN cannot be reformed. Most leaders in the revolutionary Left realize and acknowledge the potential benefits their parties can reap by emphasizing gender equality. Sectors within the women's movement, on the other hand, have questioned whether it still makes sense to fight to transform the parties of the Left. Political parties throughout the world are confronted with a crisis of credibility. This crisis has been most evident in the Central American context. Female leaders have seriously been considering whether they should continue to focus their energies on established parties, a strategy that, at best, will have limited results. An eloquent minority has argued for the creation of alternative modes of political representation. In their opinion, the revolutionary Left is beyond redemption and has hardly distinguished itself from the traditional parties.

Any evaluation of gender equality and democratization within the URNG has to emphasize the enormous task facing the URNG leadership and its female members and supporters. At the dawn of the new millennium, the Guatemalan peace process is still in its early stages and the URNG has yet to complete its transition from a political-military organization into a democratic political party. In this context, gender equality has simply not been a priority in the minds of many key officials. Female leaders have affirmed that the URNG and Guatemala's society at large, lack gender awareness.

URNG militants have debated many of the key issues that their counterparts in Nicaragua and El Salvador encountered, such as doble militancia and the autonomy of the women's movement. In addition to these debates, however, URNG women have confronted problems specific to the Guatemalan situation. Most importantly, party members of both sexes have been overwhelmed by the demands that the demobilization and the creation of a political party placed on them. A central challenge facing the women who have sought to advance gender equality within their emerging party structures was that they are still in the process of getting to know each other. The problem has two roots: first, the majority of the female URNG members have only recently acknowledged their militancy publicly; and, second, despite advances in the unification process and the dissolution of the historic structures of the four constituent groups, many activists are only slowly shedding their identities as members of the subgroups in order to assume full membership in the URNG. Female activists from these subgroups have had to overcome years of mutual distrust in their efforts to find a common platform for their struggle. It appears that women have been the vanguard in the effort to forge a URNG identity. In the eyes of some leaders, the bonds of solidarity among women from the four groups helped to heal the divisions among the organizations.

Practical gender interests continue to be of paramount interest to the FMLN's female constituents. Nevertheless, there has been growing awareness among women, that the time has come to fight for women's emancipation, starting with gender equality in the party and the society at large. Overall the record of the FMLN's female members has been impressive. Arguably the greatest impact came from the adoption of quotas in 1994 and the 1996 implementation of a gender policy perspective by the party. This created the overall context that made everything else possible. At the end of the last millennium, one-third or more of the positions in the party's decision-making bodies were held by women. In addition, a similar proportion of those FMLN officials who held public office were female. At the local and regional levels, however, there is ample room for improvement. Yet even there, the FMLN's record compares well with parties from other countries.

Despite these important achievements, the FMLN Women's Secretariat continues to function under precarious conditions. By 2000, the Secretariat was still not fully institutionalized because its status was not determined in the party's statutes. Also, the 1997 convention brought changes to the leadership of the Secretariat. From the perspective of some of the long-serving members, the newcomers, including Mercedes Peña, the new head, have showed little interest in the Secretariat's work and lack a commitment to implement a feminist agenda. In their eyes, the new members are party hacks whose loyalty is not with the female militants. As a consequence, there has been discord in the Secretariat, and its work has suffered. In addition to these problems, structural constraints persist.

A central problem has been the lack of financial resources. At the end of the 1990s, the Secretariat still lacked a regular budget. Instead it had to finance its activities in an ad hoc fashion. Financial support came mostly from international sources.[134] There was also a tremendous lack of qualified people to fill leadership positions. This combination of material and personnel deficits has made it particularly difficult for the FMLN to reach out to its membership. For example, the Secretariat sought to increase significantly the number of women affiliated with the party. Yet as its leaders acknowledged, it failed to accomplish this objective.[135] Also, a series of workshops and seminars designed by the Secretariat to strengthen gender awareness within the party had to be cancelled or postponed for financial reasons.

The Secretariat's leadership has criticized local and national party authorities for not embracing the gender perspective wholeheartedly and abdicating all responsibility for its implementation. In effect, the burden for achieving gender equality has been put on the Secretariat.[136] As female leaders have pointed out, the lack of concrete measures to implement the commitment to achieve gender equality and the failure of women in leadership positions to take full advantage of the opportunities they have had has impeded further advances. These limitations help to explain why substantive gender equality remains elusive. Final success needs a transformation of the male vision whose "schedules, evaluations and established procedures" continue to hold women back.[137] The Secretariat's leadership recognizes that men and women need to come together to implement the party's gender policy and the necessary economic resources have to be allocated for the policy's successful execution.[138]

The analysis of women's advancement or the lack thereof within the revolutionary Left demonstrates one thing clearly: the fight for formal gender equality is but the first step in a long, protracted struggle. The experience of the three parties leads to the conclusion that only the mainstreaming of the gender agenda will ultimately lead to success. It is the lack of support for such an agenda by the predominantly male leadership and by female leaders who are too compliant that has held back the FMLN, the FSLN, and the URNG. Mainstreaming would put the responsibility for advancing gender equality where it belongs—in the hands of women and men.

6

Gender Equality and Recent Elections

*Cuando una mujer llega a la política cambia la mujer; pero . . . cuando
las mujeres llegan a la política cambia la política.*
—*Poder Feminino*, FMLN Election Pamphlet

In an excellent study of post–civil war elections in Nicaragua and El Salvador Karen Kampwirth found significant differences in the gendered content of these electoral experiences. Regarding the 1990 Nicaraguan elections, Kampwirth argues that "seen from a feminist perspective, the first
post–civil war election in Nicaragua was close to disastrous." She ac-
knowledges, however, the important role played by organized feminists in
the case of El Salvador.[1] The analysis of subsequent elections in both countries shows that women's organizing becomes more effective over time. The
first postwar elections in Guatemala emphasize how difficult it is for women
on the Left to take the initial steps toward effective participation. So how
did the Salvadoran and Nicaraguan women's movements try to put gender
equality on the political agendas of their parties and how successful were
they in getting women on the candidate lists and increasing their representation in parliament?

Putting Gender Equality on the Agenda

El Salvador

The FMLN's Women's Secretariat in El Salvador fought for the introduction of measures of positive discrimination, such as quotas. As discussed
in Chapter Five, female leaders argued that the strong participation of

women during the war had gained them the right to participate in the party's leadership structures. An extension of this fight was the struggle to increase the number of FMLN women holding public office. The leadership of the Secretariat began to work for this in the months leading up to the 1994 elections. They fought for a 30 percent female quota of the candidates selected for the 1994 parliamentary elections. This initial effort was unsuccessful.

In January 1993, representatives of a number of Salvadoran women's organizations began to build "a broad-based coalition to press for women's demands."[2] Having concluded that women had been marginalized in the peace accords, they attempted to exert pressure on the political parties competing in the 1994 elections to support a platform advocating women's rights. Upon realizing that "the political parties were no more interested in women's issues than the peace negotiators had been," they launched Mujeres '94 (Women '94), a multipartisan coalition of women that worked to increase female voter turnout, persuade parties to include women's demands in their platform, and elect female candidates.[3] FMLN women played a key role in this organizing effort. Although women made some progress in putting gender equality on the national agenda, the experience of the 1994 elections convinced them of the need to elaborate a more effective strategy for the next elections.

In 1997, the FMLN's Women's Secretariat obtained an important agreement from the party leadership giving the female candidates complete autonomy in conducting their campaigns. This was done in an effort to make sure that the party's precarious financial situation would not negatively affect the current female candidates, who expected to be allocated fewer resources than their male counterparts. To give an idea of the limited resources available for the campaign, Nidia Díaz, then the FMLN's deputy coordinator, was given less than $900 to run the party's campaign in the department of San Vicente.

The FMLN women set up the Comando Electoral de Mujeres (Women's Electoral Command) to coordinate their efforts. The Comando was led by four women, representing the female candidates and the Women's Secretariat. Its strategy aimed to achieve three goals: to design a women's platform to make clear to the voters what the female candidates stood for, to pressure the party to give the female candidates as much visibility as possible in the election campaign, and to lobby within the FMLN to make sure that the overall election campaign promoted women's issues.

The Comando composed a campaign song, designed propaganda and campaign posters, and produced radio and television advertisements. It also set up brigades, consisting of three to five women who lobbied door to door for female mayoral candidates. Furthermore, the women were so successful at obtaining favorable prices from female heads of advertising agencies that their male colleagues pleaded with them to negotiate on their behalf also.[4] Male candidates were so eager to use the propaganda designed by the Comando in their own election campaigns that the Comando finally had to refuse them so as to keep enough resources available for the female candidates. The Comando's success was evident in the streets of the capital, where the faces of the FMLN's female candidates were omnipresent, while male candidates had little exposure.

Members of the Comando were also involved in a more comprehensive effort—launched by representatives of the Salvadoran women's movement—to put women's issues on the electoral agenda. This initiative was designed to build on the experience of Mujeres '94. Mujeres '94 had not been without its problems. In 1994, the central dividing issue among the women had been *doble militancia*. The question was whether women who participated in Mujeres '94 as representatives of the women's movement could also be active party militants. The main opponents in this debate were the Movimiento de Mujeres "Mélida Anaya Montes" and the Mujeres por la Dignidad y la Vida. Las Dignas considered party militancy incompatible with maintaining autonomy as an activist of the women's movement, while the MAM argued that these roles could be combined. This controversy had its roots in the struggle for autonomy, a salient issue for several women's groups that emerged in the 1990s and had close ties to the FMLN.[5]

In February 1996, representatives of the women's movement held a meeting to evaluate the experience of Mujeres '94. The first task of the Iniciativa de Mujeres por la Igualdad en la Participación Política (Women's Initiative for Equality in Political Participation, its cumbersome official name) was to revise and update the 1994 platform.[6] The group of women who worked consistently on this task was rather small.[7] Over the course of 1996, it became evident that several key issues divided the women involved in the project.

The question of impartiality had replaced the problem of the doble mil-itancia. Women affiliated with Las Dignas argued that the Women's Coali-tion had to work impartially and promote female candidates regardless of their ideology. The majority of participants in the Initiativa de Mujeres, however, held the view that they were all women supporting parties on the left of the ideological spectrum and therefore they could not work on be-half of their political rivals. One woman put it succinctly: "We are women of the Left and we can't call on people to vote for the women of ARENA." This position particularly made sense from the MAM point of view. Not only was Irma Amaya, the movement's coordinator, herself a candidate for parliament, but four other female FMLN candidates were members of the MAM. (All five of them were elected.)

In the end, the group settled on a nonpartisan approach embodied in the slogan "Woman, vote for yourself," although many participants still questioned its effectiveness. Because of this infighting, the crucial task of agreeing on a common agenda was not completed until February 1997, a whole year after the organizing effort began. In the words of Deysi Cheyne, a key protagonist, "This was a wall that we never managed to surmount. We could never reach an agreement, which left us discussing for weeks and weeks."[8] This delay defeated the organizing effort's main purpose—to get the parties to sign the platform and commit themselves to implementing an agenda benefiting women's rights. Indeed, the final version of the plat-form was first available on March 10 (six days before the election)—the day representatives of all parties were invited for its presentation. Only three parties, ARENA, the FMLN, and the Coalition (three parties sup-porting a joint candidate for mayor of San Salvador), bothered to show up; and not surprisingly, all three refused to sign the protocol of commitment. The obvious argument was that the representatives could not commit their parties to a document no one had even seen yet. The disappointed women had no one to blame but themselves.

Nicaragua

In Nicaragua, female FSLN militants confronted difficult conditions in their struggle to increase the number of women holding elected office. As we have seen, during the revolutionary period, the fight for gender equality within the party was given a low priority. Awareness that the party had to move toward more equal gender relations increased dramatically after the FSLN's 1990 electoral defeat. In 1994, FSLN women succeeded in persuading the party leadership to revise the party statutes and allocate a minimum of 30 percent of all party positions to women. This same quota was also to be applied in the selection of the candidates for the 1996 elections. In their struggle for gender equality, the militants were supported by the Asociación de Mujeres Nicaragüenses, Luisa Amanda Espinoza, the Sandinista women's organization. This movement played a key role in fighting for increased female participation within the party. AMNLAE, which had lacked autonomy under the Sandinista government, was making an effort to evolve into a broad-based, nonpartisan movement. As part of this strategy it reached out to other sectors of the women's movement and became a participant in the Nicaraguan Coalición Nacional de Mujeres (Women's Coalition).

The Coalition began as an initiative by a group of women who were working in various capacities for the government of Violeta Chamorro. They considered it important for women affiliated with the political Right to reconsider their view of the women's movement, which those women had dismissed as being controlled by the Sandinista party. The group held several seminars to help the different groups get acquainted. The idea was for all participants to join forces to combat discrimination against women. According to María Teresa Blandón, who helped organize these first encounters, initially it was even a challenge to obtain a consensus that women were indeed discriminated against in Nicaraguan society. For example, Azucena Ferrey, a former leader of the Nicaraguan Resistance and a member of parliament, took the position that she was not subordinated, that she had power, and that she had always been able to achieve what she had wanted.[9] Ferrey's position reflected her distrust of the views held by "Sandinista feminists" rather than any lack of recognition of Nicaraguan society's discrimination against women.

On March 8, 1987, Ferrey convoked a rally to commemorate Women's Day and to protest the plight of women who did not favor the Sandinista revolution. This demonstration was brutally repressed by the Sandinista police, headed by Doris Tijerino, one of the historical female FSLN commanders. Only in the early 1990s, when both Ferrey and Tijerino were serving in the Nicaraguan parliament, could the two women start a dialogue that made it possible to bridge ideological boundaries and unite in the fight for women's emancipation.[10] Until these women with diverse backgrounds agreed on a strategy to "fight for women's rights and transformation of the traditional ways to make politics," the process was, indeed, slow.[11]

In 1996, the women of the Coalition were working to overcome the past. They developed an *agenda mínima* (basic platform) that included the call for women's rights in the political and socioeconomic arena.[12] All demands that were part of the agenda were based on consensus. Despite this cumbersome process, the participants managed to include even controversial demands, such as the delivery of reproductive health services.[13] The Coalition's first official task was to organize the celebration of Women's Day on March 8, 1996. For the first time, women from across the ideological spectrum joined forces with feminists, lesbians, and autonomous women's groups to celebrate this event. Subsequently, the Coalition held meetings with representatives of the various political parties to obtain their commitment to implement the agenda mínima if their candidates were elected. Several parties, including the FSLN, the Nicaraguan Resistance Party, and the Alliance UNO '96, signed a protocol of commitment. Most notably, the Liberal Alliance refused to sign. The Liberal Alliance supported Arnoldo Alemán, the eventual winner of the election, for president.

As in El Salvador, one of the key debates for the Women's Coalition was whether to support individual female candidates or to promote women's participation in the elections regardless of party. Coalition members who were party militants refused to support candidates nominated by ideological opponents. Many feminists had little interest in supporting female candidates at all, since in their opinion, "not a single candidate was a feminist."[14] This conflict was never resolved, and it limited the Coalition's effectiveness. Ironically, the female candidates, fully immersed in their own campaigns, had little time available to advance the Coalition's goal; thus the Coalition's work was carried out mainly by the feminists. Feminists organized public events and wrote the speeches to be given, but the female candidates fearing that they "would get burned" from being associated with "radical" groups, told the feminists to remain invisible.[15]

The Nicaraguan experience was not free from conflict. In contrast to their Salvadoran counterparts, however, the members of the Women's

Coalition were effective in forging a pluralistic alliance that presented a united front to the political parties. More important, their agenda was finalized more than six months before the elections, giving the movement ample time to lobby the political establishment. In particular contrast to the Salvadoran case, the Coalition's efforts received financial support, mainly from governments and nongovernmental organizations in the Scandinavian countries.[16] Eivor Halkjaer, the Swedish ambassador, whom the Coalition considered "our godmother," was a key figure in this effort.[17] Moreover, the funds received from the U.S. Agency for International Development constitute evidence that the Coalition was indeed considered to be a pluralist, multipartisan effort.[18]

Candidate Selection: Women's Innovative Strategies

The female militants of the FMLN and FSLN developed innovative strategies to increase their representation on the candidate lists.[19] The first line of attack was to get the party leadership to adopt a quota for female candidates. The next step was to make sure that the quota was observed in the selection of departmental and municipal candidates.

In addition, women were well aware of the central requirement for a successful candidate under a system of proportional representation: to hold a top position on the candidate list. Under proportional representation, the number of votes a party receives corresponds to the number of seats it wins in parliament. Thus, a party that wins 10 percent of the vote gets about 10 percent of the seats in the legislature. Only the top candidate on most departmental lists had a good chance of getting elected. Most departments have fewer than five representatives in parliament. Thus, no major party can expect to win more than two or three seats in any department. The higher a candidate is on the candidate list, the better his or her chances of getting elected. For the national list, a "safe" position for a candidate of the Left was to be among the first five candidates. Only a candidate in such a position was assured election, assuming that the party came in first or second in the electoral contest.[20] The party's male militants could concede the numerical quotas and claim adherence to formal equality without incurring any real cost in terms of increased competition from women if women's names appeared near the bottom of the lists. So women had to fight to be ranked at the top in the department lists and very high in the national list. In general, the women in both countries benefited under their countries' electoral systems, in that "proportional representation electoral systems lead to better representation of women than majoritarian electoral systems."[21]

In the 1994 parliamentary elections in El Salvador, the female militants succeeded in getting 21 women, representing 25 percent of the 84 candidates, onto the party lists (see Table 6.1). Although the FMLN's Women's Secretariat had argued unsuccessfully for a 30 percent female quota in the selection of the candidates for parliament, the gender composition of the FMLN candidates demonstrates that women had considerable success in getting the attention of the party hierarchy. Women were most successful at the national level, where they represented 35 percent of the candidates and 40 percent of the substitutes. Female representation in the municipal elections was not as strong. Of the 240 candidates for mayor that were officially registered one week before the elections, only 23 were women. The candidate lists were established in a difficult bargaining process between the five groups then constituting the FMLN.

In terms of gender distribution, the Communist Party had the highest number of female candidates with six, representing 27.3 percent of its candidates and the ERP had the lowest rate with 20 percent. The absolute number of candidates gives us some information regarding the bargaining power of the female membership. Yet it is much more important to examine the number of safe seats allocated to women, since under a system of proportional representation, being a candidate by no means guarantees success. Before the 1994 elections, senior FMLN officials were confident that the new party would gain at least twenty seats. Women were allocated four seats considered safe.[22]

Ana Guadalupe Martínez and Lorena Peña, who had held the second and third spot, respectively, were elected from the national list. In addition, Norma Guevara and Sonia Aguinada, who had occupied positions four and five in the department of San Salvador, were elected, as was Nidia Díaz— the only women heading a department list. Thus, women performed somewhat better than expected.

In the 1997 elections, women did considerably better in occupying top, "safe" positions on candidate lists and thus being virtually assured of elec-

Table 6.1   Gender Composition of FMLN Candidates for the 1994 Elections
by FMLN Group

A: FMLN Candidates for the Legislative Assembly

	Women		Men		Total	
Group	Candidates	Substitutes	Candidates	Substitutes	Candidates	Substitutes
ERP	3	2	12	15	15	17
PCS	6	6	16	13	22	19
FPL	5	5	17	17	22	22
PRTC	3	3	9	8	12	11
RN	3	3	10	9	13	12
Affiliation Unknown	0	0	0	1	0	1
MNR	0	0	0	2	0	2
Total	20	19	64	65	84	84

	B: FMLN Candidates for Mayor			C: FMLN Mayors		
Organization	Women	Men	Total	Women	Men	Total
ERP	7	54	61	2	3	5
PCS	2	38	40	0	0	0
FPL	12	89	101	0	10	10
PRTC	0	7	7	0	0	0
RN	1	17	18	0	0	0
MNR	0	1	1	0	0	0
CD	1	11	12	0	0	0
Total	23	217	240	2	13	15

Source: This distribution is based on candidate lists provided by the Farabundo Martí National Liberation Front.

PCS: Partido Communista de El Salvador; MNR: Movimiento Nacional Revolucionario; CD: Convergencia Democrática.

tion. These gains, however, were won after a hard fight. In June 1996, when about 50 of El Salvador's 262 municipal conventions had already selected their candidates, the FMLN's Women's Secretariat conducted a survey and found that not a single woman had been proposed as a candidate for mayor and only a few were on candidate lists for municipal councils. With this finding, several female leaders "went to scare" the FMLN's Political Commission, persuading it to "communicate to all departments that they needed to observe the quota at the municipal and departmental level."[23] This pressure had results in the national elections.

In the end, there were twenty-four female candidates (28.6%) and twenty-six substitutes (30.1%) on the FMLN candidate list for Member of Parliament. Of the five top positions considered safe on the national list, women occupied two. In the department of San Salvador, women held the top two positions as well as the fifth place, which was also considered safe. Female candidates also headed the departmental lists in Santa Ana, Chalatenango, and San Vicente. Overall, in four out of fourteen departments, women headed the ticket. Based on the 1994 election results, seven women were considered to hold safe positions. In light of the positive polls, however, female FMLN leaders expected a minimum of eight women to be elected and considered up to ten female representatives a realistic outcome. According to their calculations, they had ensured that 35 percent of the safe candidate positions were held by women.

The improvement in the female candidates' chances of election was not an accident but evidence of the female militants' hard work persuading their male counterparts to accept gender equality within the party. The record indicates that their efforts were more successful at the national than at the departmental level. Interviews with the party leadership and female candidates support the view that the issue of gender equality enjoyed sup-

Table 6.2   Gender Composition of FMLN Candidates for Parliament, 1994 and 1997

Candidacy	Candidates				Substitutes				Total			
	Women	%	Men	%	Women	%	Men	%	Women	%	Men	%
A: 1994 Elections												
Department Lists	14	21.9	50	78.1	10	15.6	54	84.4	24	18.8	104	81.2
National List	7	35.0	13	65.0	8	40.0	12	60.0	15	37.5	25	62.5
Total	21	25.0	63	75.0	18	21.4	66	78.6	39	23.2	129	76.8
B: 1997 Elections												
Department Lists	15	23.4	49	76.6	16	25.0	48	75.0	31	24.2	97	75.8
National List	9	45.0	11	55.0	10	50.0	10	50.0	19	47.5	21	52.5
Total	24	28.6	60	71.4	26	31.0	58	69.0	50	29.8	118	70.2

Source: A: Secretaría Electoral del FMLN, in Las Dignas, Las mujeres, p. 28. B: Based on data provided by the FMLN.

port at the national level, while considerable resistance to any kind of positive discrimination programs for women prevailed at the departmental and local levels. The situation cannot be generalized, however, because there were considerable differences among departments. In several of them, especially San Salvador, women forged effective alliances with male party members and employed a variety of innovative strategies to get female candidates on the lists.

The department of San Salvador had a total of sixteen candidates. It was considered a difficult department for women to get elected in, because they had to compete with male leaders of great renown. Realizing that the FMLN could not expect to win more than eight seats in this department, the departmental leadership took the position that women needed to occupy at least three of the first eight positions. To ensure that all delegates voted for at least three women, the leadership of the department agreed that any ballot that did not include the names of three female candidates would be declared invalid. The rank order of the candidates was based on the total number of votes received.

According to Violeta Menjívar, who eventually headed the department's slate, the reaction of many men was vehement: "This is a violation of human rights. This is an imposition of the women. What are these quotas about? Women are no good for leadership positions; when they are elected they don't deliver."[24] This position, however, was more than counterbalanced by those males in the department leadership who were interested, not in window dressing, but in achieving substantive equality for female militants. Thus the voting proceeded as planned. Women did even better than expected, with four female candidates among the first seven names on the list. Most surprising was that the women outdistanced important male leaders, such as Gerson Martínez, then the FMLN's parliamentary whip, who enjoyed an excellent reputation among the party faithful yet came to occupy only the fourth position on the list.

The victory of the female candidates was the result of an astute strategy. A group of female delegates got together and decided to nominate fewer candidates in order to concentrate the vote. While only five women ran for the first eight positions, there were twenty male candidates. Indeed, several female delegates, urged by their male counterparts to run, declined to do so. They suspected that this was a ruse by their male competitors intended to dilute the vote.

While San Salvador was a success story for female candidates, other departments had problems. In Ahuachapan, one of the leading male candidates started a defamation campaign against Aída Herrera, the nominee of the women's movement. Herrera was accused of being a wealthy and loose woman, wearing miniskirts, smoking, and drinking. These charges created a furor among some delegates. According to one account, an old peasant almost suffered a heart attack and announced, "We can't have a prostitute as a deputy." To no one's surprise, divisions emerged among the delegates, and Herrera was not elected. This enraged several female leaders and they insisted that she be included on the national ticket. The "misogynist views" that had carried the day in Ahuachapan, they argued, should be countered immediately. Herrera, fearing another humiliation, was at first reluctant to be a candidate; but after much discussion she agreed that a point had to be made. Eventually she was nominated to the seventh position on the national list. With her nomination, the FMLN's National Council (whose members played a key role, choosing the candidates) sent a strong message of support for gender equality.

In Chalatenango's departmental convention, María Ofelia Navarrete displaced Eduardo Linares, the incumbent from 1994. Navarrete, a charismatic figure with a long history of struggle in the FMLN, faced considerable opposition from within her own party. Her candidacy was opposed by FMLN members who had joined the party following the 1992 peace accords and did not share the ideological views of those FMLN cadres who had fought in the war. These newer members had joined forces with landowning interests that feared the "radical" FMLN leader.

In San Vicente, the leadership of Nidia Díaz was uncontested, but old rivalries among the groups that historically made up the FMLN raised problems. Díaz, a leader of the old Revolutionary Party of Central American Workers, faced opposition from a sector previously affiliated with the Popular Forces of Liberation, led by Facundo Guardado. Elected FMLN president in December 1997, Guardado advocated *renovación*, in the belief that the party should nominate "new faces" instead of historical leaders. His position did not carry the day. The resistance to Díaz's candidacy was overcome when women identified with the FPL convinced their male friends that Díaz was an ideal candidate. Recent surveys, they argued, had shown that she was one of the most popular FMLN leaders, and the FMLN would lose votes if she were not nominated.

As in 1994, women did best at the national level, where they accounted for 45 percent of the candidates and 50 percent of the substitutes (see Table 6.2). While department lists were determined by the FMLN delegates elected to the departmental conventions, the national list was voted on by the fifty-two-member National Council, the highest decision-making body after the fifteen-member Political Commission. In light of the success women had achieved in several departments, particularly in San Salvador, several male leaders were apprehensive when it came time to choose the national list. The women argued for *la trenza* ("the braid"), an arrangement whereby males and females would alternate on the list, but this was not approved. Instead the voting proceeded in several rounds. Candidates were elected in slates of five, with separate ballots for men and women. Of the five top positions, two were allocated to female candidates.

In the first round of voting, Ileana Rogel received the most votes, and Lorena Peña came in fourth. Unlike the voting procedures used in San Salvador, however, a subsequent round of voting established the rank order of the first five candidates. Schafik Hándal, one of the historic FMLN commanders, was voted into first place, displacing Rogel, while Peña was dropped to the fifth position. In her case, eleven of the fifty-two ballots gave her zero votes. Peña, probably the most outspoken feminist in the party, had apparently antagonized a considerable number of male leaders. The same procedure was employed to determine the remaining fifteen positions. At the national level, a total of nine women were nominated.

In 1997, women constituted 29.8 percent of all candidates and substitutes compared with 23.2 percent in 1994 (Table 6.2). This was a substantial improvement and was only slightly below the relative strength of women in the party. The success of the candidates for parliament was not replicated at the municipal level, however. Out of 262 FMLN candidates for mayor, only 16 (6%) were female, as were about 20 percent of the candidates for city council. It was evident that women had been most successful in mobilizing their forces at the national level and for the high-profile parliamentary elections. Female leaders also acknowledged that their efforts met with greater success in urban areas than in the countryside. A main obstacle to increasing the number of women elected to municipal office was many women's expressed reluctance to be nominated. This, in turn, was the result of traditional gender relations, which relegated women to the private sphere. Nevertheless, the FMLN record was impressive, particularly when compared to that of the other parties.

The governing party, the Alianza Republicana Nacionalista, by comparison, had a total of sixteen females on its 1997 party lists for seats in the parliament. Gloria Salguero Gross, then president of the parliament and one of the three ARENA legislators elected in 1994, headed the national list. She was, however, the only woman in a prominent list position. Not a single department list was headed by a female, and only three of the twenty ARENA candidates on the national list were women. As a consequence of women's weak positions on the candidate lists, only four female ARENA candidates were elected to parliament. ARENA's record indicates that the support FMLN women received from their national leadership was not replicated in the governing party. According to female FMLN leaders, Gloria Salguero Gross acknowledged as much: in private conversations with her FMLN counterparts, she expressed admiration for the strong positions female candidates held on the FMLN lists.

The challenges that confronted FSLN women in Nicaragua were very similar to those that faced FMLN militants in El Salvador. Despite the strong participation of women in the revolutionary struggle, women were given only limited representation on the Council of State, Nicaragua's corporatist, colegislative body, which was established in 1981. Of its fifty-one initial members, who represented different sectors of Nicaraguan society, only four were women. Women increased their representation on the 1984 FSLN candidate lists for the first democratic elections following the insurrection. That year, the FSLN presented 16 female candidates and 18 substitutes, 19 percent of the 180 candidates and substitutes it put forward for parliament (see Table 6.2). Only a few women, however, headed the candidate lists for regional positions.[25] Among the few were Dora María Téllez and Leticia Herrera, historic FSLN leaders who headed the ticket in Managua, and Gladys Báez, who led the list of candidates in Boaco-Chontales.[26]

Table 6.3   Gender Composition of FSLN Candidates for Parliament, 1984–1996

	Candidates				Substitutes				Total			
Year	Women	%	Men	%	Women	%	Men	%	Women	%	Men	%
1984	16	17.8	74	82.2	18	20.0	72	80.0	34	18.9	146	81.1
1990	19	21.1	71	78.9	15	16.7	75	83.3	34	18.9	146	81.1
1996												
Department Lists	23	32.9	47	67.1	24	34.3	46	65.7	47	33.6	93	66.4
National List	9	45.0	11	55.0	8	40.0	12	60.0	17	42.5	23	57.5
All Candidates	32	35.6	58	64.4	32	35.6	58	64.4	64	35.6	116	64.4

Source: Calculated from candidate lists published by the Consejo Supremo Electoral and the FSLN.

In Zelaya Norte, one of the three Atlantic Coast electoral districts, all three candidates were female, with Dorotea Wilson heading the ticket; the other two districts had no female candidates at all.

For the national elections of 1990, the FSLN presented nineteen female candidates and fifteen substitutes. Only in region six (Matagalpa and Jinotega) did a woman, Doris Tijerino, lead the list of candidates. In Managua, Dora María Téllez and Leticia Herrera had been placed after Carlos Núñez Téllez, then president of parliament; Gladys Baéz was running in region two, where she was ranked fourth; Dorotea Wilson was not up for re-election.

On the candidate lists for 1996—when the 30 percent quota for women was applied for the first time—the women of the FSLN substantially increased their representation. In these elections for parliament, women represented 35.6 percent of all candidates and substitutes, as compared to 18.9 percent in 1990. Of the ninety candidates, thirty-two were female. As in El Salvador, women were more successful in getting on the national list than the departmental lists. In Nicaragua, the composition of the national list was decided by delegates elected to a National Congress. This body included the Sandinista Assembly, the highest party authority after the National Directorate. While female candidates held about one-third of the positions on the department lists, they held 45 percent of the twenty seats on the national slate.

This positive picture is deceptive, however. Considering the department lists from the perspective of order of names, it is evident that few female

FSLN candidates occupied secure spots. Only in two instances were the lists of the country's fifteen departments and two autonomous zones headed by women. In Managua, Mónica Baltodano held the top spot on the ticket as did Edna Stubbert in Boaco. At the municipal level, the situation was even worse, with few women even being proposed as candidates.

This situation had three main roots. First, "the good will on behalf of the male *compañeros* was missing," and the intent of the 30 percent quota mandated in the party statutes was subverted by putting women in positions from which they could not be elected.[27] Second, many women in the FSLN were simply not willing to accept a candidacy. For many of them, particularly at the local level, cultural prejudices and harsh economic realities raised the cost of assuming a leadership position to a prohibitive level. According to Dorotea Wilson, this problem was compounded by the 1995 split in the FSLN. Many educated, highly qualified members left the party when Sergio Ramírez established the Movimiento Renovador Sandinista.[28] Finally, the efforts of female militants to increase women's participation on the candidate lists lacked coordination. As discussed in Chapter Five, the Sandinista party did not have a women's secretariat to oversee these kinds of activities.

By the time the FSLN convened the 1996 National Congress to establish the national list, female leaders were outraged that so few women were in safe positions on the departmental lists. They argued that in compensation women should receive special consideration at the national level. To secure good positions, the female militants persuaded the party leadership to adopt "the braid," alternating males and females. Women used the metaphor of a braid to argue that only if they were given equal consideration on the candidate lists would the party represent all its members. Through this procedure, four women obtained safe positions.

Despite obvious shortcomings, the Sandinista record compared favorably to the gender composition of the candidate lists established by other Nicaraguan parties. For example, the Liberal Alliance had only eight female candidates and fourteen substitutes in its lists, none of them in a prominent position. As a result, despite winning the elections and gaining forty-two seats in parliament, the Liberal Alliance had only a single female representative. Three minor parties—the MRS, the Nicaraguan Unity Party, Workers, Peasants and Professionals and the Democratic Nicaraguan

Alliance—had female candidates heading their national lists. The last two did not gain a single seat, while the sole seat won by Sergio Ramírez's MRS went to Jorge Samper, a party heavyweight who headed the ticket in Managua. (Samper is the husband of Rosa Marina Zelaya, the president of Nicaragua's Supreme Election Council. This fact led to speculation that the seat allocated to Samper was actually won in another department.)[29] The dissident Sandinistas of Ramirez's MRS obtained so few votes that Dora María Téllez, who headed the national ticket, failed to win election. It is also interesting that of the twenty-two presidential candidates, only one was a woman: The Partido Alianza Popular Conservadora supported Miriam Arguello Morales. One other minor party had a female vice-presidential candidate.

Election Results from a Gender Perspective

The 1994 Salvadoran elections for president, parliament, and municipal councils were indeed remarkable, since the FMLN, a former guerrilla movement, participated for the first time. While the participation of the revolutionary Left lent legitimacy to the electoral process, the elections suffered from serious shortcomings. The FMLN presidential candidate, Rubén Zamora (he headed a ticket supported by the FMLN, the Democratic Convergence, and the Democratic Revolutionary Movement), was soundly defeated in the second round run-off of the 1994 elections. ARENA's Armando Calderon Sol won with 68 percent of the vote.

In the legislative elections, on the other hand, the FMLN's results were respectable. The former guerrillas obtained 287,811 votes out of a total of 1.3 million and won twenty-one out of the eighty-four seats in parliament. The gender distribution of the FMLN's legislators showed that of the five groups that formed the FMLN at the time, the Revolutionary Army of the People had the highest number of women. Of the ERP's five representatives in parliament, two were female. Three of the other groups had one female legislator each. Only the National Resistance had none of its three female candidates elected.

Following the elections, disagreements among the five groups intensified, resulting in the December 1994 exodus of parts of two of the historic FMLN groups, the Ejército Revolucionario del Pueblo and the Resistencia

Table 6.4   Gender Composition of FMLN Representatives in the Legislative Assembly (until December 1994)

Group	Women		Men		Total	
	Candidates	Substitutes	Candidates	Substitutes	Candidates	Substitutes
ERP	2	1	3	4	5	5
PCS	1	2	4	3	5	5
FPL	1	1	5	4	6	5
PRTC	1	1	1	1	2	2
RN	0	1	3	2	3	3
MNR	0	0	0	1	0	1
Total	5	6	16	15	21	21

Source: Distribution based on data provided by the FMLN.

Nacional.[30] This breakup had only a minor impact on the gender distribution of the FMLN's bench.

As discussed in Chapter Four, those that left formed their own political party, the Partido Demócrata. All female legislators and substitutes of the ERP and RN joined the new party. In the case of the male parliamentarians, only Eugenio Chicas, the previous number two of the RN, remained with the FMLN. Since this split reduced the number of female representatives within the FMLN from five to three, and the number of male representatives from sixteen to eleven, the relative strength of women on the FMLN bench remained basically unchanged.

ARENA won thirty-nine seats in parliament and thus did not have an absolute majority (see Table 6.6). At the municipal level, however,

Table 6.5   Gender Composition of Partido Demócrata in the Legislative Assembly, 1994–1997

Group	Women		Men		Total	
	Candidates	Substitutes	Candidates	Substitutes	Candidates	Substitutes
ERP	2	1	3	4	5	5
RN	0	1	2	2	2	3
Total	2	2	5	6	7	8

Source: Distribution based on data provided by the FMLN.

ARENA swept the elections, gaining control of 207 of the 262 municipal councils. The FMLN was victorious in only 15 towns. This setback was particularly significant because local elections were conducted according to the winner-take-all system. Thus the FMLN was largely left out of local government. Nevertheless, FMLN leaders considered the party's first electoral performance "a partial but important victory."[31] They argued that taking circumstances into account, the FMLN did reasonably well, becoming the second strongest political force in the country and attracting close to 300,000 votes in the parliamentary elections.

Calderon Sol, elected president of El Salvador, characterized the 1994 elections as "another step toward the definitive consolidation of democracy."[32] His own mandate, however, was in question, since 54.5 percent of the registered voters abstained in the second round of the presidential elections. In Central America, only Guatemala had a worse participation record.

Of those voters in possession of voting cards, only 29.9 percent endorsed the ARENA candidate.[33] In addition, judging from the reports of election observers, the elections were fraught with irregularities, which leaves one to wonder about the meaning of Calderon's statement. It appears that once again, thousands of Salvadoran voters were unable to cast their votes. It has been estimated that "the total number unable to vote may have been nearly 20 percent of those who did cast ballots."[34] Although the inclusion of these potential voters would not have changed the outcome of the presidential election, it did make a difference in the parliamentary and municipal elections. FMLN officials argued that their party lost several townships because so many of their supporters could not vote. The elections results lend credibility to this view. The FMLN came in second in sixty-nine municipalities. In eighteen of those, the new party trailed the winner by less than 10 percent of the vote.[35]

There is evidence that women were particularly affected by the irregularities surrounding the elections. A survey found that one month before the elections, 58 percent of those who complained of not having voting cards were women.[36] Female voters experienced greater difficulties than males in their efforts to obtain cards. Many of them lacked the required records (for example, birth certificates), and their domestic responsibilities made it difficult if not impossible to resolve their problems. Similarly, on the day of the elections, those women who were in possession of voting cards experienced difficulties in exercising their right to vote. Many lacked transportation to the polls, and those who did get there were faced with complicated procedures that could present hurdles impossible for illiterate peasants to overcome. Adding this group of female voters to the ones without voting cards, one can estimate that about 275,000 women could not vote.

In 1994, the comparative success rate for male and female FMLN candidates was almost the same. Five of the twenty-one women and sixteen of the sixty-three men who ran on the FMLN ticket were elected. Women thus constituted 23.8 percent of the FMLN's representatives in parliament, a rate that is quite high by international standards. The party's record also compared favorably with its domestic competitors. Of a total of nine women in the Salvadoran parliament, five belonged to the FMLN. ARENA had three female legislators including the president of the National Assembly, Gloria Salguero Gross, and the Christian Democratic Party had one female representative. This meant that less than 11 percent of all seats in parliament were held by women. Similarly, few women were elected as mayors. Out of a total of 262 mayors, only 32 were female. Of all the political parties in El Salvador, only ARENA and the FMLN had any female representatives at that level.

Women made considerable progress in the 1997 parliamentary elections. Nine of the twenty-four female candidates were elected. Although female leaders were jubilant, they were also saddened that Aída Herrera, who had occupied the seventh position on the national list, missed joining her friends in parliament by a mere 1,414 votes (0.4% of the FMLN vote). On the male side, eighteen of the sixty candidates were successful. The electoral success of 37.5 percent of the women, compared to 30 percent of the men, indicates that the female militants had indeed managed to place their candidates in safe list positions. A crucial part of their success was their strategy of fighting for one-third of the safe positions and not being satisfied with merely securing their quota on the list as a whole. With women representing 33.3 percent of the FMLN members of parliament (as opposed to 28.6% of the candidates), the political commitment made by the FMLN leadership to ensure women's representation had become a reality. The FMLN increased the number of its deputies from fourteen to

Table 6.6   Female Candidates Elected in 1994 and 1997 Salvadoran Elections

Party	Legislative Assembly			Mayors		
	Women	%	Total Seats	Women	%	Total Number of Mayors
A: Women Elected in 1994 Elections						
ARENA	3	7.7	39	30	14.5	207
FMLN	5	23.8	21	2	13.3	15
PDC	1	5.6	18	0	0.0	29
PCN	0	0.0	4	0	0.0	10
CD	0	0.0	1	0	0.0	0
Unidad	0	0.0	1	0	0.0	0
Total	9	10.7	84	32	12.2	262[1]
B: Women Elected in 1997 Elections						
ARENA	4	14.3	28	16	9.9	162
FMLN	9	33.3	27	6	12.5	48
PDC	0	0.0	7	0	0.0	15
PCN	0	0.0	11	1	5.6	18
CD	0	0.0	2	0	0.0	0
MU	0	0.0	1	0	0.0	3
PD	0	0.0	0	0	0.0	1
PLD	1	50.0	2	0	0.0	0
PRSC	0	0.0	3	0	0.0	6
PDC-PD[2]	0	0.0	3	0	0.0	4
FMLN-CD[2]	0	0.0	0	0	0.0	2
FMLN-Unidad[2]	0	0.0	0	0	0.0	3
Total	14	16.7	84	23	8.8	262

Sources: FLACSO, El proceso electoral en El Salvador, pp. 189, 193; Movimiento Salvadoreño de Mujeres (MSM), "Las mujeres salvadoreñas y los resultados electorales," in Las Dignas, Las mujeres, p. 29; Tribunal Supremo Electoral.

[1] The total includes one township gained by a candidate of the Movimiento Auténtico Christiano (MAC).

[2] These parties formed an election alliance in several departments.

twenty-seven, more than making up for the seven it had lost to the Partido Demócrata. Of the thirteen new members, six were women. Thus female representation on the FMLN bench was effectively tripled.

Again, the accomplishment of the FMLN militants becomes more impressive when one compares it to ARENA's record. While only four of the sixteen female candidates of the governing party gained a seat in parliament, this represented a gain of one compared to 1994. The male candidates suffered a debacle: only twenty-four of the sixty-eight candidates were elected, a loss of twelve representatives. For this reason the relative influence of women on the ARENA bench actually increased from 7.7 percent in 1994 to 14.3 percent, while the total number of successful women candidates only increased by one. Of the remaining parties represented in parliament, only the Partido Liberal Demócrata had a female representative. At the municipal level, women won only 8.8 percent of the 262 mayoralties. Although the FMLN did somewhat better than ARENA in getting its female mayoralty candidates elected, the success of female FMLN militants was largely limited to the national level. Only six of the fifty-four towns controlled by the FMLN (six of those in coalition) had female mayors. Nevertheless, four FMLN women were elected mayors of large, important municipalities in the department of San Salvador.

Overall, the FMLN performed exceptionally well in 1997. It almost doubled its number of representatives in parliament. The FMLN gained thirteen seats for a total of twenty-seven. ARENA, on the other hand, was reduced from thirty-nine to twenty-eight seats. Compared to 1994, the former guerrillas gained 82,000 votes, while the governing party lost about 210,000.

One of the key victories for the Left was to gain control of the capital and several other important cities. Indeed, although the FMLN controlled only 53 of the country's mayoralities compared to ARENA's 162, more people lived under its municipal government.[37] In the 1997 election, the FMLN obtained more votes in every department than it had in 1994, with the sole exception of Morazán, where it received 678 fewer votes. The FMLN's weak performance in this department was probably a consequence of the internal struggle and subsequent division that resulted in the formation of the PD. During the war, the ERP had its social base in Morazán. Personal interviews with ERP supporters revealed that they had difficulty com-

Table 6.7   Results of 1994 and 1997 Salvadoran Legislative Elections (valid votes)

Party	1994		1997	
	Number of Votes	%	Number of Votes	%
ARENA	605,775	45.03	396,301	35.39
FMLN	287,811	21.39	369,709	33.02
PDC	240,451	17.87	93,545	8.35
PCN	83,520	6.21	97,362	8.69
CD	59,843	4.45	39,145	3.49
MU	33,510	2.49	25,244	2.25
MNR[2]	9,431	0.70		
MAC[2]	12,109	0.90		
MSN	12,827	0.97	7,012	0.62
PLD			35,279	3.15
PRSC			40,039	3.57
PD[1]			13,533	1.20
MAS[1]			132	0.01
PL[1]			2,302	0.20
PUNTO[1]			0	0.00
Total	1,345,277	100.00	1,119,603	100.00

Source: Tribunal Supremo Electoral as reported in FLACSO, El proceso electoral 1994, p. 175; Tribunal Supremo Electoral (1997).

[1]Party did not participate in 1994 elections.

[2]Party did not participate in 1997 elections.

prehending the struggle within the FMLN leadership and were therefore alienated from politics. The only department where the FMLN won no parliamentary seats was Usulután, where it had also failed to win any seats in 1994.

The revolutionary Left in Nicaragua was not as successful as its Salvadoran counterpart in increasing women's representation on its parliamentary bench. Of the thirty-six FSLN deputies elected in 1996, only eight were female (see Table 6.8). Only four candidates were elected from department lists. In addition to the two women who headed the lists in Managua and Boaco, one other candidate was elected to parliament from Managua, and Angela Ríos was elected from the Chinandega list. Ríos's success was a surprise, since she had held the weak fourth position on her list. In the

opinion of a member of the Sandinista directorate, Ríos's electi
result of manipulations by the Supreme Electoral Council. The c
posedly distributed residual votes in an arbitrary fashion. In th
opinion, the FSLN lost a seat in the Autonomous Region Atlantic North,
while gaining the seat of Ríos. The maneuvers were alleged to have secured
the election of Jorge Samper.

In the case of the FSLN, the "braid" resulted in the election of four
women from the national list, giving female candidates at that level the
same success rate as their male counterparts.[38] At the departmental level,
however, the poor performance of FSLN women was pronounced. Out of
twenty-three female candidates only four were elected, whereas twenty-
four of the forty-seven male candidates were successful. On paper, FSLN
women had been in a strong position, representing 32.9 percent of the departmental candidates. Yet the lack of safe positions meant that only 17
percent of these women were elected as opposed to 51 percent of the men.
The electoral results were a setback for the female militants trying to increase their influence in the legislature. Indeed, the relative strength of
FSLN women in parliament actually declined, from 23.1 percent in 1990
to 22.2 percent in 1996 (see Table 6.8).

The FSLN's record is evidence that guaranteeing a quota for women is
not enough. Instead, more energy needs to be devoted to securing safe positions for women on the lists of nominees. Nevertheless, the FSLN record
is quite good when compared with those of its political rivals. Only two

Table 6.8 Gender Composition of FSLN Members of Parliament, 1980–1996

	Members of Parliament				Substitutes				Total			
Year	Women	%	Men	%	Women	%	Men	%	Women	%	Men	%
1980[1]	4	7.8	47	92.2	8	15.7	43	84.3	12	11.8	90	88.2
1984	13	21.3	48	78.7	13	21.3	48	78.7	26	21.3	96	78.7
1990	9	23.1	30[2]	76.9	8	20.5	31	79.5	17	21.8	61	78.2
1996	8	22.2	28[2]	77.8	15	41.7	21	58.3	23	31.9	49	68.1

Sources: Calculations based on membership lists provided by FSLN; data for 1990 reported in Olivera, de Montis, and Meassick (1992), 169.
[1]In 1980, the members of the Council of State were appointed by the FSLN leadership.
[2]Includes the losing presidential candidate, Daniel Ortega.

other parties represented in the new parliament had any female legislators. The Liberal Constitutionalist Party and the Liberal Independent Party each had one. Women also were left out of municipal government. Of the 145 Nicaraguan towns, the FSLN won the mayoralty in 52 and the Liberal Alliance in 91; among these the FSLN had 3 female mayors, and the governing party had 6.

The Liberal Alliance was the big winner of the 1996 elections. Arnoldo Alemán won the presidency, and his party gained forty-two of the ninety-three seats in parliament. The FSLN, which had documented a myriad of irregularities, charged election fraud. In the end, however, the Sandinistas accepted the verdict of the Supreme Election Council and conceded the legality of the new government while continuing to question its legitimacy. The FSLN decided to oppose the Alemán administration in the legislative arena where the FSLN controlled thirty-six seats. More than half the parties participating in the elections failed to win a single seat. Indeed, the 1996 elections moved Nicaragua further toward domination by two parties.

It is important to note that in a regional context, the record of the revolutionary Left in Nicaragua and El Salvador for women's representation looked quite good. The number of female legislators in Central American parliaments is generally low, although it does not differ that much from the records of many industrialized societies. Costa Rica and El Salvador in particular have a competitive record by international standards. In Latin America as a whole (as of June 1994), an average of 10 percent of the legislators in the various countries are women, with Cuba, a revolutionary society, reporting 23 percent. If one looks at the overall international standards, the FMLN also compared well. Only 10 percent of parliamentary seats are held by women in the United States, only 7 percent in Japan, 6 percent in France, 15 percent in Spain, and 20 percent in Germany. Only the Nordic countries with an average of 35 percent, the Netherlands with 29 percent, and the Seychelles with 27 percent, had a better record.[39] For the purpose of our discussion it is significant to note that the parties on the political Left in these countries had an even higher proportion of female legislators.

There is, however, a matter that is of great concern for the future of democratic consolidation in Nicaragua and El Salvador. This is the decreasing number of people who vote in elections. Nicaragua's figures for the 1996

Table 6.9   Nicaraguan Legislative Elections, 1996

Party	No. of Valid Votes	%	Seats
Alianza Liberal	789,533	45.97	42
Frente Sandinista de Liberación Nacional	629,178	36.64	36
Camino Cristiano Nicaragüense	63,867	3.72	4
Proyecto Nacional	40,656	2.37	3
Partido Conservador de Nicaragua	36,543	2.13	2
Movimiento Renovador Sandinista	22,789	1.33	1
Partido Resistencia Nicaragüense	21,068	1.23	1
Alianza Unidad	14,001	0.82	1
Partido Liberal Independiente	12,459	0.73	1
Alianza UNO 96	10,706	0.62	1
Acción Nacional Conservadora	9,811	0.57	1
Alianza Pan y Fuerza	9,724	0.57	0
Partido Justicia Nacional	8,155	0.47	0
Partido de Unidad Liberal	7,531	0.44	0
Partido Alianza Popular Conservadora	6,726	0.39	0
Partido Comunista de Nicaragua	6,360	0.37	0
Partido Unidad Nicaragüense Obreros, Campesinos y Profesionales	5,641	0.33	0
Partido Acción Democrática	5,272	0.31	0
Movimiento de Renovación Nacional	4,988	0.29	0
Partido Socialista Nicaragüense	2,980	0.17	0
Partido Integracionista de América Central	2,834	0.17	0
Movimiento de Acción Popular Marxista-Leninista	2,446	0.14	0
Movimiento Acción Renovadora	2,418	0.14	0
Alianza Democrática Nicaragüense	1,730	0.10	0
Total	1,757,775	100.00	93

Source: Data provided by Consejo Supremo Electoral (Supreme Electoral Council), Nicaragua.

elections still represent a decent turnout by international standards, but in El Salvador, the lack of interest in the electoral process has reached crisis proportions. In the presidential elections of 1989, 48 percent of eligible voters failed to vote, and in the first postwar elections only half the electorate participated.[40] In the 1997 elections, however, 62 percent of the voters decided not to go to the polls or cast invalid ballots. This phenomenon was described as "the first important result of the elections."[41] Female leaders in both countries maintain that women constituted the majority of these nonparticipating voters, a development that raises serious questions about the overall role and involvement of women in the Central American transitions. As discussed above, institutional barriers explain why women are disenfranchised in greater numbers than men. This problem is now compounded by increased apathy among the female electorate.

The Guatemalan Experience

Historically, Guatemala's voting record is the worst in the region, with poor turnout rates that rival those of the 1997 Salvadoran elections. For example, in the presidential elections of 1995, 53 percent of the voters chose to stay at home in the first round, while 63 percent did not vote in the second round. There was considerable hope that the 1996 peace accords, which made it possible for the revolutionary Left to participate in the electoral process, would strengthen the legitimacy of the political system in the eyes of the electorate and lead to increased turnout. These expectations proved to be justified. In the November 1999 elections, 53 percent of the electorate went to the polls.

Alfonso Portillo, the candidate of the Frente Republicano Guatemalteco gained almost 48 percent of the vote, just shy of the majority required to be elected in the first round. Oscar Berger, the candidate of the governing Partido de Avanzada Nacional (Party for National Advancement, or PAN), came in second with 30 percent. The candidate of the left-wing Alianza Nueva Nación, Alvaro Colom, came in a distant third with 12 percent. The Alliance, centered around the URNG, obtained 270,891 votes in the presidential elections, gained nine seats in the legislature, and controlled twenty-nine townships. Eleven towns were won outright by the Alliance, while civic committees with affinities for the Alliance won the others. This was substantially better than had been expected. No poll conducted prior to the elections had predicted that the ANN candidate would win more than 7 percent of the vote. The ANN's poor showing in the polls and respectable showing at the polls indicated to many observers that, almost three years after the signing of the peace accords, many Guatemalans were still reluctant to publicly state their support for the former guerrillas.

In the legislative elections the picture was similar. Of the 113 parliamentary seats contested, the FRG secured an absolute majority of 62 . The PAN won 38 seats, while the ANN secured 9. Compared to the 1995 election results, the FRG improved dramatically, tripling its seats from the original 21. The PAN lost 5 of the 43 seats it held previously, while the FDNG which had represented the Left in the 1995 election lost all of its 6 seats. Since the number of deputies was increased to 113 from the 80 deputies who constituted Congress in 1995, the changes in public support were most dramatic in the case of the PAN. The governing party's share of the vote declined from 54 to 30 percent. The FRG, on the other hand, improved its share from 42 to 48 percent. The PAN paid the price for the public's discontent with the limited results of the peace accords, the high crime rate, the difficult economic situation, and the corruption scandals engulfing PAN politicians.

Female candidates did not do well in the 1999 elections. The election results demonstrated that Guatemala was lagging behind its neighbors in increasing women's participation in public office. The two female presidential candidates, Ana Catalina Soberanis of the FDNG, and Flor de María Alvarado of the National Reconciliation Alliance gained 1.3 and 0.1 percent of the vote, respectively. In the legislature, only eight female deputies were elected. Five of them belonged to the FRG, two were PAN deputies, and one came from the ANN. This represented a decline from 1995, when eleven women representatives had been elected. The majority of the 1999 female representatives (five of the eight) were elected in the capital, the central district. This abysmal result is no surprise if one examines the candidate lists of the various parties. The candidate lists show ninety-one people running in the country's twenty-three districts. An additional twenty-two deputies were chosen from a national list. With few exceptions, women were placed in noncompetitive positions on the candidate lists, making it clear from the outset that they would not be elected.

The governing party did not have a single female candidate heading either its national list or any of its twenty-three district lists. The record of the FRG was only marginally better. It had one woman, Aura Otzoy, heading the list in the department of Chimaltenengo. Among the parties of the Left, the ANN had only one woman among its top candidates. Nineth Montenegro was ranked as the first candidate on the capital's list. The

FDNG was the only party whose candidate lists showed a gender composition that was not as lopsided. The top two candidates on its national list and on the list of the department of Santa Rosa were female, as was the leading candidate in Chiquimula. As noted above, however, not a single FDNG candidate was elected to parliament.

The struggle over the composition of the candidate lists was complex, particularly in the case of the URNG. Having barely completed its transformation into a legal political party, it was faced with the task of selecting its candidates for the 1999 elections. The URNG leadership had to balance the interests of its four historic groups with the demands of its coalition partners in the ANN. All parties wanted to secure top list positions for their candidates. This inevitably led to conflict. The ANN, formed in February 1999, brought together the URNG, the FDNG, DIA, and Unid (a party in formation). By the end of July, however, the FDNG had pulled out of the coalition.

A main reason for the fracture of the initial Alliance was the position of Rafael Arriaga, the FDNG's secretary general, who wanted to impose militants from the Partido Revolucionario on the candidate lists of the ANN. When the FDNG decided to run its own separate campaign, Nineth Montenegro, one of the key FDNG leaders, left her old party and ran on the ANN ticket. She was the only one of the six FDNG deputies who was reelected to parliament. The great majority of the FDNG base also chose to support the ANN over their old party. Soberanis, the FDNG presidential candidate, attracted barely more than 1 percent of the vote. Amilcar Méndez, an FDNG deputy, acknowledged after the elections that "personal ambitions had damaged the party."[42] Méndez himself, elected to Congress as a FDNG deputy for Quiche in 1995, failed even to be renominated by the party's grass roots.

The controversy between the FDNG and the other members of the Left Alliance made it even more difficult for female militants to advance their agenda of gender equality. As in El Salvador, ideological disputes took precedence over building coalitions to favor women's rights. There was great disappointment that the parties on the Left failed to take advantage of a historic opportunity to join forces for the first postwar elections. Women were divided in their support between the URNG, which remained in the ANN, and the FDNG, which pulled out, although the majority of women supporting the Left voted for the ANN. In the end, URNG militants managed to get some statements supporting women's rights into the ANN's electoral program but failed to get women into strong positions on the candidate lists.

Conclusion

From a gender perspective, the strategies FMLN and FSLN militants employed to increase the representation of women in public office were impressive. The Guatemalan experience, on the other hand, showed that the fight for gender equality within the URNG is still inchoate. The status of women within the revolutionary Left of Nicaragua and El Salvador has undoubtedly improved significantly, yet excessive optimism is premature. The Salvadoran legislative elections of March 2000 demonstrate how quickly initial gains in formal gender equality can erode.

The FMLN's electoral success in the March 1997 parliamentary elections surprised many. Most astonishing was the success of the female FMLN candidates, who outperformed their male colleagues. Women tripled their numbers from three to nine representatives, greatly encouraging those militants advocating greater gender equality within the party. The substantial gains by FMLN women had an immediate impact in the legislature. FMLN representatives introduced legislation in parliament that forced Salvadoran society to take note of gender issues. For example, as a small but significant sign of a changed climate, all male representatives elected to the legislative assembly in the 1997 elections had to present evidence that they were up-to-date on their child-support payments before they were allowed to assume office.

Yet female militants failed to maintain the high levels of organization achieved in 1997. The reason for this decline is to be found in the infighting among the two main FMLN currents. At the time of the 2000 election campaign, internal squabbles had destroyed the effective organization that women had built in 1997 to advance female candidates. Women were not united behind female candidates. This lack of unity, in turn, prevented them from forging effective coalitions with men. Ideological disputes were given priority over advancing the gender equality agenda. Candidates who were not identified with either of the main FMLN currents paid a high price for their independence. For example, Violeta Menjívar, who had gained the top position on the FMLN candidate list for the department of San Salvador in 1997, failed to be supported by either reformers or revolutionary socialists, since she refused to commit to either group. As a consequence she obtained only the seventh position on the list for the March 2000 election, despite having served effectively as the FMLN's deputy coordinator and having been a respected member of the parliament's executive council for the past three years. While the number of female candidates did not decline substantially in 2000—only two fewer female members were nominated—not a single woman obtained the top position on any of the candidate lists. Predictably, the result was a decline in female representation. While the FMLN increased its number of deputies from twenty-seven to thirty-one, only seven women were elected to the FMLN bench, a loss of two seats. This outcome reduced female representation on the FMLN bench from 33.3 percent to 22.6 percent.

Women's representation also declined in ARENA, the governing party, from four to one representative. Although ARENA gained one seat in the elections overall, the party's showing was considered a defeat. ARENA had won a convincing victory in the 1999 presidential election, but by 2000 it failed to maintain its status as the strongest party in parliament. Gloria Salguero, a former president of ARENA, called the election result "catastrophic" and publicly criticized her party for having included only one female candidate. In her opinion the "low presence of women" had contributed to ARENA's election defeat.[43]

The national political climate in Nicaragua following the 1996 elections did not favor women's emancipation. In February 1997, President Alemán attempted to railroad the National Assembly into creating a Family Ministry, which was supposed to replace the Instituto Nicaragüense de la Mujer (Nicaraguan Women's Institute). Only the rapid mobilization of the women's movement in opposition to this proposal—considered a threat to the institutions favoring women's rights—prevented the immediate approval of this initiative. The measure was referred instead to a congressional committee, which gave the women's movement time to convince the legislators that the Women's Institute must be preserved.

Despite the forces mounted against it, the Nicaraguan women's movement is growing stronger and more cohesive, while the female FSLN militants are still struggling to extend their organizing efforts from the national level to intermediate party structures. It is interesting to observe that the situation in El Salvador presents a different picture. FMLN women who were initially very successful in their fight for gender equality within the party, are now struggling to preserve these achievements. Compared to its Nicaraguan counterpart, the Salvadoran women's movement failed in the last elections to mount a strong organizing effort. This raises the question of what lessons may be learned from the comparative study of the Salvadoran and Nicaraguan experiences.

At present, it appears that only the Left is prepared to accept the challenge of gender equality and revise party doctrine and structures accordingly. Continuing efforts by party militants are therefore likely to bear fruit. These partisan efforts need to be broadened, however, and incorporated into pluralist alliances to have an impact on gender relations in society at large. Unity and lack of infighting are preconditions for the women's movement to become an effective advocate of women's rights and to exert pressure on political parties to take up the banner of gender equality. Furthermore, although the implementation of quantitative measures of positive discrimination, such as quotas, is an essential part of the struggle to increase women's representation in the public sphere, too much emphasis on this strategy can easily trap women in mere statistical equality and not lead to a truly equal presence in public office. It also indicates that the struggle is still at the stage of ensuring formal equality only. At this point, party leaders often pay attention to women's issues out of concern for their image in the eyes of the female electorate. Positive developments in terms of formal equality must be distinguished from a fundamental rethinking of traditional gender relations, a precondition for the realization of substantive equality.

On the basis of the candidate selection process in both El Salvador and Nicaragua, it is evident that, at this juncture, the fight for gender equality continues to be a basically urban phenomenon. The discussion in Chapter Three emphasized that the women's movement needs to reach out to its rural constituents and bring the debate on women's rights to the countryside. It is evident that the center of resistance to women's emancipation is located in the departmental and local party structures. While men resist because they feel threatened, women are reluctant to assume the burden of public office without the necessary network of support. In light of their difficult economic conditions, they can not afford the luxury of being active within the party. Our interviews showed that although female members professed support for the FMLN, they had little or no knowledge of what was happening at the national level, a situation that contrasted starkly with their male counterparts.

Finally, the fight for gender equality is a long-term project. Accumulated experience is what allows effective strategies to emerge. In Nicaragua, many women began to rethink their role in society during the Sandinista revolution. The expertise in grass-roots organizing on behalf of the revolution, acquired during the 1980s, proved helpful in creating a strong women's movement. Similarly, the current success of FMLN militants in making gender equality a central issue within the party has its roots in the "extensive network of organizations and personal contacts" female FMLN members cultivated during the war.[44] Militants of the revolutionary Left are aware that the struggle for gender equality has just begun. In this light, the advances made so far are encouraging.

Conclusion

Gender Equality and Democratization

Si la mujer no está, la democracia no va

The Central American experience discussed in this book teaches us that a focus on gender politics can indeed illuminate the process of democratic consolidation. Gender equality and meaningful democratization are inextricably linked. From a normative point of view, the democratization of the region requires the full incorporation of women as voters, candidates, and office holders. Looking through the lens of gender equality, we have seen the revolutionary Left's strengths and weaknesses as it struggles to establish itself as a force for democracy in the region. The Central American guerrilla movements have accepted the challenge of transforming themselves from hierarchical military organizations into democratic political parties. By doing so, they have made an important contribution to the consolidation of formal, representative democracy, which requires a party system that is capable of representing voters across the political spectrum. An emphasis on gender equality sheds light on the Left's incipient democratization that transcends adherence to formal norms and procedures of democracy and focuses on the substance of this transformation.

The revolutionary Left has started to institute a gender perspective in its policies, particularly as they relate to internal party development and electoral politics. Women are the key advocates behind the drive for the institutionalization of gender equality. In their struggle for equality between men and women, they have sought to change traditional gender relations and to strengthen the internal democratic decision-making processes of the former guerrilla movements of El Salvador, Nicaragua, and

Guatemala. A distinction between formal and substantive gender equality reveals the accomplishments of female party members and the hurdles they have yet to overcome on the road to full, substantive equality. Female militants advocating gender equality share an inherent interest in the internal democratization of their political parties. Standing to benefit from party rules favoring measures of positive discrimination, they are natural advocates for strict adherence to formal rules and procedures, a prerequisite for democratic decision-making.

When we focus on formal gender equality, it becomes evident that women have increased their participation in the new parties that grew out of the Central American guerrilla movements. The evidence presented in this book strongly supports the thesis that measures of positive discrimination are indispensable tools in the fight to strengthen female participation in political party structures and increase the number of women holding public office. The Salvadoran experience, in particular, demonstrated that quotas and gender-based candidate lists can be effective mechanisms to open previously closed doors for women. Yet such measures are by no means sufficient to guarantee greater access for women to positions of authority and power. Measures of positive discrimination are ultimately mere tactical tools to be used by committed women and men in the fight for gender equality. The most effective tools are of no value if the environment for their successful application does not exist. In the final analysis, it is the level of organization and coordination that women achieve that determines whether these measures can be used effectively. In particular, coalition-building with open-minded men who can be enlisted in the struggle is essential. In the case of Guatemala, the tools for increasing the percentage of women in the party's decision-making structures were put in place, but a male-dominated leadership lacked the political will to apply them. In Nicaragua, male FSLN militants who opposed any effort to increase female representation successfully managed to subvert women's efforts to guarantee the effective implementation of measures of positive discrimination at the local and regional level.

The importance of positive discrimination to increase women's representation in leadership positions at the national level entered the realm of public discussion in Latin America in 1991, when Argentina introduced compulsory gender quotas for candidates for political office. The new quota law required that female candidates would be allocated at least 30 percent of the positions on candidate lists. By 2000, ten other Latin American countries had joined Argentina and adopted quota laws, which established minimum participation rates for female candidates ranging from 20 to 40 percent.[1] In Central America, the revolutionary Left supported the cause of gender quotas. Although women across the ideological spectrum have come to recognize the importance of quotas and have sought to emulate the example of Argentina, neither El Salvador, Nicaragua, nor Guatemala passed national quota laws. By the end of 2000, only El Salvador had made a serious effort to introduce national quotas.

The day after the March 2000 Salvadoran elections, Gloria Salguero, president of the Salvadoran parliament and head of the governing ARENA party during the 1990s, met with several colleagues from the Left and proposed collaboration. She wanted to use the waning days of the legislature to introduce a constitutional amendment modeled after the Argentine law that would require all political parties to institute a 30 percent female quota for candidates for public office. In her view, a simple law was not good enough, since it could too easily be reversed. Realizing that the votes were not there for a constitutional amendment, Salguero introduced a law in the next to last session of the legislature that would have established a minimum quota of 30 percent for either sex for all public office and party leadership positions. The women behind this effort had obtained fifty-six (out of eighty-four) supporting signatures from their colleagues.[2] In the end the effort failed. The proposed law obtained only forty-one of the forty-three required votes. The unexpected defeat shocked the advocates of gender equality. In a victory for male chauvinism, several female ARENA and Christian Democrat legislators who had signed on in support changed their position under pressure from influential male colleagues. Further, two male FMLN deputies who had committed themselves to vote for the law engaged in a last minute political maneuver and left the session without casting their votes. Nidia Díaz, one of the initiative's supporters, admitted that the backers of the legislation had committed a vital error in failing to involve the women's movement in the effort to get it passed. She recognized that jointly they might have been able to exert sufficient pressure on the legislature to succeed.[3] Despite this setback, the coalition-building by female legislators was an excellent sign that women had started to transcend ideological differences and were joining forces in the struggle for gender equality.

The gender distribution in the national decision-making structures of the Salvadoran FMLN and the FSLN in Nicaragua indicated that women had made progress in obtaining formal representation that corresponded to their numerical strength in the party membership. However, more time is needed to assess the quality of this representation. While there is no doubt that women have made substantial progress in their fight for gender equality, much remains to be done. The FMLN's Women's Secretariat summarized its achievements and remaining challenges in 1998:

> Progress has been made in [women's] quantitative participation and in the organization of women's committees at the party's grass-roots level. Through the gender policy and internal rules, the quota has been institutionalized as a tool, as have been the National, the Departmental, and the Municipal Women's Secretariats. The statutes have been reformed. But we need to make progress in increasing the skills and sensibility of men and women and in the creation of mechanisms that improve the conditions of women's participation in relation to men. We need to increase the power of the National Women's Secretariat with economic and material resources and guarantee that the whole party apparatus supports the execution of the gender policy.[4]

In general, the relative success in the area of formal gender equality has yet to translate into substantive change. Women confront a difficult situation when they seek to win substantive equality within the revolutionary Left. Some significant changes notwithstanding, traditional gender relations continue to characterize relations between male and female party members. Recent developments in Nicaragua and El Salvador suggest that the fight for gender equality is suffering a backlash. Male leaders see their privileges threatened. This indicates that the strategies to strengthen formal gender equality have been effective. Women have to defend their gains in the fight for formal gender equality and establish alliances with their male colleagues in order to transform party cultures in the direction of substantive equality.

A central battle concerns the fight to address male chauvinism within the ranks of the revolutionary Left. A vocal minority within the male leadership and among rank-and-file members, has resisted attempts to institute effective policies that would ensure greater gender equality. "Gender" is a concept that has only recently begun to be used to address the societal inequalities between men and women. It is often misinterpreted and tends to polarize men and women. For this reason, it is hardly the best way to communicate the issue of equality between women and men in the Central American context, yet female leaders are reluctant to abandon it, having struggled too long to achieve its current level of acceptance. Nevertheless, there needs to be greater emphasis on the fact that the goal is a societal transformation that liberates both women and men from the fetters of traditional norms.

The road to this new social order is a long and difficult one, considering the limited progress that has been made worldwide in achieving formal equality between men and women. According to the 1999 *Human Development Report*, in only five of the world's countries do women hold more than 30 percent of the seats in parliament.[5] It is important that we keep this in mind when we assess the record of the revolutionary Left. While it is true that the Left has made limited progress toward achieving gender equality within its ranks, the record of the Central American Left looks quite good when compared with the rest of the world. With the exception of the Nordic countries, few parties in Western Europe or North America can point to a similar level of accomplishment.

There have been some encouraging signs that the gains in the area of formal gender equality were being translated into substantive gender equality. Male and female militants were starting to build alliances that challenged traditional gender relations. For example, the candidate-selection process for the 1997 Salvadoran elections demonstrated that a number of male leaders had revised long-held stereotypical views regarding women. At the same time, female militants exhibited a newly gained confidence that indicated they no longer felt confined by traditional boundaries.

The struggle for gender equality will be greatly shaped by the degree to which party militants can build alliances with the women's movement. For a constructive partnership to be possible, the controversy over *doble mili-*

tancia, which is rooted in the question of autonomy, needs to be resolved. Infighting over the issue whether a woman can be loyal to both party and the women's movement has plagued all three countries.

In Nicaragua during the 1980s, the FSLN subordinated the fight for women's rights to the survival of the revolution. As a result female militants have had only limited success in their struggle to transform gender relations within their party and their society. Following the 1990 electoral defeat of the Sandinistas, an autonomous women's movement emerged, and female militants renewed their efforts to achieve gender equality within the FSLN. Although they could point to some positive results, female leaders faced great challenges in their efforts to transform party structures. At the same time, the Nicaraguan women's movement was increasingly successful in putting women's rights on the national agenda. Nicaragua confirms that it is difficult to advance the struggle for gender equality on both fronts—party and society—simultaneously. The price of the independence the women's movement gained from the Sandinistas was the arrested development of gender equality inside the FSLN. When many of the best minds among the female FSLN militants chose to focus their energy on building a strong women's movement, female leaders who remained in the party were left without the support they needed to make substantial progress.

El Salvador presents yet another picture. There, female FMLN militants have demonstrated a remarkable ability to increase their representation in the party's decision-making structures and in the Salvadoran parliament. Having observed women's subordination in the FSLN, female militants began their fight for autonomy even before the final peace accords were signed. Although some key leaders broke with the FMLN to ensure their full autonomy, most remained in the party, committed to fighting the battle for gender equality from within. The Salvadoran women's movement supported the efforts of FMLN cadres during the 1990s to change the party. Although the issue of doble militancia has come up, it has not had the same prominence as it has in Nicaragua. Problems, however, have emerged in a different arena. The controversy over the nomination process for the FMLN's presidential candidate in the 1999 elections destroyed the alliance between the women's movement and FMLN militants. Key leaders of the movement, albeit sympathetic to the FMLN, were so disgusted with the machinations surrounding the nomination process that they distanced themselves from the party. A number of high-profile leaders abstained from voting in order to protest what they perceived as discrimination against Victoria Marina de Avilés, the female nominee. The fallout from this episode was a general weakening of the forces for gender equality within the FMLN.

The URNG would benefit from paying close attention to the experiences of the revolutionary Left in El Salvador and Nicaragua. Two key lessons can be derived from these experiences for Guatemala. Efforts by female URNG militants to strengthen gender equality in the party will bear fruit if measures of positive discrimination are strictly enforced during the early stages of the fight for women's rights. For this to happen, female militants need to be well organized and prepared to seek alliances with male party leaders. Simultaneously, these partisan efforts need to be broadened and incorporated into pluralist coalitions to affect gender relations in society at large. Unity and lack of infighting are preconditions for success. Guatemalan women who seek to strengthen gender equality in political parties and society need to keep this in mind.

The women of Central America confront the necessity of broadening the struggle for gender equality. For too long it has been essentially an urban, middle-class issue. The fight has to be moved from its elitist quarters to encompass the great majority of poor, rural women. It is essential that progress made at the national level filters down to the grass roots. A significant gap has prevailed between the opportunities and support available to women who participate in national politics and those working within the departmental and municipal party structures. In this fight, international solidarity is of importance.

Gloria Salguero argued recently that international pressure is both needed and very effective in moving recalcitrant parties toward adopting a platform of gender equality. This is an important statement coming from a representative of the political Right, which has traditionally objected to any meddling by international agencies or groups in El Salvador's internal affairs. The Central American experience discussed in this book supports the view that the international context has been an important factor in the fight for gender equality. Nevertheless, recent developments force us to reflect on the relevance of international meetings and the resulting conventions favoring women's rights. The state needs resources to guarantee second generation human rights. It appears that in the age of neoliberalism and a shrinking state, governments are more willing than ever before to sign conventions committing them to institute important changes favoring women. There is justified suspicion that this change of heart can be explained by the fact that government officials know full well that they will lack the resources to carry out their commitments.

The quest for the most effective strategy to consolidate democracy and advance gender equality continues. Two main schools of thought have surfaced. One advocates fighting within the existing parties of the Left to transform them into effective vehicles for greater gender equality. In the opinion of Deysi Cheyne, one of the foremost Salvadoran women's leaders, this strategy requires that female militants succeed in establishing "emotional independence" from the Left. This permits women to support the revolutionary Left when they consider it in their interest, instead of lending unconditional support to the Left's agenda out of a sense of historic commitment. Female leaders are becoming increasingly sophisticated in their struggle for women's rights. In the eyes of many women the events of the 1990s confirmed that the fight for formal gender equality could only take them so far. For example, after having succeeded to greatly increase the number of female deputies in the Salvadoran parliament, the women's movement was disappointed when these new women leaders failed to support an agenda for women's rights. This situation, while painful, was also liberating. Women, whether they were active in the party or the movement, were free to explore new and better ways to reach their goals. Sofía Montenegro from Nicaragua, one of the most lucid theoreticians of the women's movement, has already taken the next logical step. She advocates the building of a new political movement, convinced that the current parties on the Left are beyond reform. At this point it is not obvious which argument will carry the day. A likely outcome is a combination of both strategies. The traditional parties require the threat of popular alternatives to reform themselves.

The beginning of the new millennium saw Ricardo Rosales and Schafik Hándal, who once headed the Communist parties of Guatemala and El Salvador, respectively, as the leaders of their parliamentary benches. In 1994 it was still unusual to see former guerrilla commanders in the Salvadoran

Legislative Assembly sharing a bench with their former military enemies. By the end of the decade, however, this situation raised nobody's eyebrows. FMLN legislators, who were novices in 1994, had evolved into influential figures in parliament, often dominating the legislative agenda together with other opposition parties. Similarly, Guatemalan revolutionaries were now challenging their former enemies in the political arena. Nine URNG deputies, elected in November 1999, opposed the legislative agenda of the majority party headed by the URNG's nemesis, former dictator Ríos Montt. In Nicaragua, the Sandinista revolutionaries, who had governed the country during the 1980s, were the main opposition party in the 1990s. This situation serves as a reminder that the struggle has moved from the military to the political arena and that the revolutionary Left has transformed itself into a political actor. With this transformation, the Left has strengthened the legitimacy of the region's political structures. Apart from this important contribution, however, has the Left been capable of defending the interests of its constituents?

The revolutionary Left encountered an extremely difficult socioeconomic and political situation during the 1990s. In the face of this challenge, the Left was frequently its own worst enemy. The electoral success of the former guerrilla movements was respectable, but it could have been greater had it not been for the internal conflicts that disrupted party-building. Even at moments of victory, internal divisions could not be overcome. Following the March 2000 Salvadoran elections, which saw the FMLN become the largest political force in the country, there was speculation that the FMLN would once again officially divide into two parties. In many regards, the two main factions were already operating as distinct political forces. They operated separate headquarters in many towns, held their meetings apart, supported opposing political agendas, and no longer socialized together. The few important party figures who were not clearly identified with either faction faced increased pressures to align themselves and became increasingly isolated. It is symbolically important that the March 2000 election victory was celebrated in two distinct venues, with revolutionary socialists in the streets outside the party headquarters and the reformers joining the victory party of Hector Silva, reelected to a second term as mayor of the capital. In the opinion of the latter group, it had "won San Salvador." The reformers vowed to use the capital as their power base in the struggle over control of the party. Thus, the inability to find common ground that had led to the FMLN's division in 1994 threatened to lead once again to a break-up of the party. This time the consequences would be truly devastating. Joaquín Villalobos's exit in 1994 affected only a small group of party militants. The threat of his challenge to the FMLN leadership was more symbolic than substantive. A parting of the revolutionary socialists and the reformers would have far greater consequences. Had the leadership learned the right lessons, or was history to repeat itself?

Similar problems plagued the FMLN's counterparts in Nicaragua and Guatemala. The Sandinistas had survived the 1995 exodus of the reformers led by Sergio Ramírez, albeit at high cost. A united FSLN would have been a formidable contender in the 1996 elections. Instead the weakened Sandinistas had to resign themselves to their position as the strongest opposition party. The scandals that permanently blackened the image of the FSLN leadership at the end of the decade paralyzed the party and reduced it to a vehicle for the political ambitions of Daniel Ortega. Under attack, the FSLN abandoned incipient democratic practices and reverted to an authoritarian style. Legitimate dissent became anathema as demonstrated when Tomás Borge threatened FSLN leaders who opposed the party's pact with the Alemán government with expulsion. Deprived of many of its best minds, the Sandinistas faced an uncertain electoral future, despite the FSLN's comeback in the 2000 municipal elections, when the Sandinistas won Managua, the capital, and many of the other most important cities. One could not escape the irony that the FSLN, which had strengthened representative democracy in Nicaragua during its decade in power, had failed to make similar progress in democratizing its internal decision-making process.

The URNG survived its first anniversary as a legal political party without public splits. Yet disagreements were raging behind the façade of unity. The disintegration of the electoral coalition formed for the 1999 elections indicated that the Guatemalan Left was unable to reconcile differences among its constituent groups, even though the failure to do so had a clear impact on its strength as a political player. Only the future will tell whether the URNG has been able to learn from the mistakes it observed in Nicaragua and El Salvador.

The cost of these internal problems was considerable. The fight in all

three countries between reformist and orthodox factions over party hegemony restricted the ability of the Left to effectively confront its political
enemies and to consolidate its transformation into a democratic political
force. It also adversely affected the struggle for greater gender equality. In
the final analysis, the revolutionary Left had yet to learn how to deal with
dissent. Legitimate disagreements over the role of the Left following the
peace accords were considered too divisive and threatening to be aired in
open, frank discussion. The legacy of the war days where similar disputes
had resulted in conflicts with deadly outcomes continued to shape the view
of key players. This inability to compromise and integrate opposing views
into a new powerful vision indicated the limits of the Left's progress toward
a truly democratic movement.

During the days of the revolutionary struggle the Left offered society the
vision of an alternative model of development. Now, however, it has to
demonstrate that it can convert its newly gained political power and implement constructive proposals that address the region's problems. The
Left's future credibility, in the eyes of its current constituents and the electorate in general, will to a great extent depend on the degree to which it
can be an effective agent for social change and reinvent itself ideologically.
The FMLN and its counterparts need to diffuse the frequently voiced crit-
icisms that revolutionaries are good at taking power but lack the skills to
administer it efficiently. Two central questions need to be resolved: will the
revolutionary Left assume the modernizing role that the traditional parties
have failed so far to carry out; and can this role be assumed successfully
while protecting the interests of the Left's core constituency, or will the parties on the Left be reduced to the status of more efficient administrators of
neoliberalism. For decades the revolutionary Left waged civil war under the
banner of achieving social justice for all. Now it faces the challenge of continuing its fight for substantive democracy while being a part of an established system that emphasizes formal democracy but is becoming increasingly unjust.

The peace agreements of Guatemala and El Salvador failed to resolve
the fundamental problems that led to the wars in the first place. In
Nicaragua, the Contras contributed to the Sandinista electoral defeat but
were marginalized in postrevolutionary society. The success of the armed
movements in reintegrating their former combatants into civilian life var-

ied from country to country. The relative success of the Salvadoran process emphasizes the importance for guerrilla movements of entering the political process as a cohesive force capable of effectively representing the interests of their constituents. The timing of the peace process appears to be of great importance. It is essential for armed movements to complete their evolution into political parties in time for the first postconflict elections. Yet even under the relatively favorable conditions for the FMLN prevailing in El Salvador, Herculean efforts were required during the reintegration phase. The Salvadoran situation posed important challenges for the FMLN and its supporters. The party's electoral successes in 1997 and 2000 tended to obscure important problems. Many supporters of the revolutionary Left, including former combatants, were disillusioned. FMLN militants and supporters were struggling economically and felt abandoned by the FMLN leadership. As the FMLN was positioning itself to attract support from new sectors of the electorate, it was running the risk of losing its historic base. A general problem for ex-combatants in all three countries were rising, unmet expectations. Many questioned whether their sacrifice had been worth it. Although they had received some material benefits, particularly land, as a result of the peace accords, their standard of living continued to be abysmal. The former fighters were pleased to have escaped the harsh reality of the war, yet many emphasized that peace brought a host of new challenges they were ill-equipped to deal with.

When we examine the reintegration process through the lens of gender, it is evident that it was especially difficult for women, who suffered both open and hidden forms of discrimination. Women paid a high price for being perceived as having violated societal norms by joining the armed struggle. Female combatants, seeking to retake their place in family structures they had abandoned during the war, were treated as outcasts by their own parents, siblings, and children. They were accused of having neglected their children and having chosen the revolutionary struggle over their families. In addition to these societal pressures, female militants faced special challenges evident when one analyzes the implementation of the reinsertion programs. Although an evaluation of the Salvadoran programs shows no evidence of open discrimination, women's gender-specific needs were seldom taken into account. The true story of the peace programs can not be read in the statistics. The accounts of female combatants indicate that we need to study the daily problems that female beneficiaries confront, if we are to comprehend the situation of women in the peace process. If we listen to what these women have to say, the crucial difference between formal and substantive equality is impossible to ignore.

The ex-combatants shared their difficult economic circumstances with the great majority of the citizens in the three countries. Hope for a better life had seemed realistic in the wake of the peace accords. Unfortunately, these hopes remained unfulfilled. While government officials and international lending agencies celebrated the macroeconomic indicators that showed growing economies, people in the villages and towns of Central America faced hunger, illness, and crime. The assumed benefits of neoliberal economic policies could not be detected at the grass-roots level.

The harsh economic situations in postwar Nicaragua, El Salvador, and Guatemala, together with an abundance of cheap weapons, led to extremely high levels of violent crime. In a 1997 report, the Nicaraguan government acknowledged that 19,821 violent crimes against people had taken place in 1996, an increase of more than 10 percent over 1995.[6] El Salvador, on the other hand, had the dubious distinction of having "the highest murder rate in the Western Hemisphere."[7] In 1996, more than 8,000 people died violent deaths, surpassing the civilian casualty rate during most civil war years. The capital, San Salvador, witnessed 359 murders in 1999, making it a truly dangerous place. Political violence continued to be of major concern. Between 1992 and 1996, 2 former FMLN commanders who had served on the party's Political Commission together with 57 FMLN ex-combatants were assassinated.[8] The most publicized case was the murder of former FMLN commander Francisco Véliz. At the time of his assassination on October 25, 1993, he was a candidate for a seat in parliament. Véliz's murder, which had a chilling effect on the FMLN's 1994 election campaign, has not been solved.[9] In the early 1990s, political violence was also rampant in Nicaragua, where hundreds of ex-members of the Resistance and Sandinista militants were killed. A particularly high-profile victim was Enrique Bermúdez, the former Contra commander. The record of Guatemala was not much different. According to World Bank data, both Guatemala and El Salvador had a murder rate fourteen times as high as that of the United States. The crime waves that engulfed the three countries were symptomatic of the difficult socioeconomic conditions and imperiled the consolidation of democracy.

What we observe in Guatemala, Nicaragua, and El Salvador is, at best, the consolidation of formal, representative democracy. Yet this transition to more democratic forms of government taking place in the political arena is linked to the implementation of structural adjustment programs guided by the dominant paradigm of neoliberalism. These economic policies carry a high price for the poor majorities of Central America, who have experienced deteriorating living conditions instead of improvements. Little remains of the promise of a popular program, based on participatory democracy that was the rally cry of the revolutionary Left during the 1980s.

Not surprisingly, many citizens have become cynical and have lost faith in the institutions of government. This is confirmed by increasingly low voter turnout and polls showing low levels of approval for the main institutions of government. In the elections of Guatemala and El Salvador, about half the electorate routinely abstains from voting. An abstention rate of this magnitude does not bode well for the future. Whereas voters did turn out in large numbers in the 1996 Nicaraguan elections (officially the participation rate was 76%), the electoral process was marred by extensive irregularities that led the FSLN to reject "the legitimacy of the election." In the opinion of knowledgeable observers, "the 1996 elections were a step backward from achieving [democratic] legitimacy."[10]

The citizens of the three countries have chosen different political solutions to their predicaments. Guatemalans chose the party of Ríos Montt, a right-wing dictator from the early 1980s, in the October 1999 elections, while the Salvadoran electorate made the FMLN the strongest party in parliament in the March 2000 electoral contest. The results of the March 2000 elections present a great opportunity as well as an enormous challenge for the FMLN. In 1996, Nicaraguan voters gave the Right another chance at fixing the country's political and economic woes and endorsed the Sandinistas as the main opposition. Four years later, the electorate punished the Alemán government for its failure to deliver on its promises and significantly strengthened the Sandinista party in the municipal elections.

In their struggle to transform current realities, Latin America's female leaders have begun to build important alliances. The organizing capabilities acquired during the days of armed struggle and civil opposition to authoritarian rule served women well in their efforts to assume a greater role in the construction of more democratic societies. Female leaders have made great strides in the building of a strong women's movement. In other areas, however, alliance building is still in its beginning phases. Female leaders are increasingly aware that they need new strategies to defend their hard-won gains in the struggle for gender equality and to take the fight to new arenas. In particular, old alliances need to be reinforced and new ones built: the women's movement must join with militants of political parties; party militants across the ideological spectrum must join together; the women's movement must find allies in other sectors of civil society; alliances must be formed among women's organizations throughout Central America; and Central American women's groups must join with women's groups in South America and find allies worldwide. The most significant effort, however, needs to be directed toward establishing the missing link—an alliance between the sexes.

The new millennium poses a central challenge for female leaders in Central America fighting for greater gender equality. They need to work on building a new alliance that includes men. Only the joint efforts of both sexes can lead to a successful transformation of society based on democratic governance and gender equality. This is obviously a long-term process. The discussion of gender equality needs to be politicized differently—men have to be brought into the dialogue, understanding that the concept of gender includes them and is not a synonym for woman. At the same time that men need to be reeducated, women have to modify exclusionary positions. Only a coming together of both sexes will permit the successful mainstreaming of gender equality.

Notes

Preface & Acknowledgments

1. See the debate on the Rigoberta Menchú–David Stoll controversy in *Latin American Perspectives* 26, no. 6 (November 1999).

2. See for example, Gilbert, *Sandinistas*; Walker, *Nicaragua in Revolution, Nicaragua: The First Five Years, Reagan versus the Sandinistas*, and *Revolution and Counterrevolution in Nicaragua*; Harris and Vilas, eds., *Nicaragua: A Revolution under Siege*; Spalding, *The Political Economy of Revolutionary Nicaragua*; Enríquez, *Harvesting Change*; Vanden and Prevost, *Democracy and Socialism in Sandinista Nicaragua*; and Luciak, *The Sandinista Legacy*.

3. Carver, *Gender Is Not a Synonym for Women*, 120.

4. Parvikko, "Conceptions of Gender Equality," 48.

5. Agüero and Stark, *Fault Lines of Democracy in Post-Transition Latin America*, v.

6. Lowenthal and Domínguez, "Introduction: Constructing Democratic Governance," in *Constructing Democratic Governance*, edited by Domínguez and Lowenthal, 7–8.

7. This point is illustrated in Chapters Four and Five, where I discuss the selection process of the FMLN's presidential candidates.

8. Huntington, *The Third Wave*.

9. Waylen, *Gender in Third World Politics*, 118.

10. Recent examples include: Domínguez and Lindenberg, *Democratic Transitions in Central America*; Domínguez and Lowenthal, *Constructing Democratic Governance*; Tulchin, *The Consolidation of Democracy in Latin America*; Linz and Stepan, *Problems of Democratic Transition and Consolidation*; and Diamond et al., *Consolidating the Third Wave Democracies*.

11. Diamond, "Introduction: In Search of Consolidation," xiv.

12. Domínguez and Lindenberg, *Democratic Transitions in Central America*, 2.

13. Agüero and Stark, *Fault Lines of Democracy in Post-Transition Latin America*, 9.

14. Ibid.

15. Navarro and Bourque, "Fault Lines of Democratic Governance," 175.

16. Ibid., 176.

17. Ibid., 182.

18. Arnson, ed., *Comparative Peace Processes in Latin America.*

19. Spalding, "From Low-Intensity Warfare to Low-Intensity Peace," 20.

20. Luciak, *The Sandinista Legacy*, 17–21.

21. Lowenthal and Domínguez, "Introduction: Constructing Democratic Governance," in *Constructing Democratic Governance*, edited by Domínguez and Lowenthal, 3.

22. Vilas, *Between Earthquakes and Volcanoes*, 184.

23. Jonas, "Electoral Problems and the Democratic Project in Guatemala," 25–44.

24. McCleary, "Guatemala's Postwar Prospects," 129.

25. Lowenthal and Domínguez, "Introduction: Constructing Democratic Governance," in *Constructing Democratic Governance*, edited by Domínguez and Lowenthal, 6.

26. Angell, "Incorporating the Left into Democratic Politics," 25.

27. Torres-Rivas, "Guatemala," 55.

28. Ibid., 56.

29. Gramajo, "Political Transition in Guatemala," 135.

30. Waylen, *Gender in Third World Politics*, 124–26.

31. Inter-American Development Bank, *Women in the Americas*, 87.

32. Vilas, *Between Earthquakes and Volcanos*, 185.

33. Angell, "Incorporating the Left into Democratic Politics," 24.

34. Interview with María Candelaria Navas, Blacksburg, Virginia, May 1, 1997.

Chapter One   The Gender Composition of the Central American Guerrilla Movements

1. Wickham-Crowley, *Guerrillas and Revolution in Latin America*, 21.

2. Che Guevara, *Guerrilla Warfare*, 132.

3. Anderson, *Che*, 234.

4. Ibid., 275.

5. Che Guevara, *Guerrilla Warfare*, 132.

6. Ibid., 132.

7. Ibid., 133.

8. Montgomery, *Revolution in El Salvador*, 123. See also Mason, "Women's Participation in Central American Revolutions," 65, for references.

9. ONUSAL, *Proceso de desmovilización del personal del FMLN*, 2–7.

10. First, the data provide a snapshot of those members of the FMLN forces who chose to go through the official registration process at the time of the 1992 demobilization. Although the great majority of the guerrilla membership was indeed registered, the records are by no means complete. Not surprisingly, it is impossible to obtain accurate figures on the number of people who were not officially demobilized. If the FMLN leadership were to acknowledge that a substantial number of its members did not participate in the official demobilization process, the former guerrillas would open themselves up to the charge of having violated the peace accords. For exactly this reason,

right-wing forces have had an obvious interest in exaggerating these figures. Apart from the problem of FMLN personnel remaining outside of the process, there were also deficiencies in the ONUSAL data of those who had registered. Following the closure of the demobilization process in 1993, the records were purified in order to correct several anomalies. Initially, FMLN members had little confidence in the registration process and were reluctant to provide personal data, citing security reasons. There were cases of combatants who were processed as *políticos* and vice versa, while others managed to register twice under different names in order to receive another of the packages of tools and food that every registered person was entitled to. According to ONUSAL, a total of 588 FMLN militants never bothered to pick up their identification papers, which eventually were declared invalid. Over time, however, the former combatants gained confidence in the integrity of the process, and data collection became an easier task. ONUSAL published the updated and revised final data in 1994.

11. ONUSAL, *Proceso de desmovilización del personal del FMLN*, 6.

12. Telephone conversation with Gerson Martínez, September 24, 1995.

13. Montgomery, *Revolution in El Salvador*, 123; interview with Norma Guevara, San Salvador, May 2, 1995.

14. Data in the Guatemalan records are not separated by sex. Age data are only available for demobilized combatants and political cadres.

15. URNG, "Personal Incorporado," 4.

16. For this observation I am indebted to an anonymous reviewer of this manuscript.

17. ONUSAL, *Proceso de desmovilización del personal del FMLN*, 8.

18. Interview with Medardo González, San Salvador, December 12, 1995.

19. Fundación 16 de Enero, "Diagnóstico de la situación actual de la mujer ex-combatiente," 10.

20. Vázquez et al., *Mujeres-montaña*, 23.

21. Ibid., 63.

22. Interview with Jackeline Noemi Rivera, San Salvador, February 5, 1996.

23. Vázquez et al., *Mujeres-montaña*, 16.

24. Ramírez-Horton, "The Role of Women in the Nicaraguan Revolution," 152.

25. Chuchryk, "Women in the Revolution," 143.

26. Vilas, *The Sandinista Revolution*, 108–9.

27. See Reif, "Women in Latin American Guerrilla Movements," 158; Ramírez-Horton, "The Role of Women in the Nicaraguan Revolution," 152; and Collinson, *Women and Revolution in Nicaragua*, 154. On the topic of the number of female combatants in the FSLN, I have benefited from discussions with Karen Kampwirth.

28. Interview with Mónica Baltodano, Managua, November 13, 1997.

29. Interview with Gladys Báez, Managua, June 9, 1998.

30. Ibid.

31. Interview with Dorotea Wilson, Managua, February 5, 1997.

32. Interview with Leticia Herrera, Managua, November 12, 1997.

33. Ibid.

34. Interview with Mónica Baltodano, Managua, November 13, 1997.

35. Ibid.

36. FSLN, *Programa histórico del FSLN*, 32.

37. Interview with Leticia Herrera, Managua, November 12, 1997.

38. Interview with Mónica Baltodano, Managua, November 13, 1997.

39. Ibid.

40. Interview with Azucena Ferrey, Managua, November 12, 1997.

41. According to Joaquín Lovo, vice-minister of government, the number of demobilized fighters is inflated by about 5,000. It appears that several thousand poor peasants who were not part of the Resistance joined the demobilization process in order to receive the benefits (food, building material, etc.) that were handed out to each processed fighter.

42. Kampwirth, "Women in the Armed Struggles in Nicaragua," 1.

43. Ibid., 1–2.

44. CIAV-OEA, "Cuadros estadísticos del proceso de desmovilización y repatriación en Nicaragua."

45. Spence et al., "Promise and Reality," 11.

46. United Nations, *Acuerdo sobre el definitivo cese al fuego*.

47. Due to the close relations between the Guatemalan government and Taiwan, China opposed the deployment of a United Nations peacekeeping mission in the UN Security Council. China withdrew its veto on January 20, 1998. Thus China's position delayed the starting day of the demobilization.

48. Interview with Araujo Lima, Esquintla, April 23, 1997.

49. These data are based on information provided by Lieutenant Colonel Carlos Tanco, UN military observer group in Guatemala, November 21, 1997.

50. McCleary, "Guatemala's Postwar Prospects," 138.

51. Interviews with Wilson Romero, Guatemala City, March 3, 1999, and Ricardo Rosales, Guatemala City, March 4, 1999.

52. Interview with Ricardo Rosales, Guatemala City, March 4, 1999.

53. Data are based on information provided by Lieutenant Colonel Carlos Tanco.

54. United Nations and URNG officials were generally reluctant to discuss membership statistics. Unlike in El Salvador, there are also no official data indicating the gender composition of the three groups making up the URNG combatants.

55. An anecdote will illustrate this point: In April 1997, I dined out with three women active in the Guatemalan women's movement. During the course of the evening they "confessed" to each other (and the author) for the first time that all three of them had been active in the URNG for several years. Although they had been close friends for years, they had not considered it prudent to reveal their political work. The three friends also maintained that no one in their family knew about their URNG membership.

56. Since many URNG combatants were brought back from refugee camps in Mexico, it is reasonable to assume that some of the women that were demobilized were not actual combatants. This is probably also the case for a number of the male URNG members.

57. These statements are from interviews conducted in 1997 and 1998.

58. Interview with Aura Marina Arriola, in Stoltz Chinchilla, *Nuestras Utopías,* 102.

59. Hurtado Paz y Paz, "Elementos de la historia del movimiento revolucionario guatemalteco," *Africa América Latina,* 12.

60. Yvon Le Bot, *La guerra en tierras mayas,* cited in Gutiérrez, "Quién quiso asaltar el cielo?" 72.

61. Interview with "Comandante Lola" (Alba Estela Maldonado), Guatemala City, November 20, 1997.

62. Yvon Le Bot, in Gutiérrez, "Quién quiso asaltar el cielo?" 72.

63. Interview with Silvia Solórzano, Guatemala City, March 3, 1999.

64. Interview with Comandante Lola, Guatemala City, November 20, 1997.

65. Ibid.

66. Yvon Le Bot, in Gutiérrez, "Quién quiso asaltar el cielo?" 72.

67. URNG, "Personal Incorporado," 2.

68. Interview with Captain Hernan, Frente Unitario, Finca Claudia, Esquintla, April 23, 1997. See also McCleary, "Guatemala's Postwar Prospects," 139.

69. For background to this incident, see Spence et al., "Promise and Reality," 19.

70. See Chapter Three for case studies elaborating this point.

71. For this point, as for several others, I am indebted to the anonymous reviewers of this manuscript.

72. Interview with Ana Gertrudis Méndez, San Salvador, December 12, 1995.

73. Anderson, *Che,* 750. Anderson reports that the house is filled with "necromantic ornaments" of Rodriguez's career in the CIA, among them a "brassiere he confiscated from a Salvadoran female *comandante.*" Nidia Díaz confirmed Anderson's account in conversation with the author.

Chapter Two   Gender Equality and the Central American Peace Accords

Epigraph: I encountered this quote at an exhibition at the Universidad Centroamericana in San Salvador on occasion of the eleventh anniversary of the assassination of the Jesuits.

1. Huntington, *The Third Wave.*

2. Some writers employ the term *Contras* to refer to those groups that opposed the Sandinistas militarily. *Resistance,* on the other hand, "refers to the formal organization that most Contra troops, to a greater or lesser extent, were affiliated with at the time of the 1990 election and the subsequent demobilization." Spalding, "From Low-Intensity Warfare to Low-Intensity Peace," n. 3. Both terms have strong ideological connota-

tions. In order to avoid identification with either side, I use the two terms as synonyms.

3. Walker, ed., *Nicaragua Without Illusions*, 12.

4. Historical Clarification Commission, *Guatemala*.

5. Ibid. See also Spence et al., "Promise and Reality," 4.

6. Broder, "Clinton Apologizes for U.S. Support of Guatemalan Rightists," *New York Times*, March 10, 1999.

7. See the review article by Gary Hoskin, "Democratization in Latin America," for a similar point of view.

8. Luciak, *The Sandinista Legacy*, 17–21.

9. For a discussion of electoral versus "real" democracy, see Vanden and Prevost, *Democracy and Socialism in Sandinista Nicaragua*, 129–51; Vilas, *Between Earthquakes and Volcanos*, 171–89; and Luciak, *The Sandinista Legacy*, 13–46.

10. Spalding, "From Low-Intensity Warfare to Low-Intensity Peace," 7.

11. Ibid., 20.

12. This section draws on the chronology of the negotiations between the Central American governments and their opponents, as presented in Núñez, *La guerra en Nicaragua*, 463–70; Child, *The Central American Peace Accords;* and various Guatemalan sources.

13. Núñez, *La guerra en Nicaragua*, 467.

14. Ibid., 469.

15. Internal struggles were endemic within and between the Contra forces. The Contras consisted of three major groups: the Fuerza Democrática Nicaragüense (Nicaraguan Democratic Force, or FDN) led by former members of Somoza's National Guard; indigenous groups integrated into the Yapti Tasba Masraka nanih Aslatakanka, or the Organization of the Nations of the Motherland; and the Alianza Revolucionaria Democrática (Revolutionary Democratic Alliance) created by former Sandinista commander Edén Pastora.

16. Child, *The Central American Peace Accords*, 90.

17. Spalding, "From Low-Intensity Warfare to Low-Intensity Peace," 9.

18. Interview with Sergio Caramagna, Managua, August 9, 1993. Caramagna, the head of CIAV's verification and follow-up program emphasized that the original mandate of the commission covered all of Central America, with the United States providing funding for its activities. Subsequently, CIAV's mandate was reduced to assisting the Nicaraguan Contras and repatriated refugees. Almost 100,000 refugees were attended by the commission.

19. CAHI, "Behind the Birth of the Recontras," 21.

20. Rodríguez, "Serán una realidad los polos de desarrollo?" 30.

21. Interview with Agenor López, Managua, July 23, 1992.

22. Interview with Joaquín Lovo, Managua, July 20, 1992.

23. CRIES, *Proceso de paz en El Salvador*, 48.

24. Interview with Morena Herrera, San Salvador, April 24, 1996.

25. LeoGrande, "After the Battle of San Salvador," 121.

26. CRIES, *Proceso de paz en El Salvador*, 48.

27. Child, *The Central American Peace Accords*, 86.

28. Ibid., 132–35.

29. McCleary, "Guatemala's Postwar Prospects," 137.

30. Gutiérrez, "Quién quiso asaltar el cielo?" 80.

31. Spence et al., "Promise and Reality," 12.

32. Gutiérrez, "Quién quiso asaltar el cielo?" 81.

33. Interviews with Lorena Peña, San Salvador, July 29, 1993, and May 4, 1995.

34. Interviews with Nidia Díaz, San Salvador, February 10 and March 18, 1997.

35. Interview with Ana Guadalupe Martínez, San Salvador, May 2, 1995.

36. Romero, "La reinserción de la mujer ex-combatiente," 370–71.

37. Interview with Nidia Díaz, San Salvador, March 9, 1994.

38. Interview with Lorena Peña, San Salvador, July 29, 1993.

39. Ibid., July 29, 1993, and April 25, 1996.

40. Fundación 16 de Enero, "Diagnóstico de la situación actual de la mujer ex-combatiente."

41. Seligson, "Thirty Years of Transformation in the Agrarian Structure of El Salvador," 2–3.

42. Seligson, "Agrarian Inequality and the Theory of Peasant Rebellion," 141.

43. Pelupessy, "Agrarian Reform in El Salvador," 44; and Segundo Montes, *El Agro Salvadoreño (1973–1980)*, 240–41.

44. Montes, *El Agro Salvadoreño*, 253–54.

45. Pelupessy, "Agrarian Reform in El Salvador," 47.

46. Ibid., 48.

47. Spence et al., "The Salvadoran Peace Accords and Democratization," 12.

48. FMLN, *Acuerdos Hacia Una Nueva Nación*, 84–85.

49. Vickers and Spence, "Endgame," 22.

50. Interview with Antonio Tapia, San Salvador, July 28, 1993.

51. USAID officials insisted that funds for the purchase of a particular property would only be authorized if all legal problems had been solved to its satisfaction.

52. The account of the Land Transfer Program is based on interviews with officials from the government, the FMLN, ONUSAL, and USAID, conducted between August 1993 and May 1996.

53. After April 1995, the ONUSAL mission remained in El Salvador under the new name MINUSAL and with greatly reduced staff. MINUSAL left in 1997, but UN officials continued to visit the country to observe the implementation of the accords.

54. *La Prensa Gráfica*, April 29, 1995, 37A.

55. Interview with Antonio Alvarez, San Salvador, July 28, 1993.

56. The low number of final beneficiaries was apparently due to demobilized soldiers' lack of interest in going into farming.

57. Interview with Antonio Tapia, San Salvador, July 28, 1993.

58. Interview with Antonio Alvarez, San Salvador, February 6, 1996.

59. Saint-Germain, "Mujeres '94," 20–22.

60. Mujeres por la Dignidad y la Vida, "Transferencia de tierras," 19.

61. Interviews with Alvarez, San Salvador, February 6 and April 22, 1996.

62. Ibid.

63. Mujeres por la Dignidad y la Vida, "Transferencia de tierras," 13–16.

64. Saint-Germain, "Mujeres '94," 19.

65. Ibid., 22.

66. Mujeres por la Dignidad y la Vida, "Transferencia de tierras," 19.

67. Montgomery, *Revolution in El Salvador*, 123.

68. Interview with Morena Herrera, San Salvador, April 24, 1996.

69. Ibid., March 17, 1997.

70. Fundación 16 de Enero, "Diagnóstico de la situación actual de la mujer ex-combatiente," 11.

71. FMLN–Secretaría Nacional de la Mujer, "Conclusiones del encuentro nacional de mujeres del FMLN, 21 de agosto 1993," 1.

72. I am indebted to Margaret Leahy for this important observation.

73. Fundación 16 de Enero, "Diagnóstico de la situación actual de la mujer ex-combatiente," 10.

74. Stanfield, "Insecurity of Land Tenure in Nicaragua," 20.

75. 1 manzana = 0.7 hectares = 1.75 acres.

76. CIERA, *La Reforma Agraria en Nicaragua, 1979–1989*, 39.

77. Wheelock, *La verdad sobre La Piñata*, 26.

78. These figures are calculated based on data presented in Wheelock, *La verdad sobre La Piñata*, 111–12.

79. Stanfield, "Insecurity of Land Tenure in Nicaragua," 13.

80. Wheelock, *La verdad sobre La Piñata*, 67.

81. Dye et al., "Contesting Everything, Winning Nothing," 25.

82. Ibid.

83. *Productores*, "Violencia política o delincuencia en el campo," 6.

84. Dye et al., "Contesting Everything, Winning Nothing," 25.

85. Interview with Ariel Bucardo, Managua, July 7, 1992.

86. Dye et al., "Contesting Everything, Winning Nothing," 34.

87. ATC, "Estabilidad laboral con libertad sindical," 14.

88. CIPRES, "La inestabilidad política y su impacto socio-económico en el campo," 7.

89. Interview with José Boanerges Matus, Managua, July 20, 1992.

90. Interview with Marta Heriberta Valle, Managua, July 10, 1992.

91. Dye et al., "Contesting Everything, Winning Nothing," 27.

92. *La Prensa*, February 2, 1997.

93. This section is based on interviews with several participants in the National Di-

alogue. I particularly benefited from the account given by María Teresa Blandón, one of the Dialogue's coordinators in an interview in Managua on November 11, 1997.

94. Interview with Henry Ruiz, Managua, November 12, 1997.

95. Henry Ruiz did not renounce his membership in the FSLN; instead he manifested his disapproval by refusing to attend meetings of the National Directorate.

96. Aguilar, "Un movimiento de mujeres embrionario."

97. Interview with Luz Méndez, Guatemala City, April 4, 1997.

98. Interview with Comandante Lola, Guatemala City, November 20, 1997.

99. Universidad de San Carlos de Guatemala, Programa Universitario de Investigación en Estudios de Género, "Proyecto: Mujeres y Acuerdos de Paz."

100. United Nations, "Acuerdo para el reasentamiento de las poblaciones desarraigadas por el enfrentamiento armado," 1994, chap. 2, art. 2.

101. Ibid., chap. 3, art. 8.

102. United Nations, "Acuerdo sobre identidad y derechos de los pueblos indígenas." 1995, chap. 2, art. 1.

103. United Nations, "Acuerdo sobre fortalecimiento del poder civil y función del ejército en una sociedad democrática." 1996, art. 59.

104. Interview with Luz Méndez, Guatemala City, April 4, 1997.

105. United Nations, "Acuerdo sobre aspectos socioeconómicos y situación agraria" 1996, arts. 12–13.

106. Gobierno de Guatemala, *Política nacional de promoción y desarrollo de las mujeres guatemaltecas plan de equidad de oportunidades 1997–2001*.

107. Spence et al., "Promise and Reality," 14.

108. Holiday, "Guatemala's Precarious Peace."

109. URNG, "Personal Incorporado," 2–3.

110. McCleary, "Guatemala's Postwar Prospects," 138.

111. World Bank, *Guatemala: An Assessment of Poverty*, 1–4, in Spence et al., "Promise and Reality," 47.

112. URNG, "Personal Incorporado," 8.

113. Ibid., 5.

114. World Bank, *Development 1997*, table 5, in Spence et al., "Promise and Reality," 47.

115. URNG, "Personal Incorporado," 9.

116. "Demandas de las mujeres y acuerdos de paz," *La Cuerda*, 1, no. 0 (March 8, 1998), 11.

117. Ibid.

118. URNG, "Cumplimiento de los acuerdos de paz: Período mayo-agosto," 19.

119. URNG, "Personal Incorporado," 9.

120. Ibid., 11.

121. Spence et al., "Promise and Reality," 8.

122. Ibid., 8.

123. Ibid., 54.

124. URNG, "Cumplimiento de los acuerdos de paz: Período mayo-agosto," 29.

125. These interviews were conducted by the author and by a team of researchers in August 1997 in Guatemala City and in two departments. They included both female and male political cadres and ex-combatants. A total of twenty-eight people were interviewed, seventeen in 1997 and eleven in 1998.

126. Holiday, "Guatemala's Precarious Peace."

127. Interview with a regional coordinator of the peasant group CONIC.

128. Grupo Mega, "Evaluación del impacto global de los programas y proyectos realizados, como parte del programa de incorporación de la URNG a la legalidad."

129. Interview with Comandante Lola, Guatemala City, March 2, 1999.

130. Interview with Amanda Carrera, Guatemala City, March 3, 1999.

131. La Prensa Gráfica, May 19, 1999 (Internet edition).

132. Holiday, "Guatemala's Precarious Peace."

133. Interview with Eduardo Stein, La Prensa Gráfica, May 24, 1999 (Internet edition).

134. See Chapter Three for an analysis of the reintegration of the FMLN's rank and file.

135. Interview with Francisco Jovel, San Salvador, May 5, 1995.

Chapter Three　Voices from the Salvadoran Grass Roots
Epigraph: Interview with Arsenio Carrillo, San Esteban Catarina, August 17, 1996.

1. FMLN–Fundación 16 de Enero, "Diagnóstico de la situación actual de la mujer ex-combatiente."

2. Ibid., 1.

3. See Chapter Four for an analysis of the FMLN split.

4. This account is based on Spence and Vickers, "A Negotiated Revolution," 2, and Spence et al., "Chapúltepec," 36–37.

5. Spence et al., "Chapúltepec," 37.

6. FMLN–Fundación 16 de Enero, "Diagnóstico de la situación actual de la mujer ex-combatiente," 11.

7. Interview with Rosa Elia Argueta, Meanguera, February 11, 1996.

8. Ibid.

9. FMLN–Fundación 16 de Enero, "Diagnóstico de la situación actual de la mujer ex-combatiente," 9.

10. Interview with Antonio Tapia, San Salvador, March 8, 1994.

11. Interview with Arsenio Carrillo, San Esteban Catarina, August 17, 1996.

12. Ibid.

13. Ibid.

14. Interview with Concepción Márquez, Meanguera, February 11, 1996.

15. FMLN–Fundación 16 de Enero, "Diagnóstico de la situación actual de la mujer ex-combatiente," 10.

16. Ibid.

17. Ibid, 11.

18. United Nations, *El Salvador*, 29.

Chapter Four   The Vanguard in Search of a New Identity

1. Vilas, *Between Earthquakes and Volcanoes*, 185.

2. Colburn, *The Vogue of Revolution in Poor Countries*, 14.

3. The PCS was dissolved in August 1995, as part of the process of unifying the FMLN. Its membership reconstituted itself as the Communist faction within the FMLN.

4. Interview with Schafik Hándal, San Salvador, February 10, 1996.

5. Interview with Francisco Jovel, San Salvador, March 10, 1994.

6. Interview with Schafik Hándal, San Salvador, February 10, 1996.

7. Ibid.

8. Interview with Gerson Martínez, San Salvador, April 28, 1995.

9. Interview with Francisco Jovel, San Salvador, March 10, 1994.

10. Ibid.

11. FMLN, *Documentos Políticos*, 41. The Council had sixty-six members. In anticipation of the 1994 elections, the future coordinator of the FMLN's parliamentary bench and the head of the mayor's council were also allocated seats.

12. See Chapter Six for a further explanation of the electoral process.

13. The Truth Commission, established under the peace accords to investigate crimes committed during the war, found Villalobos responsible for the ERP policy of assassinating mayors. See United Nations, *El Salvador*.

14. For an elaboration of the election see Chapter Six.

15. Vickers and Spence, "Elections," 11.

16. This account is based on interviews with Eduardo Sancho, Ana Guadalupe Martínez, Francisco Jovel, Norma Guevara, Eugenio Chicas, Gerson Martínez, and Salvador Sánchez conducted during 1994–95.

17. Interview with Salvador Sánchez, San Salvador, May 3, 1995.

18. Interview with Eugenio Chicas, San Salvador, May 5, 1995.

19. Interview with Salvador Sánchez, San Salvador, May 3, 1995.

20. Interview with Eduardo Sancho, San Salvador, May 4, 1995.

21. Interview with Ana Guadalupe Martínez, San Salvador, May 2, 1995.

22. Interview with Francisco Jovel, San Salvador, May 5, 1995.

23. Interview with Norma Guevara, San Salvador, May 2, 1995.

24. FMLN–Secretaría Nacional de la Mujer, "Con respecto a la situación actual del FMLN."

25. Interview with Salvador Sánchez, San Salvador, May 3, 1995.

26. These rules were to be approved at the Third National Convention.

27. FMLN, *Documentos Políticos*, 51.

28. Ibid., 52.

29. Interview with Salvador Sánchez, May 3, 1995. See also Spence et al., "The Salvadoran Peace Accords and Democratization," 27.

30. FMLN, *Documentos Políticos*, 29.

31. Ibid., 25.

32. I had the privilege of being invited to observe this historic event.

33. Interview with Salvador Sánchez, San Salvador, April 29, 1996.

34. See articles 25 and 32 of "Estatutos del Frente Farabundo Martí para la Liberación Nacional," in FMLN, *Documentos Políticos*, 25, 29.

35. FMLN, *Documentos Políticos*, 47.

36. FMLN, "Estatutos del FMLN con reformas," art. 82.

37. For an elaboration of the 1997 election, see Chapter Six.

38. Interview with Schafik Hándal, San Salvador, February 10, 1996.

39. Interview with Eduardo Sancho, San Salvador, April 24, 1996.

40. Spence, "Post War Transitions," 20.

41. Interview with Facundo Guardado, San Salvador, June 4, 1998.

42. Ibid.

43. "Sobre el rumbo actual del FMLN," May 1998 (internal FMLN document).

44. "Reglamento para la elección de candidatos y candidatas a la presidencia y vicepresidencia de la republica," *Cambio*, May 1998, 11.

45. This account is based on interviews with key protagonists, including Victoria Marina de Avilés, Nidia Díaz, and Norma Guevara.

46. *La Prensa Gráfica*, August 17 and 18, 1998 (Internet edition).

47. There were reports that Arias did in fact obtain the required 518 votes. This would have disqualified Silva automatically from the contest because of the requirement that a woman had to be on the ticket. Some observers charged that the FMLN leadership manipulated the results to prevent Silva's premature exit. Personally, I have no reason to question the veracity of Norma Guevara.

48. Interview with Salvador Arias in *El Diario de Hoy*, August 17, 1998 (Internet edition).

49. See Chapter Five for the implications of this selection process from a gender perspective.

50. Facundo Guaradado, quoted in *El Diario de Hoy*, March 16, 1999 (Internet edition).

51. *CoLatino*, May 10, 1999 (Internet edition, emphasis added).

52. Interview with Vilma Núñez, Managua, June 8, 1998.

53. See Luciak, *The Sandinista Legacy*, for an analysis of the evolution of Sandinista democracy.

54. Vanden and Prevost, *Democracy and Socialism in Sandinista Nicaragua*, 109.

55. Invernizzi et al., *Sandinistas*, 66.

56. Vanden and Prevost, *Democracy and Socialism in Sandinista Nicaragua*, 114.

57. Ibid., 109.

58. For this view by Moisés Hassan, a member of Nicaragua's original governing junta in 1979, see Luciak, *The Sandinista Legacy*, 43.

59. Gilbert, *Sandinistas*, 49. Gilbert's book was the best analysis of the FSLN published during the 1980s.

60. Interview with Mónica Baltodano, Managua, November 13, 1997.

61. Ibid.

62. See Chapter Five for a discussion of the implementation of the female quota.

63. Hoyt, *The Many Faces of Sandinista Democracy*, 153.

64. Prevost, "The FSLN," 159.

65. Interview with Henry Ruíz, Managua, November 12, 1997.

66. Prevost, "The FSLN," 156. The full text of the document is in *Barricada Internacional* (July 14, 1990).

67. Ibid., 159.

68. Vanden and Prevost, *Democracy and Socialism in Sandinista Nicaragua*, 126.

69. See Chapter Five for a discussion of these events.

70. Vanden and Prevost, *Democracy and Socialism in Sandinista Nicaragua*, 126.

71. Ibid., 120.

72. Interview with Mónica Baltodano, Managua, November 13, 1997.

73. Vanden and Prevost, *Democracy and Socialism in Sandinista Nicaragua*, 121.

74. Ibid., 123.

75. Interview with Vilma Núñez, Managua, June 8, 1998.

76. See Chapter Six on electoral politics for a discussion of the Women's Coalition.

77. Prevost, "The FSLN," 156–57.

78. Ibid., 158.

79. Ibid., 160.

80. Hoyt, *The Many Faces of Sandinista Democracy*, 151.

81. Ibid., 160.

82. Ibid., 153.

83. Interview with Sergio Ramírez, Managua, January 31, 1996.

84. Prevost, "The FSLN," 162.

85. Interview with Victor Hugo Tinoco, Managua, June 10, 1998.

86. Interview with Dora María Téllez, Managua, June 8, 1998.

87. See Chapter Five for an elaboration of the Zoilamérica controversy.

88. Zoilamérica Narváez Murillo, "Testimonio de Zoilamérica." Zoilamérica dropped "Ortega" from her name after she pressed charges against her stepfather.

89. Interview with Vilma Núñez, Managua, June 8, 1998.

90. Vilma Núñez, "En el 103 aniversario del nacimiento de Augusto C. Sandino," Managua, May 18, 1998 (emphasis added).

91. Estrella de Alba Treto, "En política, lo real es lo que no se dice . . . ," *7 Días*, 151 (May 27–June 3, 1998).

92. Interview with Victor Hugo Tinoco, Managua, June 10, 1998.

93. Orlando Núñez, Bayardo Arce, and René Núñez, "Congreso fue el inicio de cambios," *7 Días*, 10–11.

94. Tomás Borge, quoted in *La Prensa*, May 24, 1998 (Internet edition).

95. See Chapter Five for a discussion of this issue.

96. Interview with Victor Hugo Tinoco, Managua, June 10, 1998.

97. Interview with Marta Heriberta Valle, Managua, June 9, 1998.

98. Interview with Gladys Báez, Managua, June 8, 1998.

99. Mónica Baltodano, quoted in *La Prensa*, May 24, 1998 (Internet edition).

100. Mónica Baltodano, quoted in *Bolsa de Noticias*, April 8, 1998.

101. Interview with Dora María Téllez, Managua, June 8, 1998.

102. Interview with Victor Hugo Tinoco, Managua, June 10, 1998.

103. Landau, *The Guerrilla Wars of Central America*, 160–61.

104. Torres Rivas, *Guatemala, izquierdas en transición*, 72.

105. Stoltz Chinchilla, *Nuestras Utopias*, 104–5.

106. Interview with Jorge Soto, Guatemala City, November 22, 1997.

107. Interview with Ricardo Ramírez, Guatemala City, November 22, 1997.

108. Interview with Jorge Soto, Guatemala City, November 22, 1997.

109. Ibid.

110. Interview with Ricardo Ramírez, Guatemala City, November 22, 1997.

111. Hurtado Paz y Paz, "Elementos de la historia del movimiento revolucionario guatemalteco," *Africa América Latina* 31: 15.

112. Ibid., 13.

113. Ibid., 15.

114. Gutiérrez, "Quién quiso asaltar el cielo?" 75.

115. Interview with Ramiro Abreu, Havana, February 13, 1998.

116. Interview with Ricardo Rosales, Guatemala City, March 4, 1999.

117. Interview with Comandante Abel, Finca Claudia, Esquintla, April 23, 1997.

118. Interview with Jorge Soto, Guatemala City, November 22, 1997.

119. Interview with Captain Hernán, Finca Claudia, Esquintla, April 23, 1997.

120. Soto succeeded Ramírez following the president's death on September 11, 1998.

121. Stoltz Chinchilla, *Nuestras Utopias*, 109.

122. Morales, "La izquierda en el entresiglo," 60–61.

123. Interview with Ricardo Rosales, Guatemala City, March 4, 1999.

124. Interview with Comandante Lola, Guatemala City, March 2, 1999.

125. Interview with Wilson Romero, Guatemala City, March 3, 1999.

126. Ibid.

127. Ortega did not retire until February 1995.

128. Premo, "The Redirection of the Armed Forces," 66, and O'Kane and Marín, "El reverso de la medalla," 22. Only with the Military Code, which became law in Sep-

tember 1994, did the executive branch gain greater authority over the military. Even the new code, however, "did not empower the president to appoint the chief of the armed forces directly. Instead, it limited the executive's authority to reject the nominee proposed by the Military Council" (ibid., 72).

129. Spalding, "From Low-Intensity Warfare to Low-Intensity Peace," 8.

130. Interview with Azucena Ferrey, Managua, November 12, 1998.

131. Interview with Rodolfo Ampié, Managua, August 19, 1993.

132. Ibid.

133. Interview with Luis Angel López, Managua, August 11, 1993.

134. Nicaraguan Resistance Party, "Declaración de principios de la PRN," 6.

135. Interview with Edén Pastora, Managua, August 18, 1993.

136. See Chapter Six on electoral politics for an analysis of the elections.

137. Spalding, "From Low-Intensity Warfare to Low-Intensity Peace," 8.

138. Ibid., 21.

139. Juan Ramón Medrano quoted in *La Prensa Gráfica*, December 13, 1999 (Internet edition).

140. Interview with Tinoco quoted in Hoyt, *The Many Faces of Sandinista Democracy*, 160.

141. Daniel Ortega quoted in *La Prensa*, December 10, 1999 (Internet edition).

Chapter Five   Transforming the Party

Epigraph: URNG, *"Propuesta a la sociedad. Cuatro objetivos, nueve cambios, cuatro prioridades."*

1. Randall, *Gathering Rage*, 37.

2. Ibid., 16.

3. Harris, *Marxism, Socialism, and Democracy in Latin America*, 188.

4. Stubbs, "Cuba," 196, in Waylen, *Gender in Third World Politics*, 81.

5. Rodríguez Calderón, "Queda mucho por andar," 29–30.

6. Randall, *Gathering Rage*, 152; Rodríguez Calderón, "Queda mucho por andar," 30.

7. *Granma*, October 11, 1997.

8. Official figures of the Central Committee of the PCC, in Rodríguez Calderón, "Queda mucho por andar," 30.

9. FMLN, "Carta de principios y objetivos," in *Documentos Políticos*, 19.

10. FMLN–Secretaría Nacional de la Mujer, "Conclusiones del encuentro nacional de mujeres del FMLN, 21 de Agosto, 1993."

11. FPL–Comisión Nacional de la Mujer, "Informe de la Comisión Nacional de la Mujer a la Secretaría de la Mujer FMLN."

12. Ibid.

13. Montenegro, "Who was Going to Trust a Montenegro," 286–311.

14. Stephen, *Hear My Testimony*, 206–20.

15. Interview with Irma Amaya, San Salvador, April 23, 1996.

16. Urbina, "Building a Feminist Organization inside the Social Movement," 26.

17. For a discussion of the impact of these fights on the March 1997 elections, see Chapter Six.

18. Waylen, *Gender in Third World Politics*, 133–34.

19. FMLN–Secretaría Nacional de la Mujer, "Informe evaluativo del primer año de trabajo de la Secretaría Nacional de las Mujeres del FMLN, Mayo 93 a Junio 94," July 1994.

20. Ibid.

21. Interview with Lorena Peña, San Salvador, May 4, 1995.

22. FMLN–Secretaría Nacional de la Mujer, "Informe evaluativo del primer año de trabajo de la Secretaría Nacional de las Mujeres del FMLN, Mayo 93 a Junio 94" (emphasis added).

23. Interview with Norma Guevara, San Salvador, May 2, 1995.

24. This meeting was observed by the author on April 30, 1995.

25. At the time the five factions consisted of the FPL, the PRTC, the FAL, the Tendencia Democrática (consisting of former members of the ERP), and the RN-fmlnista (representing those RN members who chose to remain part of the FMLN).

26. Interview with Violeta Menjívar, San Salvador, May 3, 1995.

27. FMLN–Secretaría Nacional de la Mujer, "Informe de los primeros 5 meses de funcionamiento de la secretaría nacional de la mujer," 2.

28. Interview with Ana Gertrudis Méndez, San Salvador, December 12, 1995.

29. FMLN–Secretaría Nacional de la Mujer, "Informe de los primeros 5 meses de funcionamiento de la secretaría nacional de la mujer," 1.

30. FPL–Comisión Nacional de la Mujer, "Informe de la Comisión Nacional de la Mujer a Secretaría de la Mujer FMLN."

31. ONUSAL, *Proceso de desmovilización del personal del FMLN*.

32. FMLN–Secretaría Nacional de la Mujer, "Políticas de género iniciales."

33. FMLN–Secretaría Nacional de la Mujer, "Documento propuesta," 3.

34. Molina, "Propuestas políticas y orientaciones de cambio en la situación de la mujer," in *Propuestas Políticas y Demandas Sociales*, vol. 3, edited by Manuel Antonio Garretón; and Lois Hecht Oppenheim, "Democracy in Post-1990 Chile and the Political Incorporation of Women," 5.

35. Jones, "Gender Quotas, Electoral Laws, and the Election of Women."

36. Htun, "Moving into Power," 34, in Jones, "Gender Quotas, Electoral Laws, and the Election of Women," 5.

37. Interview with Francisco Jovel, San Salvador, June 1, 1998.

38. Interview with Nidia Díaz, San Salvador, May 3, 1995.

39. Spence et al., "Chapúltepec: Five Years Later," 25.

40. Interview with Catalina Rodríguez de Merino, San Salvador, May 1, 1995.

41. Interview with Aída Herrera, San Salvador, May 5, 1995.

42. FMLN–Secretaría Nacional de la Mujer, "Conclusiones del encuentro nacional de mujeres del FMLN."

43. See Chapter Three for a discussion of these issues.

44. Montgomery, *Revolution in El Salvador*, 123.

45. Subsequently Mirna Perla resigned in order to accept a judgeship. This reduced the number of women on the commission to three.

46. Interview with Nidia Díaz, San Salvador, May 3, 1995.

47. Interview with Salvador Sánchez, San Salvador, May 3, 1995.

48. The membership of the National Council was reduced from sixty-six in 1994 to fifty in 1995. From then on, departmental representatives were an integral part of the fifty-member Council. In addition to the fifty members elected by the convention, the coordinator of the FMLN's parliamentary bench and the coordinator of the Council of Mayors were part of the National Council.

49. FMLN–Secretaría Nacional de la Mujer, "Programa de fortalecimiento y desarrollo político de las mujeres desde el nivel de base" (emphasis added).

50. Interview with Eugenio Chicas, San Salvador, May 5, 1995.

51. FPL–Comisión Nacional de la Mujer, "Informe de la Comisión Nacional de la Mujer a Secretaría de la Mujer FMLN."

52. Interview with Salvador Sánchez, San Salvador, April 29, 1996.

53. Interviews with Nidia Diaz, San Salvador, April 26, 1996, and February 2, 1997.

54. Interview with Deysi Cheyne, San Salvador, March 8, 1999.

55. Interview with Victoria de Avilés, San Salvador, March 9, 1999.

56. Ibid.

57. Interview with Nidia Díaz, San Salvador, March 9, 1999.

58. Interview with Victoria de Avilés, San Salvador, March 9, 1999.

59. Interview with Ana Gertrudis Méndez, San Salvador, March 8, 1999.

60. FMLN–Secretaría Nacional de la Mujer, "Informe evaluativo del trabajo de la SNM (96–97)" (emphasis added).

61. Ibid. (emphasis added).

62. FSLN, *Programa histórico del FSLN*, 32.

63. Interview with Dora María Téllez, Managua, June 8, 1998.

64. See Chapter One for a discussion of women's participation in the war.

65. Gorman, "The Role of the Revolutionary Armed Forces," 124.

66. Ramírez-Horton, "The Role of Women in the Nicaraguan Revolution," 156–57.

67. Interview with Vilma Núñez, Managua, June 8, 1998.

68. Pérez Alemán, *Organización, Identidad y Cambio*, 194–95.

69. Ibid., 195. See also Luciak, *The Sandinista Legacy*, 161–81, for an analysis of Sandinista policies toward rural women.

70. See Molyneux, "Mobilization Without Emancipation," 280–302.

71. Criquillon, "The Nicaraguan Women's Movement," 227.

72. Randall, *Sandino's Daughters Revisited*, xi.

73. Collinson, *Women and Revolution in Nicaragua*, 137.

74. Waylen, *Gender in Third World Politics*, 82.

75. Interview with Mónica Baltodano, Managua, November 13, 1997.

76. Interview with Dorotea Wilson, February 5, 1997.

77. Interview with Dora María Téllez, Managua, June 8, 1998.

78. Waylen, *Gender in Third World Politics*, 82.

79. Interview with Dora María Téllez, Managua, June 8, 1998.

80. Molyneux, "Women," 152.

81. See Luciak, *The Sandinista Legacy*, 164–66, for an elaboration of this point.

82. Interview with Dora María Téllez, Managua, June 8, 1998.

83. See Chapter Four for a discussion of these events.

84. Interview with Dora María Téllez, Managua, June 8, 1998.

85. Interview with Mónica Baltodano, Managua, November 13, 1997.

86. Ibid.

87. Interview with Vilma Núñez, Managua, June 8, 1998.

88. Gilbert, *Sandinistas*, 53.

89. CENIDH, *La política es aún un campo dominado por los hombres*, 33.

90. Interview with Dorotea Wilson, Managua, February 5, 1997.

91. Interview with Leticia Herrera, Managua, November 12, 1997.

92. CENIDH, *La política es aún un campo dominado por los hombres*, 34.

93. Ibid., 37.

94. Interview with Mónica Baltodano, Managua, November 13, 1997.

95. CENIDH, *La política es aún un campo dominado por los hombres*, 35.

96. Interview with Mónica Baltodano, Managua, November 13, 1997.

97. See the discussion in Chapter Six for an elaboration of the impact of the quota on women's participation in elections to public office.

98. Interview with Mónica Baltodano, Managua, November 13, 1997.

99. Ibid.

100. FSLN, "El FSLN y la mujer en la revolución popular sandinista," 148.

101. Chamorro, "La Mujer," 132–33.

102. Interview with Mónica Baltodano, Managua, November 13, 1997.

103. Zoilamérica Narváez Murillo, "Testimonio de Zoilamérica," Managua, May 22, 1998.

104. Ibid. (emphasis added).

105. Interview with Dorotea Wilson, Managua, February 5, 1997.

106. Interview with Vilma Núñez, Managua, June 8, 1998.

107. CENIDH, *La política es aún un campo dominado por los hombres*, 46.

108. Ibid., 39.

109. Interview with Mariela Aguilar, Guatemala City, November 19, 1997.

110. Interview with Nineth Montenegro, Guatemala City, April 24, 1997.

111. Interview with Manuela Alvarado, Guatemala City, April 24, 1997.

112. Interview with Mariela Aguilar, Guatemala City, November 19, 1997.

113. Interview with Manuela Alvarado, Guatemala City, November 19, 1997.

114. Interview with Mariela Aguilar, Guatemala City, November 19, 1997.

115. Stoltz Chinchilla, *Nuestras Utopias*, 11.

116. Interview with Comandante Lola, Guatemala City, November 20, 1997.

117. Interview with Wilson Romero, Guatemala City, March 3, 1999.

118. Interview with Comandante Lola, Guatemala City, November 20, 1997.

119. FAR, "Documento resoluciones sobre el trabajo de la mujer, Asamblea Nacional de Cuadros de las FAR."

120. FAR, "La dimension de género en nuestra concepción revolucionaria," 14.

121. Interviews with Luz Méndez, April 4 and November 20, 1997.

122. There has been heated discussion within the Central American women's movement over the issue of establishing a women's secretariat within parties of the Left. In the case of the FMLN, such a secretariat was established early on. While it had little autonomy in its first years, it is starting to evolve into an effective advocate for women's rights within the party. In the case of the FSLN, a women's secretariat was only established recently at the May 1998 party congress.

123. Méndez, "El papel de las mujeres en la URNG," 62.

124. Ibid.

125. Ibid., 61–62.

126. Interview with Comandante Lola, November 20, 1997.

127. See Chapter Six for an explanation of the electoral system.

128. Interview with Fermina López, Guatemala City, November 22, 1997.

129. Interview with Silvia Solórzano, Guatemala City, March 3, 1999.

130. Ibid.

131. Interview with Comandante Lola, Guatemala City, March 2, 1999.

132. The UNAMG was actually a re-creation of a woman's movement set up in March 1980 by URNG militants.

133. Interview with Comandante Lola, March 2, 1999.

134. FMLN–Secretaría Nacional de la Mujer, "Informe evaluativo del trabajo de la SNM (96–97)," 6.

135. Interview with Violeta Menjívar, San Salvador, February 6, 1997.

136. FMLN–Secretaría Nacional de la Mujer, "Informe evaluativo del trabajo de la SNM (96–97)," 4.

137. Ibid.

138. FMLN–Secretaría Nacional de la Mujer, "Documento propuesta," 5.

Chapter Six   Gender Equality and Recent Elections

Epigraph: When a woman enters politics the woman changes; but . . . when women enter politics, politics change.

My account of women's efforts to put gender issues on the agendas of their political parties in El Salvador and Nicaragua is based largely on interviews with Nidia Díaz, Deysi Cheyne,

Violeta Menjívar, Lorena Peña, Irma Amaya, and Sonia Cansino in El Salvador and Daisy Zamora, Alba Palacios, Esmeralda Dávila, Azucena Ferrey, María Teresa Blandón, Marta Valle, Benigna Mendiola, Mónica Baltodano, Dorotea Wilson, and Mónica Zalaquett in Nicaragua.

1. Kampwirth, "Feminism, Anti-feminism, and Electoral Politics in Post-war Nicaragua and El Salvador," 1–2.

2. Saint-Germain, "Mujeres '94," 18.

3. Ibid., 19; and Kampwirth, "Feminism, Anti-feminism, and Electoral Politics in Post-war Nicaragua and El Salvador."

4. Interview with Lorena Peña, San Salvador, February 7, 1997.

5. See the discussion in Chapter Five.

6. See Saint-Germain, "Mujeres '94," for a discussion of the 1994 platform and the organizational effort of the women's movement.

7. The main organizations involved in the 1997 effort were the Movimiento de Mujeres "Mélida Anaya Montes" (Mélida Anaya Montes Women's Movement, or MAM), the Mujeres por la Dignidad y la Vida (Women for Dignity and Life, or Las Dignas), the Instituto de Investigación, Capacitación y Desarrollo de la Mujer (Institute for Women's Research, Training and Development, or IMU), the Movimiento Salvadoreño de la Mujer (Salvadoran Women's Movement, or MSM), and the Asociación de Madres Demandantes (Association of Women Demanding Child Support). In addition, a number of independent women joined the group for its regular Wednesday breakfast meetings. For example, twenty-seven organizations were represented in a February 1997 workshop to finalize the electoral platform.

8. Interview with Deysi Cheyne, San Salvador, March 19, 1997.

9. Interview with María Teresa Blandon, Managua, February 4, 1997.

10. Interview with Azucena Ferrey, Managua, November 12, 1997.

11. Coalición Nacional de Mujeres, Agenda Mínima, 3.

12. See Chavez Metoyer, "The Women's Movement in the 1996 Nicaraguan Elections," 14, for a discussion of the content of the Minimum Agenda.

13. Coalición Nacional de Mujeres, Agenda Mínima, 10.

14. Interview with María Teresa Blandon, Managua, February 4, 1997.

15. Ibid.

16. The Scandinavian countries were among the first to incorporate gender equality as a key objective in their aid programs. The Swedish International Development Cooperation Agency (Sida) selected Nicaragua as a model country in which to implement an aid program emphasizing gender equality.

17. Interview with Mónica Zalaquett, Managua, February 4, 1997.

18. Chavez Metoyer, "The Women's Movement in the 1996 Nicaraguan Elections," 13.

19. The account of the candidate-selection process is based on interviews with Nidia Díaz, Violeta Menjívar, Lorena Peña, Gerson Martínez, Irma Amaya, and Sonia

Cansino in El Salvador; and in Nicaragua, Daisy Zamora, Alba Palacios, Esmeralda Dávila, María Teresa Blandón, Marta Valle, Benigna Mendiola, Mónica Baltodano, Dorotea Wilson, and Orlando Núñez.

20. In both countries, candidates are elected from departmental lists compiled by the parties, with the number of representatives of a particular department determined by the size of its population. In addition, each party compiles a national list for twenty seats that are allocated by the total number of votes a party has obtained.

21. Matland and Taylor, "Electoral System Effects on Women's Representation," 186.

22. Interview with Gerson Martínez, San Salvador, March 4, 1994.

23. Interview with Lorena Peña, San Salvador, February 6, 1997.

24. Interview with Violeta Menjívar, San Salvador, February 6, 1997.

25. For the 1984 and 1990 elections Nicaragua's electoral districts consisted of regions, whereas in 1996, the country was divided into departments.

26. In the 1984 and 1990 elections, Nicaragua elected its parliament from a national list and lists in six regions and three electoral districts on the Atlantic coast. Five of the six regions, with the exception of Managua, the capital, consisted of two departments. In 1996, every department had its own list and the regions ceased to function as administrative units. On election day, people voted in their respective departments for the party of their choice. The number of votes a party received determined how many of its departmental candidates were elected. The votes from all departments given to a particular party were then added up. This vote total determined how many candidates from a party's national list were elected. El Salvador and Guatemala have the same system.

27. Interview with Dorotea Wilson, Managua, February 5, 1997.

28. Ibid.

29. Under proportional representation, the total number of votes cast for candidates for parliament in a particular department are divided by the number of representatives allocated to the department. This establishes the electoral quotient. A party's total number of departmental votes divided by this quotient determines the number of seats a party wins. Because this result seldom comes out even, this procedure leaves residual votes and seats that have to be allocated by the Supreme Electoral Council. At this point, the Council's decisions are open to manipulation, since there is no clearly established procedure for allocating these seats.

30. See Chapter Four for a discussion of these events.

31. Interview with Gerson Martínez, San Salvador, April 28, 1995.

32. *Washington Post*, June 2, 1994, A25.

33. Mujeres por la Dignidad y la Vida, *Las Mujeres*, 21.

34. Spence et al., "El Salvador: Elections of the Century," 7.

35. Mujeres por la Dignidad y la Vida, *Las Mujeres*, 22.

36. Ibid., 24.

37. The FMLN was victorious in forty-eight towns and gained five additional ones as part of electoral alliances.

38. Interview with Mónica Baltodano, Managua, November 13, 1997.

39. United Nations Development Program, *Human Development Report 1995*, 60–62.

40. *La Prensa Gráfica*, September 16, 1998 (Internet edition).

41. Editorial, *Estudios Centroamericanos*, 52 (March–April 1997), 183. In "El Salvador's Extraordinary Elections," 5, Tommie Sue Montgomery has argued that the high abstention figure is misleading. She deducts an estimated 300,000 Salvadorans living abroad, the 300,000 dead persons still on the rolls, and 400,000 who never picked up their voting cards from the electoral authority. She thereby gets an abstention rate of 44 percent, close to the one in 1994. See also FLACSO, *El proceso electoral*, 173. Considering, however, that more than 350,000 voters did not pick up their cards in 1994 (Spence, Dye, and Vickers, "El Salvador: Elections of the Century," 7), and there is no evidence suggesting any differences between 1994 and 1997 in the number of Salvadorans living abroad or showing up on the electoral register posthumously, the decline in turnout appears to be real.

42. Amilcar Méndez quoted in *La Prensa Libre*, November 9, 1999 (Internet edition).

43. Gloria Salguero Gross quoted in *La Prensa Gráfica*, March 15, 2000, 6–7.

44. Hipsher, "The Micromobilization of the Feminist Movement in Democratizing El Salvador," 11.

Conclusion

Epigraph: "Without women's participation, democracy cannot go forward." This election slogan was coined in Chile. See Navarro and Bourque, "Fault Lines of Democratic Governance," 190.

1. Htun, "El liderazgo de las mujeres en América Latina," 1.

2. Apparently, Salvadoran President Flores had agreed in advance to sign the law.

3. This account is based on conversations with three key protagonists: Gloria Salguero, Nidia Díaz, and Deysi Cheyne.

4. FMLN–Secretaría Nacional de la Mujer, "Programa de fortalecimiento y desarrollo político de las mujeres desde el nivel de base."

5. UNDP, *Human Development Report 1999*.

6. Policía Nacional, *Nicaragua 1997* (Managua, 1997).

7. Spence et al., "Chapúltepec: Five Years Later," 16.

8. Interview with Eugenio Chicas, San Salvador, April 22, 1996.

9. In February 2000, Carlos Romero Alfaro was indicted for this crime.

10. Spence, "Democracy Weakened?" 19–20.

Bibliography

Author's Interviews

In this list, legal names are given first. Noms de guerre follow in parentheses in order to establish an official record.

Abreu, Ramiro. Official of the Central Committee of the Cuban Communist Party in charge of Central America. Havana, February 13, 1998.

Aguilar, Ana Leticia. Member of the Executive Committee of *La Corriente*. Guatemala City, February 11, 1997, and November 17, 1997.

Aguinada, Sonia. Former ERP official and deputy in the Salvadoran Parliament for the Partido Demócrata. San Salvador, February 7, 1997.

Alegría, Damian. President of the Foundation 16 de Enero and member of the FMLN's National Council. San Salvador, August 2, 1993.

Alvarado, Manuela. FDNG deputy in the Guatemalan parliament. Guatemala City, April 24 and November 19, 1997.

Alvarez, Antonio. Member of the FMLN's Political Council in charge of the reinsertion programs. San Salvador, July 28, 1993, and February 6 and April 22, 1996.

Amaya, Irma. Executive Director of the Mélida Anaya Women's Movement. San Salvador, April 23, 1996; March 19, 1997; and February 15, 2001.

Ampié, Rodolfo ("Comandante Invisible"). Member of the directorate of the Nicaraguan Resistance and director of the Office of Administration and Planification of Development Centers. Managua, August 19, 1993.

Argüello, Miriam. Presidential candidate for the Conservative Popular Alliance. Managua, June 8, 1998.

Argüeta, Rosa Elia. FMLN official in charge of Land Transfer Program in Meanguera. Meanguera, February 11, 1996.

Argüeta, Yanira. Executive Director of the Association of Salvadoran Women (AMS). San Salvador, April 26, 1996.

Avilés, Victoria Marina. Former Salvadoran Human Rights Ombudsperson and FMLN nominee for president. San Salvador, March 9, 1999.

Báez, Gladys. Member of the FSLN's National Directorate and Head of its Women's Secretariat. Managua, June 8, 1998.

Baltodano, Mónica. Member of the FSLN's National Directorate and head of the FSLN's Secretariat of Organization. Managua, November 13, 1997.

Blandón, María Teresa. Executive Director of *La Corriente* and coordinator of the women's collective, La Malinche. Managua, February 4, 1997; November 11, 1997; and February 19, 2001.

Bolaños, María. FSLN deputy in parliament. Managua, November 11, 1997.

Bucardo, Ariel. President of FENACOOP. Managua, July 7, 1992.

Calderón, Fidel. Head of the Special Agrarian Commission of the Comisión de Paz (COPAZ). San Salvador, July 27, 1993.

Cansino, Sonia. Member of Las Dignas. San Salvador, February 10, 1997.

Caramagna, Sergio. Head of the International Commission on Support and Verification of the Organization of American States. Managua, August 9, 1993.

Carrera, Amanda. URNG official in charge of the gender group of the Fundación Guillermo Toriello. Guatemala City, March 3, 1999.

Cheyne, Deysi. Executive Director of the Institute for Women's Research, Training and Development (IMU). San Salvador, April 27, 1996; March 19, 1997; June 2, 1998; March 8, 1999; March 11, 2000; and February 13, 2001.

Chicas, Eugenio ("Marcos Jiménez"). Vice-coordinator of the FMLN. San Salvador, May 5, 1995, and April 22, 1996.

Crespo, Alfredo. Head of public relations for the United Nations Mission in Guatemala (MINUGUA). Guatemala City, April 22, 1997.

Dalton, Aída. FMLN militant and widow of Roque Dalton. San Salvador, February 2, 1996.

Dávila, Esmeralda. Vice-president of the Association of Nicaraguan Women, Luisa Amanda Espinoza (AMNLAE). Managua, February 4, 1997.

Díaz, Nidia. Member of the FMLN's Political Commission, deputy in the Salvadoran parliament and candidate for vice-president. San Salvador, March 9, 1994; May 3, 1995; December 12, 1995; April 26, 1996; February 10, 1997; March 18, 1997; November 16, 1997; June 7, 1998; March 8, 1999; and March 15, 2000.

Domínguez, José Osmin. Executive Director of the Foundation 16 de Enero. San Salvador, March 7, 1994.

Ferrey, Azucena. Member of the directorate of the Nicaraguan Resistance and deputy in the Nicaraguan parliament (1990–96). Managua, November 12, 1998.

Flores, Rosibel. Member of the directorate of the Mélida Anaya Women's Movement. San Salvador, December 7, 1995.

Garcia, Edgardo. Member of the Sandinista Assembly and President of the Association of Agricultural Workers (ATC). Managua, January 30, 1996.

Góngora, Ana Francis. Member of the Executive Committee of the Mélida Anaya Women's Movement. San Salvador, April 29, 1995, and February 9, 1997.

González, Medardo ("Milton Méndez"). Head of the FMLN's Secretariat of Organization and a member of the FMLN's Political Commission. San Salvador, December 12, 1995.

Guardado, Facundo. President of the FMLN. San Salvador, February 5, 1996; June 4,
1998; March 13, 2000.

Guevara, Isabel. Executive Director of the Salvadoran Women's Movement (MSM).
San Salvador, April 22, 1996.

Guevara, Norma. Senior FMLN official and member of the Salvadoran parliament. San
Salvador, May 2, 1995; December 7, 1995; and March 5, 1999.

Gutiérrez, Isolina ("Marta Segovia"). Member of the FMLN's Women's Secretariat. San
Salvador, December 5, 1995.

Hándal, Schafick. Former leader of the Communist Party and a member of the FMLN's
Political Commission. San Salvador, February 10, 1996.

Hernán. Capitán in the URNG. Finca Claudia, Esquintla, Guatemala, April 23, 1997.

Hernandez, Julia María. Head of Tutela Legal. San Salvador, July 28, 1993.

Herrera, Aída. Coordinator of the PRTC and member of the FMLN's Political Council. San Salvador, May 5, 1995.

Herrera, Leticia. FSLN leader and member of parliament, (1984–96). Managua, November 12, 1997.

Herrera, Morena. Leader of Las Dignas. San Salvador, April 24, 1996, and March 17,
1997.

Jovel, Francisco ("Roberto Roca"). Coordinator of the PRTC, member of the FMLN's
Political Commission and of the Salvadoran parliament. San Salvador, March
10, 1994; May 5, 1995; June 1, 1998; and February 16, 2001.

Joya de Mena, Ana Luz. USAID Project Manager. San Salvador, April 25, 1996.

Leon, Anabela de. PAN deputy in the Guatemalan parliament. Guatemala City, November 17, 1997.

Lima, Araujo. Commander, United Nations observer mission in Guatemala. Demobilization camp located at Finca Claudia. Esquintla, April 23, 1997.

López, Agenor. President of the National Union of Farmers and Ranchers (UNAG) in
Nueva Guinea. Managua, July 23, 1992.

López, Fermina. Vice-president of URNG's Women's Secretariat. Guatemala City, November 22, 1997.

López, Luis Angel. President of the Partido Resistencia Nicaragüense. Managua, August 11, 1993.

Lorenzana, Francisco Roberto. Former official of the Communist Party of El Salvador
(PCS), vice-coordinator of the FMLN and deputy of the Salvadoran parliament.
San Salvador, May 2, 1995.

Lovo, Joaquín. Vice-minister of government in charge of police and security. Managua,
July 20, 1992.

Maldonado, Alba Estela ("Comandante Lola"). Member of the URNG's Executive

Council and head of the Women's Secretariat. Guatemala City, November 20, 1997; March 2, 1999; and May 4, 2001.

Marquéz, Concepción. Mayor of Meanguera. Meanguera, February 11, 1996.

Marroquin, María Dolores. Feminist leader. Guatemala City, April 24, 1997.

Martínez, Ana Guadalupe. Vice-president of the Salvadoran Parliament and leader of the Partido Demócrata. San Salvador, May 2, 1995.

Martínez, Gerson. Member of the FMLN's Political Commission and Speaker of the FMLN's Parliamentary Group. San Salvador, July 24, 1993; March 4, 1994; April 28, 1995; September 24, 1995 (via telephone); December 8, 1995; February 2, 1996; February 9, 1997; and February 17, 2001.

Matus, José Boanerges. Minister of Agrarian Reform. Managua, July 20, 1992.

Méndez, Ana Gertrudis ("Lety"). Head of the FMLN's Women's Secretariat and a member of the FMLN's Political Commission. San Salvador, December 12, 1995; February 11, 1996; April 24, 1996; June 5, 1998; and March 5, 1999.

Méndez, Luz. Member of the URNG's Political Council and Executive Director of the National Union of Guatemalan Women (UNAMG). Guatemala City, April 4, 1997; November 20, 1997; and March 3, 1999.

Mendiola, Benigna. Member of the FSLN's National Directorate and head of UNAG's Women's Secretariat. Managua, January 31, 1997.

Menjívar, Violeta. Member of the FMLN's Women's Secretariat, the FMLN's Political Commission, and member of the Salvadoran parliament. San Salvador, May 3, 1995; December 7, 1995; and February 6, 1997.

Montenegro, Nineth. FDNG deputy in the Guatemalan parliament. Guatemala City, April 24, 1997, and May 7, 2001.

Montenegro, Sofía. Renowned feminist and Executive Director of the Center for Information and Communication (CINCO). Managua, November 12, 1997; Blacksburg, USA; April 1, 1998; and Managua, February 18, 2001.

Montis, Malena de. Coordinator of the Red Latinoamericana y de El Caribe "Mujeres y Política." Managua, June 9, 1998.

Moran, Sandra. Feminist leader. Guatemala City, April 24 and November 19, 1997.

Navas, María Candelaria. FMLN militant and head of the Gender and Development program of the National University of El Salvador. San Salvador, February 8, 1996; and Blacksburg, USA, May 1, 1997.

Noack, Olga Camey de. PAN deputy in the Guatemalan parliament. Guatemala City, November 19, 1997.

Núñez, Daniel. Member of the Sandinista Assembly and President of the National Union of Farmers and Ranchers. Managua, January 30, 1996.

Núñez, Orlando. FSLN leader and sociologist. Managua, February 3, 1997, and June 8, 1998.

Núñez, Vilma. President of the Centro Nicaragüense de Derechos Humanos. Managua, July 21, 1992; June 8, 1998; and February 20, 2001.

Orrellana, Rolando. Head of the FMLN's Human Rights Secretariat. San Salvador, July 30, 1993.

Palacios, Alba. Member of the Sandinista Assembly and member of the Central American Parliament. Managua, January 30, 1996; February 3, 1997; and Guatemala City, April 21, 1998.

Pastora, Edén. Ex-Sandinista commander, former leader of the Southern Front, and president of the Movimiento de Acción Democrática. Managua, August 18, 1993.

Peña, Lorena ("Rebeca Palacios"). Member of the FMLN's Political Council, cofounder of the Mélida Anaya Montes Women's Movement, and member of the Salvadoran parliament. San Salvador, July 29, 1993; May 4, 1995; December 11, 1995; April 25, 1996; and February 7, 1997.

Ramírez, Ricardo ("Rolando Moran"). Former head of the EGP and president of the URNG. Guatemala City, November 22, 1997.

Ramírez, Sergio. Former vice-president of Nicaragua and leader of the Sandinista Renovation Movement. Managua, January 31, 1996.

Rodríquez de Merino, Catalina. Senior FPL official and former vice-rector of the National University. San Salvador, May 1, 1995.

Romero, Wilson. Former official of the PGT and member of the URNG's Executive Committee. Guatemala City, March 3, 1999.

Rosales Ricardo ("Carlos Gonzáles"). Former secretary general of the PGT and member of the URNG's Executive Committee. Guatemala City, March 4, 1999.

Ruíz, Henry. Member of the FSLN's National Directorate. Managua, November 12, 1997.

Salazar, Bernardo ("Comandante Abel"), URNG. Finca Claudia. Esquintla, Guatemala, April 23, 1997.

Sánchez, Guadalupe. FSLN deputy in the Nicaraguan parliament. Managua, November 12, 1997.

Sánchez Cerén, Salvador ("Leonel González"). Coordinator of the FMLN. San Salvador, May 3, 1995; April 29, 1996; and February 16, 2001.

Sancho, Eduardo ("Ferman Cienfuegos"). Secretary of the Salvadoran parliament and leader of the Partido Demócrata. San Salvador, May 4, 1995, and April 24, 1996.

Senteno, Humberto. Member of the FMLN's National Council and head of the National Unity of Salvadoran Workers (UNTS). San Salvador, July 29, 1993, and December 6, 1995.

Sintes, Luis Alejandro. Head of the Military Division of the United Nations observer mission in El Salvador (ONUSAL). San Salvador, August 3, 1993.

Solórzano, Silvia. Member of URNG's International Relations Secretariat. Guatemala City, March 3, 1999, and May 4, 2001.

Soto, Jorge ("Pablo Monsanto"). Former head of the FAR and vice-president of the URNG, Guatemala City, November 22, 1997.

Tanco, Carlos. United Nations military observer group in Guatemala. Guatemala City, November 21, 1997.

Tapia, Antonio. ONUSAL official in charge of political matters. San Salvador, July 28, 1993, and March 8, 1994.

Téllez, Dora María. Former member of the FSLN's National Directorate and leader of the Sandinista Renovation Movement. Managua, June 8, 1998.

Tinoco, Víctor Hugo. Member of the FSLN's National Directorate. Managua, June 10, 1998.

Tulio, Lima. Executive Director of the Cooperative Association of El Salvador (COACES). San Salvador, August 2, 1993.

Valle, Marta Heriberta. Member of the FSLN's National Direcorate, member of UNAG's national executive committee, and head of the woman's section in region VI. Managua, July 10, 1992; February 1, 1997; and June 9, 1998.

Villagran, Arnoldo ("Daniel Ruíz"). FAR commander and URNG leader. Guatemala City, November 21, 1997.

Wilson, Dorotea. Member of the FSLN's National Directorate. Managua, February 5, 1997.

Zalaquett, Mónica. Coordinator of the Women's Coalition. Managua, February 4, 1997.

Zamora, Angela. Member of the FMLN's Political Commission. San Salvador, December 11, 1995.

Zamora, Daisy. Executive Director of Coordinadora Regional de Investigaciones Económicas y Sociales (CRIES). Managua, February 4, 1997.

Zeledon, Dora. FSLN deputy in the Nicaraguan parliament. Managua, November 10, 1997.

Published and Unpublished Sources

Agüero, Felipe, and Jeffrey Stark, eds. *Fault Lines of Democracy in Post-Transition Latin America*. Miami: North-South Center Press, 1998.

Aguilar, Ana Leticia. "Un movimiento de mujeres embrionario." In *El movimiento de mujeres en Centroamérica*, edited by María Teresa Blandón and Sofía Montenegro. Managua: La Corriente, 1997.

Alegría, Claribel, and D. J. Flakoll. *No me agarran viva: La mujer salvadoreña en la lucha*. San Salvador: UCA, 1992.

Alvarez, Sonia. *Engendering Democracy in Brazil: Women's Movements in Transition Politics*. Princeton: Princeton University Press, 1990.

Americas Watch. *Fitful Peace: Human Rights and Reconciliation in Nicaragua under the Chamorro Government*. New York: Americas Watch, 1992.

Anderson, Jon Lee. *Che*. New York: Grove Press, 1997.

Angell, Alan. "Incorporating the Left into Democratic Politics." In *Constructing Democratic Governance: Latin America and the Caribbean in the 1990s—Themes and Issues*, edited by Jorge I. Domínguez and Abraham F. Lowenthal. Baltimore: Johns Hopkins University Press, 1996.

Arnson, Cynthia, ed. *Comparative Peace Processes in Latin America.* Stanford: Stanford University Press, 1999.

Asociación de Trabajadores del Campo. "Estabilidad laboral con libertad sindical: Informe central 1991–1992." Managua: ATC, 1992 (mimeographed).

Asociación Salvadoreña de Cientistas Sociales. *Tendencias actuales de la resolución del conflicto salvadoreño.* San Salvador: ASACS, 1993.

Babb, Florence. "After the Revolution: Neoliberal Policy and Gender in Nicaragua." *Latin American Perspectives* 88 (Winter 1996): 27–48.

Bendaña, Alejandro. *Una tragedia campesina: Testimonios de la resistencia.* Managua: Editora de Arte, Centro de Estudios Internationales, 1991.

Bose, Christine E., and Edna Acosta-Belén. *Women in the Latin American Development Process.* Philadelphia: Temple University Press, 1995.

Carver, Terrell. *Gender Is Not a Synonym for Women.* Boulder, Colo.: Lynne Rienner, 1996.

Central American Historical Institute. "US demands devaluation of the FSLN." *Envío,* no. 119 (June 1991): 3–9.

———. "The contra war, part II." *Envío,* no. 120 (July 1991): 19.

———. "Reconciliation and stability: Still an unreachable dream." *Envío,* no 123 (October 1991): 3–11.

———. "Behind the birth of the recontras." *Envío,* no 123 (October 1991): 20–27.

———. "The 'revueltos': Just the tip of the iceberg." *Envío,* no 131 (June 1992): 27–38.

Central American Revolutionary Workers Party. *El Nuevo Reto.* San Salvador: PRTC, 1993.

Centro de Investigación y Estudios de la Reforma Agraria. *La Reforma Agraria en Nicaragua, 1979–1989: Cifras y Referencias Documentales.* Managua: CIERA, 1989.

Centro Nicaragüense de Derechos Humanos. *Derechos humanos en Nicaragua: Informe Anual. Abril 1992–Abril 1993.* Managua: CENIDH, 1993.

———. *La política es aún un campo dominado por los hombres.* Managua: CENIDH, 1997.

Centro para la Promoción, la Investigación y el Desarrollo Rural y Social. "La inestabilidad política y su impacto socio-económico en el campo." *Cuadernos Agrarios* 6 (October 1990): 1–104.

Chamorro, Amalia. "La Mujer: Logros y límites en 10 años de revolución." *Cuadernos de Sociología* 9–10 (January–June 1989): 117–43.

Chavez Metoyer, Cynthia. "The Women's Movement in the 1996 Nicaraguan Elections." Paper presented at the Latin American Studies Association meeting, Guadalajara, Mexico, April 17–19, 1997.

Child, Jack. *The Central American Peace Accords, 1983–1991: Sheathing Swords, Building Confidence.* Boulder, Colo.: Lynne Rienner, 1992.

Chuchryk, Patricia M. "Women in the Revolution." In *Revolution and Counterrevolu-*

tion in Nicaragua, edited by Thomas W. Walker. Boulder, Colo.: Westview Press, 1991.

Coalición Nacional de Mujeres. *Agenda Mínima*. Managua, March 1996.

Colburn, Forrest. *The Vogue of Revolution in Poor Countries*. Princeton: Princeton University Press, 1994.

Collinson, Helen, ed. *Women and Revolution in Nicaragua*. London: Zed, 1990.

Comisión Internacional de Apoyo y Verificación. "Informe sobre homicidios de desmo-bilizados de la ex-RN." Managua: CIAV-OEA, 1992 (mimeographed).

————. "Cuadros estadísticos del proceso de demobilización y repatriación en Nicaragua." Managua: CIAV-OEA, 1993.

Communist Party of El Salvador. *Construyendo la Utopia*. San Salvador: Ediciones Alternativa, 1993.

Coordinadora Nacional Campesina. "Comunicado." Matagalpa: CNC, 1992 (mimeographed).

Coordinadora Regional de Investigaciones Económicas y Sociales. *Proceso de paz en El Salvador*. Managua: IDESE/CRIES, 1992.

Cordero, Virginia and Ricardo Pereira. "Recompas y recontras ponen fin a la guerra." *L'Avispa* 8 (January–February 1992): 23–31.

Creative Associates International. "Program Options for Reintegrating Ex-Combatants into Civilian Life: Final Report." Submitted to USAID/El Salvador, San Salvador, April 1991.

————. "Other Country Experiences in Demobilization and Reintegration of Ex-Combatants." Washington, D.C., April 1995.

Criquillon, Ana. "The Nicaraguan Women's Movement: Feminist Reflections from Within." In *The New Politics of Survival: Grassroots Movements in Central America*, edited by Minor Sinclair. New York: Monthly Review Press, 1995.

Development Associates. "Final report: Evaluation of the Peace and National Recovery Project–El Salvador." Prepared for USAID, Washington D.C., January 1994.

Diamond, Larry, Marc F. Plattner, Yun-han Chu, and Hung-mao Tien. *Consolidating the Third Wave Democracies*. Baltimore: Johns Hopkins University Press, 1997.

Díaz, Nidia (María Marta Valladares). *Nunca estuve sola*. El Salvador: UCA Editores, 1993.

Domínguez, Jorge I., and Marc Lindenberg, eds. *Democratic Transitions in Central America*. Gainesville: University Press of Florida, 1996.

Domínguez, Jorge I., and Abraham Lowenthal, eds. *Constructing Democratic Governance: Mexico, Central America and the Caribbean in the 1990s*. Baltimore: Johns Hopkins University Press, 1996.

————. *Constructing Democratic Governance: Latin America and the Caribbean in the 1990s—Themes and Issues*. Baltimore: Johns Hopkins University Press, 1996.

Dye, David R., Judy Butler, Deena Abu-Lughod, Jack Spence, with George Vickers. "Contesting Everything, Winning Nothing: The Search for Consensus in Nicaragua, 1990–1995." Cambridge, Mass.: Hemisphere Initiatives, 1995.

Editorial. *Estudios Centroamericanos* 52 (March–April 1997).

Enríquez, Laura. *Harvesting Change: Labor and Agrarian Reform in Nicaragua, 1979–1990.* Chapel Hill: University of North Carolina Press, 1991.

Facultad Latinoamericana de Ciencias Sociales (FLACSO). *El Proceso Electoral de 1994.* San Salvador: UCA, 1995.

Farabundo Martí National Liberation Front. *Acuerdos Hacia una Nueva Nación.* San Salvador: FMLN, 1992.

———. *Documentos Políticos.* San Salvador: Ediciones Alternativa, 1993.

———. *Documentos Políticos.* San Salvador: Ediciones Alternativa, 1995.

———. "Sobre el rumbo actual del FMLN," May 1998 (internal FMLN document).

———. "Estatutos del FMLN con reformas," n.d. (internal FMLN document)

Farabundo Martí National Liberation Front–Secretaría Nacional de la Mujer. "Con respecto a la situación actual del FMLN." San Salvador, n.d. (internal FMLN document).

———. "Conclusiones del encuentro nacional de mujeres del FMLN, 21 de Agosto, 1993." San Salvador, n.d. (internal FMLN document).

———. "Informe evaluativo del primer año de trabajo de la Secretaría Nacional de las Mujeres del FMLN, Mayo 93 a Junio 94." San Salvador, July 1994 (internal FMLN document).

———. "Políticas de género iniciales a ser incorporadas al FMLN en su desarrollo interno y proyección nacional." San Salvador, July 1994 (internal FMLN document).

———. "Informe de los primeros 5 meses de funcionamiento de la secretaría nacional de la mujer, FMLN (Mayo–Septiembre 15 de 1995)." San Salvador, n.d. (internal FMLN document).

———. "Documento propuesta: Reglamento interno para nombrar el proceso de equidad en la participación de hombres y mujeres en todos los espacios de decisión del partido y a todos los niveles." San Salvador, Junio 1997 (internal FMLN document).

———. "Informe evaluativo del trabajo de la SNM (96–97)." San Salvador, n.d. (internal FMLN document).

———. "Programa de fortalecimiento y desarrollo político de las mujeres desde el nivel de base." San Salvador, February 1998 (internal FMLN document).

Fonseca, Roberto. "El precio del desarme." *Pensamiento Propio* 89 (April 1992): 38.

Frente Sandinista de Liberación Nacional. *Programa histórico del FSLN.* Managua: Departamento de Propaganda y Educación Política del FSLN, 1984.

———. "El FSLN y la mujer en la revolución popular sandinista." *Revolución y Desarrollo* 5 (July 1989): 145–50.

Fuerzas Armadas Revolucionarias. "Documento resoluciones sobre el trabajo de la mujer, Asamblea Nacional de Cuadros de las FAR." May 1991 (internal FAR document).

———. "La dimensión de género en nuestra concepción revolucionaria." September 1996 (internal FAR document).

Fuerzas Populares de Liberación–Comisión Nacional de la Mujer. "Informe de la Comisión Nacional de la Mujer a la Secretaría de la Mujer FMLN." San Salvador, n.d. (internal FPL document).

Fundación 16 de Enero. "Balance del proceso de inserción de los ex-combatientes del FMLN." San Salvador, 1993 (mimeographed).

————. "Diagnóstico de la situación actual de la mujer ex-combatiente." San Salvador, 1993 (mimeographed).

————. "Ejecución del plan de reconstrucción nacional: Balance 1993." San Salvador, 1994 (mimeographed).

Gilbert, Dennis. *Sandinistas: The Party and the Revolution*. New York: Basil Blackwell, 1988.

Gobierno de Guatemala. *Política nacional de promoción y desarrollo de las mujeres guatemaltecas plan de equidad de oportunidades 1997–2001*. Guatemala City: Government of Guatemala, 1997.

Golden, Renny. *The Hour of the Poor, the Hour of Women*. New York: Crossroad, 1991.

Gorman, Stephen M. "The Role of the Revolutionary Armed Forces." In *Nicaragua in Revolution*, edited by Thomas W. Walker. New York: Praeger, 1982.

Gramajo Morales, Hector Alejandro. "Political Transition in Guatemala, 1980–1990." In *Democratic Transitions in Central America*, edited by Jorge I. Domínguez and Marc Lindenberg. Gainesville: University Press of Florida, 1996.

Guevara, Che. *Guerrilla Warfare*. Edited by Brian Loveman and Thomas M. Davies, Jr. Wilmington, Del.: Scholarly Resources, 1997.

Gutiérrez, Edgar. "Quién quiso asaltar el cielo?" In *Guatemala, izquierdas en transición*, by Edelberto Torres Rivas. Guatemala City: FLACSO, 1997: 65–92.

Harris, Richard L. *Marxism, Socialism, and Democracy in Latin America*. Boulder, Colo.: Westview Press, 1992.

Harris, Richard L., and Carlos Vilas, eds. *Nicaragua: A Revolution under Siege*. London: Zed, 1985.

Hecht Oppenheim, L. "Democracy in Post-1990 Chile and the Political Incorporation of Women." Paper presented at the meeting of the Latin American Studies Association, Washington, D.C., September 28–30, 1995.

Herrera Morena. "Movimiento de mujeres—Estudio de Caso: El Salvador: Síntesis de Resultados." Paper presented at the II Jornada Feminista, Managua, May 14–18, 1996.

Hipsher, Patricia. "The Micromobilization of the Feminist Movement in Democratizing El Salvador." Paper presented at the Latin American Studies Association meeting, Guadalajara, Mexico, April 17–19, 1997.

Holiday, David. "Guatemala's Precarious Peace." *Current History* 99, no. 634 (February 2000): 78–84.

Holiday, David, and William Stanley. "Building the Peace: Preliminary Lessons from El Salvador." *Journal of International Affairs* 46, no. 2 (1993): 79–84.

Hoskin, Gary. "Democratization in Latin America." *Latin American Research Review* 32, no. 3 (1997): 209–23.

Hoyt, Katherine. *The Many Faces of Sandinista Democracy*. Athens: Ohio University Press, 1997.

Huntington, Samuel P. *The Third Wave: Democratization in the Late Twentieth Century*. Norman: University of Nebraska Press, 1991.

Hurtado Paz y Paz, "Elementos de la historia del movimiento revolucionario guatemalteco." *África América Latina*, no. 31: 5–17.

Htun, Mala N. "El liderazgo de las mujeres en América Latina: Retos y tendencias." Paper presented at the Inter-American Development Bank / PROLEAD seminar, "Liderazgo de la mujer: teoría y práctica." Cancún, Mexico, August 28–30, 2000.

Inter-American Development Bank. *Women in the Americas: Bridging the Gender Gap*. Washington, D.C.: Inter-American Development Bank, 1995.

Invernizzi, Gabriele, Francis Pisani, and Jesús Ceberio. *Sandinistas: Entevistas a Humberto Ortega Saavedra, Jaime Wheelock Román y Bayardo Arce*. Managua: Editorial Vanguardia, 1986.

Jonas, Susanne. "Electoral Problems and the Democratic Project in Guatemala." In *Elections and Democracy in Central America Revisited*, edited by Mitchell A. Seligson and John A. Booth. Chapel Hill: University of North Carolina Press, 1995.

Jones, Mark P. "Gender Quotas, Electoral Laws, and the Election of Women: Lessons From the Argentine Provinces." *Comparative Political Studies* 31, no. 1 (February 1998): 3–21.

Kampwirth, Karen. "Feminism, Anti-feminism, and Electoral Politics in Post-war Nicaragua and El Salvador." Paper presented at the Annual Meeting of the American Political Science Association, Chicago, August 31–September 2, 1995.

———. "From Feminine Guerrillas to Feminist Revolutionaries: Nicaragua, El Salvador, Chiapas." Paper presented at the Latin American Studies Association meeting, Guadalajara, Mexico, April 17–19, 1997.

———. "Women in the Armed Struggles in Nicaragua: Sandinistas and Contras Compared." Paper presented at the Latin American Studies Association meeting, Chicago, September 24–26, 1998.

Landau, Saul. *The Guerrilla Wars of Central America*. New York: St. Martin's Press, 1993.

LeoGrande, William M. "After the Battle of San Salvador." In *Understanding the Central American Crisis: Sources of Conflict, U.S. Policy, and Options for Peace*, by Kenneth M. Coleman and George C. Herring.Wilmington, Del.: Scholarly Resources, 1991.

Leonhard, Ralf. "Nicaragua: Conflicto sin fin." *Pensamiento Propio* 87 (January–February 1992): 7–9.

Linz, Juan J., and Alfred Stepan. *Problems of Democratic Transition and Consolidation.* Baltimore: Johns Hopkins University Press, 1996.

Lowenthal, Abraham F., and Jorge I. Domínguez. "Constructing Democratic Governance." Introduction to *Constructing Democratic Governance: Mexico, Central America and the Caribbean in the 1990s,* edited by Jorge I. Domínguez and Abraham F. Lowenthal. Baltimore: Johns Hopkins University Press, 1996.

Luciak, Ilja A. *The Sandinista Legacy: Lessons From a Political Economy in Transition.* Gainesville: University Press of Florida, 1995.

Luxemburg, Rosa. *The Russian Revolution and Leninism or Marxism?* Ann Arbor: University of Michigan Press, 1982.

Mahling Clark, Kimberly. "Mozambique's Transition from War to Peace: USAID's Lessons Learned." Washington, D.C.: USAID, April 1996.

Martínez, Ana Guadalupe. *Las cárceles clandestinas de El Salvador.* San Salvador: UCA, 1992.

Mason, David T. "Women's Participation in Central American Revolutions." *Comparative Political Studies* 25, no. 1 (April 1992): 63–89.

Matland, Richard and Michelle Taylor. "Electoral System Effects on Women's Representation: Theoretical Arguments and Evidence from Costa Rica." *Comparative Political Studies* 30, no. 2: 186–210.

McCleary, Rachel. "Guatemala's Postwar Prospects." *Journal of Democracy* 8, no. 2 (April 1997): 129–43.

Méndez, Luz. "El papel de las mujeres en la URNG." *Africa América Latina,* no. 31: 60–62.

Ministerio de Gobernación. "Datos estadísticos generales sobre la desmovilización de la R.N. y los grupos re-contras y re-compas en Nicaragua." Managua: Government of Nicaragua, 1992 (mimeographed).

Misión de las Naciones Unidas para la Verificación de los Derechos Humanos en Guatemala. *Acuerdo sobre el definitivo cese al fuego.* Guatemala City: MINUGUA, 1996.

Molina, N. "Propuestas políticas y orientaciones de cambio en la situación de la mujer." In *Propuestas Políticas y Demandas Sociales,* vol. 3, edited by Manuel Antonio Garretón. Santiago: FLACSO, 1989.

Molyneux, Maxine. "Mobilization Without Emancipation? Women's Interests, State and Revolution." In *Transition and Development: Problems of Third World Socialism,* by Richard R. Fagen et al. New York: Monthly Review Press, 1986.

———. "Women." In *Nicaragua: The First Five Years,* edited by Thomas W. Walker. New York: Praeger, 1995: 145–62.

Montenegro, Sofía. "Who Was Going to Trust a Montenegro." In *Sandino's Daughters Revisited: Feminism in Nicaragua,* edited by Margaret Randall. New Brunswick, N.J.: Rutgers University Press, 1994.

Montes, Segundo. *El Agro Salvadoreño (1973–1980).* San Salvador: UCA, 1996.

Montgomery, Tommie Sue. *Revolution in El Salvador: From Civil Strife to Civil Peace*. Boulder, Colo.: Westview Press, 1994.

———. "El Salvador's Extraordinary Elections." *LASA Forum* 27, no. 1 (Spring 1997): 5.

Morales, Mario R. "La izquierda en el entresiglo." In *Guatemala, izquierdas en transición*, by Edelberto Torres Rivas. Guatemala City: FLACSO, 1997: 53–64.

Movimiento de Mujeres "Mélida Anaya Montes." "Buscando caminos: Abriendo puertas y caminos." San Salvador: MAM, 1993.

Movimiento Salvadoreño de Mujeres. "Las Mujeres salvadorenas y los resultados electorales." San Salvador: MSM, n.d. (mimeographed).

Mujeres por la Dignidad y la Vida. "Transferencia de tierras: Discriminación hacia las Mujeres." San Salvador: Las Dignas, 1993.

———. *Las mujeres: ante, con, contra, desde, sin, tras . . . el poder político*. San Salvador: Las Dignas, 1995.

Narváez Murillo, Zoilamérica. "Testimonio de Zoilamérica." Managua, March 1998 (unpublished paper).

Navarro, Marysa, and Susan C. Bourque, "Fault Lines of Democratic Governance: A Gender Perspective." In *Fault Lines of Democracy in Post-Transition Latin America*, edited by Felipe Agüero and Jeffrey Stark. Miami: North-South Center Press, 1998.

Navas, María Candelaria. "Los movimientos femeninos en Centroamérica: 1970–1983." In *Movimientos Populares en Centroamérica*, coordinated by Daniel Camacho and Rafael Menjívar. San José: EDUCA, 1985.

Nicaraguan Resistance Party, "Declaración de principios de la PRN." Managua: PRN, 1993.

Núñez, Orlando, ed. *La guerra en Nicaragua*. Managua: Centro para la Investigación, la Promoción y el Desarrollo Rural y Social, 1991.

Núñez, Vilma. "En el 103 aniversario del nacimiento de Augusto C. Sandino." Managua, May 18, 1998 (unpublished paper distributed by author).

O'Kane, Trish, and Raul Marín. "El reverso de la medalla." *Pensamiento Propio* 88 (March 1992): 21–22.

Olivera, Mercedes, Malena de Montis, and Mark Meassick. *Nicaragua: El poder de las mujeres*. Managua: Cenzontle, 1992.

Parvikko, Tuija. "Conceptions of Gender Equality: Similarity and Difference." In *Equality Politics and Gender*, edited by Elizabeth Meehan and Selma Sevenhuijsen. London: Sage, 1991.

Pastora, Edén. "Movimiento de Acción Democrática." Managua: M.A.D., August 18, 1993.

Pelupessy, Wim. "Agrarian Reform in El Salvador." In *A Decade of War: El Salvador Confronts the Future*, edited by Anjali Sundaram and George Gelber. New York: Monthly Review Press, 1991.

Pérez Alemán, Paola. *Organización, Identidad y Cambio*. Managua: CIAM/Editorial Vanguardia, 1990.

Policia Nacional–Nicaragua. *Anuario Estadístico*. Managua: Government of Nicaragua, 1997.

Premo, Daniel. "The Redirection of the Armed Forces." In *Nicaragua Without Illusions: Regime Transition and Structural Adjustment in the 1990s*, edited by Thomas W. Walker. Wilmington, Del.: Scholarly Resources, 1997.

Prevost, Gary. "The FSLN." In *Nicaragua Without Illusions: Regime Transition and Structural Adjustment in the 1990s*, edited by Thomas W. Walker. Wilmington, Del.: Scholarly Resources, 1997.

Przeworski, Adam. *Democracy and the Market: Political and Economic Reforms in Eastern Europe and Latin America*. Cambridge: Cambridge University Press, 1991.

Ramírez-Horton, Susan E. "The Role of Women in the Nicaraguan Revolution." In *Nicaragua in Revolution*, edited by Thomas W. Walker. New York: Praeger, 1982.

Randall, Margaret. *Sandino's Daughters: Testimonies of Nicaraguan Women in Struggle*. Vancouver: New Star Books, 1981.

———. *Gathering Rage: The Failure of 20th Century Revolutions to Develop a Feminist Agenda*. New York: Monthly Review Press, 1992.

———. *Sandino's Daughters Revisited: Feminism in Nicaragua*. New Brunswick, N.J.: Rutgers University Press, 1994.

Reif, Linda L. "Women in Latin American Guerrilla Movements." *Comparative Politics* 18, no. 2 (January 1986): 147–69.

República de Nicaragua-Ministerio de Finanzas Vice-Ministerio de la Propiedad. "Estadísticas y visión del tema de la propiedad." Managua: Government of Nicaragua, 1997 (mimeographed).

Rodríguez, Isabel. "Serán una realidad los polos de desarrollo?" *Pensamiento Propio* 78 (August 1990): 30–31.

Rodríguez Calderón, Mirta. "Queda mucho por andar." United Nations–Cuba office, n.d. (unpublished report).

Romero, Irene. "La reinserción de la mujer ex-combatiente. Un legado de guerra." *Realidad* 44 (March–April 1995): 369–83.

Saint-Germain, Michelle A. "Mujeres '94: Democratic Transition and the Women's Movement in El Salvador." Unpublished manuscript, n.d.

Saint-Germain, Michelle A., and Martha I. Morgan. "Equality: Costa Rican Women Demand 'The Real Thing.'" *Women and Politics* 11 (1991): 23–75.

Schedler, Andreas. "Concepts of Democratic Consolidation." Paper presented at the Latin American Studies Association meeting, Guadalajara, Mexico, April 17–19, 1997.

Seligson, Mitchell. "Thirty Years of Transformation in the Agrarian Structure of El Salvador." San Salvador: Fundación Dr. Guillermo Manuel Ungo, 1994.

———. "Agrarian Inequality and the Theory of Peasant Rebellion." *Latin American Research Review* 31 no. 2 (1996): 140–57.

Spalding, Rose J. *The Political Economy of Revolutionary Nicaragua*. Winchester, Mass.: Allen and Unwin, 1987.

———. *Capitalists and Revolution in Nicaragua: Opposition and Accommodation, 1979–1993*. Chapel Hill: University of North Carolina Press, 1994.

———. "From Low-Intensity Warfare to Low-Intensity Peace: The Nicaraguan Peace Process." Paper prepared for the Woodrow Wilson International Center for Scholars Conference, "Comparative Peace Processes in Latin America," Washington, D.C., March 13–14, 1997.

Spence, Jack. "Democracy Weakened? A Report on the October 20, 1996 Nicaraguan Elections." Cambridge, Mass.: Hemisphere Initiatives, 1997.

———. "Post War Transitions: Elections and Political Parties in El Salvador and Nicaragua." Paper presented at the Latin American Studies Association meeting, Guadalajara, Mexico, April 17–19, 1997.

Spence, Jack, David R. Dye, Mike Lanchin, and Geoff Thale with George Vickers. "Chapúltepec: Five Years Later. El Salvador's Political Reality and Uncertain Future." Cambridge, Mass.: Hemisphere Initiatives, 1997.

Spence, Jack, David R. Dye, and George Vickers. "El Salvador: Elections of the Century." Cambridge, Mass.: Hemisphere Initiatives, 1994.

Spence, Jack, David R. Dye, Paula Worby, Carmen Rosa de Leo-Escribano, George Vickers, and Mike Lanchin. "Promise and Reality: Implementation of the Guatemalan Peace Accords." Cambridge, Mass.: Hemisphere Initiatives, 1998.

Spence, Jack, George Vickers, and David Dye. "The Salvadoran Peace Accords and Democratization: A Three Year Progress Report and Recommendations." Cambridge, Mass.: Hemisphere Initiatives, 1995.

Spence, Jack, and George Vickers with Margaret Popkin, Philip Williams, and Kevin Murray. "A Negotiated Revolution: A Two Year Progress Report on the Salvadoran Peace Accords." Cambridge, Mass.: Hemisphere Initiatives, 1994.

Stanfield, David. "Insecurity of Land Tenure in Nicaragua." Madison: Land Tenure Center, University of Wisconsin, 1992.

Stephen, Lynn, ed. and trans. *Hear My Testimony: Maria Teresa Tula–Human Rights Activist of El Salvador*. Boston: South End Press, 1994.

Stoltz Chinchilla, Norma. *Nuestras Utopias: Mujeres guatemaltecas del siglo XX*. Guatemala City: Magna Terra, 1998.

Torres Rivas, Edelberto. "Guatemala: Democratic Governability." In *Constructing Democratic Governance: Mexico, Central America and the Caribbean in the 1990s*, edited by Jorge I. Domínguez and Abraham F. Lowenthal. Baltimore: Johns Hopkins University Press, 1996.

———, ed. *Guatemala, izquierdas en transición*. Guatemala City: FLACSO, 1997.

Tulchin, Joseph S., ed. *The Consolidation of Democracy in Latin America*. Boulder, Colo.: Lynne Rienner, published with the Woodrow Wilson Center, 1995.

Ueltzen, Stefan. *Como salvadoreña que soy: Entrevistas con mujeres en la lucha*. San Salvador: Editorial Sombrero Azul, 1993.

"La UNAG antes era mi enemiga ahora mi aliada dice excontra." *Productores* (Managua) 13 (1992): 23–25.

Unidad Revolucionaria Nacional Guatemalteca. "Propuesta a la sociedad. Cuatro objetivos, nueve cambios, cuatro prioridades." Guatemala City: URNG, 1995.

———. "Personal Incorporado: Diagnóstico Socio-Economico." Guatemala City: URNG, 1997.

Unión Nacional de Agricultores y Ganaderos. "Informe evaluativo de la junta directiva nacional al II congreso de UNAG (1986–1992)." Managua: UNAG, 1990.

United Nations. "Acuerdo para el reasentamiento de las poblaciones desarraigadas por el enfrentamiento armado." Guatemala City: MINUGUA, 1994.

———. "Acuerdo sobre identidad y derechos de los pueblos indígenas." Guatemala City: MINUGUA, 1995.

———. *El Salvador, 1990–1995*. New York: United Nations, 1995.

———. "Acuerdo sobre el definitivo cese al fuego." Guatemala City: MINUGUA, 1996.

United Nations Development Program. *Human Development Report 1995*. New York: Oxford University Press, 1995.

———. *Human Development Report 1999*. New York: Oxford University Press, 1999.

United Nations Observer Mission in El Salvador. *Proceso de desmovilización del personal del FMLN*. San Salvador: Imprenta El Estudiante, n.d.

United States Agency for International Development. "The First Three Years of the Peace and National Recovery Project: Lessons Learned." San Salvador: USAID, October 1994.

Universidad de San Carlos de Guatemala, Programa Universitario de Investigación en Estudios de Género. "Proyecto: Mujeres y Acuerdos de Paz." Universidad de San Carlos, n.d.

Urbina, Vance. "Building a Feminist Organization inside the Social Movement." In *Compañeras: Voices from the Latin American Women's Movement*, edited by Gaby Küppers. London: Latin American Bureau, 1994.

Vanden, Harry, and Gary Prevost. *Democracy and Socialism in Sandinista Nicaragua*. Boulder, Colo.: Lynne Rienner. 1993.

Vázquez, Norma, Cristina Ibáñez, and Clara Murguialday. *Mujeres-montaña: Vivencias de guerrilleras y colaboradoras del FMLN*. Madrid: Editorial horas y HORAS, 1996.

Vickers, George, and Jack Spence. "Endgame: A Progress Report on the Implementation of the Salvadoran Peace Accords." Cambridge, Mass.: Hemisphere Initiatives, 1992.

———. "Elections: The Right Consolidates Power." *NACLA* 38, no. 1 (July–August 1994): 10–14.

Vilas, Carlos. *The Sandinista Revolution: National Liberation and Social Transformation in Central America*. New York, Monthly Review Press, 1986.

————. *Between Earthquakes and Volcanos: Market, State, and the Revolutions in Central America*. New York: Monthly Review Press, 1995.

"Violencia política o delincuencia en el campo." *Productores* (Managua) 3 (1991): 8–12.

Walker, Thomas W., ed. *Nicaragua in Revolution*. New York: Praeger, 1982.

————. *Nicaragua: The First Five Years*. New York: Praeger, 1985.

————. *Reagan versus the Sandinistas*. Boulder, Colo.: Westview Press, 1987.

————. *Revolution and Counterrevolution in Nicaragua*. Boulder, Colo.: Westview Press, 1991.

————, ed. *Nicaragua Without Illusions*. Wilmington, Del.: Scholarly Resources, 1997.

Washington Office on Latin America. "Nicaragua Issue Brief No. 1: The Helms Report on Nicaragua." Washington, D.C., September 22, 1992.

Waylen, Georgina. *Gender in Third World Politics*. Boulder, Colo.: Lynne Rienner, 1996.

Wheelock Román, Jaime. *La verdad sobre La Piñata: Los cambios en la propriedad agraria: julio 1979–abril 1990*. Managua: Instituto para el Desarrollo de la Democracia, 1991.

Wickham-Crowley, Timothy P. *Guerrillas and Revolution in Latin America*. Princeton: Princeton University Press, 1992.

Zavatto, Daniel. "Latin America: Between the Electoral Euphoria and Democratic Disenchantment. A Balance of the 1991–1995 Period." Paper presented at the 1996 Democracy Forum, International Institute for Democracy and Electoral Assistance, Stockholm, Sweden, June 1996.

Index

(Organization of American States;
OEA), 21–22
Organización Revolucionaria del Pueblo
en Armas (Revolutionary Organization
of Armed Citizens; Guatemala; ORPA),
24, 25, 26, 28, 130–31, 133–34
Organization of American States. *See*
Organización de Estados Americanos
ORPA. *See* Organización Revolucionaria
del Pueblo en Armas
Ortega, Daniel: allegations against, 175,
179–81, 190, 236; and FSLN, 119,
121–28, 130, 143–44
Ortega, Humberto, 127, 138
Ortega (Narváez) Murillo, Zoilamérica,
125–26, 128, 144; allegations by,
179–81, 190
Otzoy, Aura, 221

PAN. *See* Partido de Avanzada Nacional
Panama, 35
Partido Alianza Popular Conservadora
(Nicaragua), 210
Partido de Avanzada Nacional (Party for
National Advancement; Guatemala;
PAN), 220–21
Partido Demócrata (Democratic Party;
El Salvador; PD), 81, 102, 109, 142,
211, 215
Partido Guatemalteco del Trabajo
(Guatemalan Workers' Party; PGT),
24, 25–26, 130–31, 133–34
Partido Humanista (Chile), 156
Partido Liberal Constitucionalista (Lib-
eral Constitutionalist Party;
Nicaragua), 175, 218
Partido Liberal Demócrata (El Salvador),
215
Partido Resistencia Nicaragüense
(Nicaraguan Resistance Party; PRN),
21, 140–41, 198–99
Partido Revolucionario de Trabajadores

Centroamericanos (Revolutionary
Party of Central American Workers;
El Salvador; PRTC), 3, 9, 68, 71, 82,
154, 158, 205; and FMLN, 96, 99–
102, 105, 165; gender composition of,
5, 7, 9
Partido Social Demócrata (Social Democratic Party; El Salvador; PSD), 142–
43
Party for National Advancement. *See*
Partido de Avanzada Nacional
Pastora, Edén, 140–41
PD. *See* Partido Demócrata
peace accords: combatants' view of, 4,
64, 91, 92, 93; and democratization,
xvii, 38, 102, 237–38; and economic
conditions, 39–45, 49–54, 59–60,
73–80, 238; in El Salvador, xii, xx, 3,
32, 61, 62, 73, 89, 96, 133, 148, 149,
162, 237–38; evolution of, 34–38;
gender dimension of, xiv, 93; in
Guatemala, xii, xxi, xxii, 23, 24, 33,
38, 55, 57, 133, 144, 145, 184, 185,
188, 189, 220, 221, 237; implementation of, 34, 93, 97; and UN, 24, 38,
93; and women, 39, 55, 63, 149, 195,
238–39
Pelupessy, Wim, 40
Peña, Lorena, 39, 158, 166, 201, 206
Peña, Mercedes, 155, 192
Pérez Aléman, Paola, 169
Perla, Mirna, 159
PGT. *See* Partido Guatemalteco del Trabajo
piñata (appropriation of government resources), 50, 124
political parties, xi, xiv; conversion of
revolutionary groups to, xi, xii, 96,
97–101, 104–7, 133, 141–43, 159,
227, 235; and democratic consolidation, xii, xv–xix, xxiii, 95; and economic conditions, 105–6, 145; in El